Wissenschaftlichen Abhandlung,   Musicological Studies,
Band XLVII   Vol. XLVII

THE AMBROSIAN CANTUS

by

Terence Bailey

The Institute of Mediaeval Music

Ottawa, Canada

The Institute of Mediaeval Music
1270 Lampman Crescent
Ottawa, Canada
K2C 1P8

ISBN 0-931902-53-3

© 1987 by The Institute of Mediaeval Music

For Bryan Gillingham

This book has been published with the help of a grant from the Canadian Federation for the Humanities, using funds provided by the Social Sciences and Humanities Research Council of Canada.

CONTENTS

	Preface	7
	Acknowledgements	10
I.	"Cantus" and "Tractus"	11
II.	"Cantus" and "Tractus" in the Ambrosian Books	16
III.	The Cantus in the Liturgy	23
IV.	The Early Usage	31
V.	The Cantus Outside Mass	40
VI.	The Singers of the Cantus	52
VII.	The Melodies	55
VIII.	The Development of the Repertory	117
IX.	Ambrosian, Gregorian, Old-Roman and Old-Beneventan	128
	Preface to the Edition	144
	The Edition	151
	Bibliography	239
	Index to The Edition	243
	List of Tables	246
	List of Musical Examples	247
	General Index	250

PREFACE

It would be difficult to exaggerate the importance of the psalms in the Christian liturgy. For nearly twenty centuries, and for innumerable men and women, their words have provided the principal idiom of the Divine Praise. In the cloister, the cycle of psalms, ceaselessly repeated, forms the substance of the Canonical Hours, the Opus Dei. But the psalms are hardly less important in the Mass, from the beginning, the central liturgical act of worship for all orthodox Christians.

The psalmody of the medieval Mass is largely choral, and although there are certainly some features of this choral psalmody – perhaps even some of the melodies – that derive from the primitive Church, there is no one, I think, who would raise serious objections to the historical precedence of solo psalms. But even though the solo psalmody between the Mass lessons is generally agreed to be "beaucoup plus primitif que celui des psaumes processionels,"[1] and even though it might seem – for that reason, if for no other – worthy of the most careful examination, it has received nothing like the attention that is warranted.

The Cantus[2] and the Tracts, as it would appear from the circumstantial evidence alone, are the chants most likely to preserve the fea-

---

[1] That is, the Introit, Offertory and Communion. The quotation is from N. M. Denis-Boulet in *L'église en prière*, edited by A. G. Martimort (Paris, 1961), p. 350.

[2] The Latin plural of Cantus (like Tractus) has the same spelling as the singular.

tures of ancient psalmody. But of all the Mass forms they are perhaps the least understood. Concerning them opinion is divided, even on the most basic questions: whether, for example, they are to be numbered among the oldest or most recent musical forms;[3] whether they replace, or have been replaced by, the Alleluia; whether their structure is oratorical or musical, regular or casual.

Circumstantial evidence suggests also that the answers to these questions are more likely to be found in the study of the relatively simple Ambrosian repertory than in the vastly more complicated Gregorian. But about the Cantus ignorance is even more general than about the Tract. The fact is, there has been almost no reliable information available. The promise implied in the title of Roy Jesson's study, "Ambrosian Chant: the Music of the Mass,"[4] was not fulfilled for the Cantus. Indeed, what he had to say about these chants was more misleading than helpful, for he suggested – and this, as the reader will see presently, is very far from the case – that the Cantus have no coherent structure. Concerning even the simplest of them he remarked, "that it is almost impossible to systematize a comparison."[5] Moreover, having compared the Gregorian and Ambrosian repertories, he concluded that, "there are few traces of actual melodic material common to both repertories, and the resemblance is chiefly confined to tonality."[6]

There is no need to enumerate Jesson's errors; I would be inclined to pass over them all if some had not become so widely known. But he had occasion to repeat a number of his opinions – to a wider audience, and more forcefully – in Willi Apel's very influential *Gregorian Chant*.[7] Jesson's chapter on the Ambrosian melodies has little to say about the

---

[3] The weight of scholarly opinion is solidly behind the antiquity of the chant, but recently one of Chant's most distinguished scholars, in a work that has perhaps more general influence than any other in English, has seen fit to question it. See Helmut Hucke, in *The New Grove Dictionary of Music and Musicians*, ed. Stanley Sadie (London, 1980), XIX, 110 (s.v. "Tract").

[4] Unpublished Ph.D. dissertation, Indiana University, 1955.

[5] Jesson, "Ambrosian Chant," p. 49.

[6] Jesson, "Ambrosian Chant," p. 48.

[7] Bloomington, (1958).

Cantus, and unfortunately almost all it does say is wrong. One reads, for example, that the Cantus "show little, if any traces of the centonization technique which is of such basic importance in the Tracts." And I find that this opinion has become part of the scholarly baggage of the growing number of scholars interested in the liturgy and chant of Milan.

It is, of course, entirely proper that scholars should be interested in the Milanese repertory, not only because of its inherent value as one of the most important manifestations of the medieval Christian culture, but also for the insights it offers into the development of the dominant Gregorian repertory and into the development of ecclesiastical chant in general. Although it would be misleading to say, without qualification, that Ambrosian Chant is older than the Gregorian (it is in various respects both older and younger), the ecclesiastical chant of Milan does preserve a number of ancient features that have been obliterated or obscured by the complicated history of its better-known neighbour.

As for the Cantus in particular, they are an especially rewarding subject for investigation. They provide, since Old-Roman, Old-Beneventan, and Gregorian versions of the standard melody have also survived, a rare opportunity to examine the musical relationship of the various Latin liturgies. But what is rarer yet, the Cantus offer an opportunity to observe the operation of the oral tradition – one of the most interesting phenomena of the musical life of the ancient world. The Ambrosian, in the twelfth century, was the last of the the great western musical repertories to be committed to writing. The relationship of the Ambrosian Cantus melodies, one to another, their relationship to the corresponding chants sung in the other Latin liturgies, and the degree to which the Cantus are seen to adhere to, or depart from, the basic structure and melody, afford excellent criteria for evaluating the successes and failures of the transmission of music before the reliance on notation.

Except only for occasional brief passages quoted by scholars, the Cantus have been generally available only in the practical edition of Gregorio Suñol, the *Antiphonale missarum iuxta ritum sanctae ecclesiae mediolanensis* (Rome, 1935). This edition was well enough suited to its purposes, but it includes no indication of the sources of its melodies (many of which can be shown to be composites of more than one version). Moreover, in order to adapt the old chants and ceremonies to modern circumstances, the editor has been obliged to include much that is recent in origin. And as, alas, the practical purpose of the book has been vitiated by recent liturgical reforms, Suñol's edition – never easily found outside the archdiocese of Milan – has become very rare indeed.

ACKNOWLEDGEMENTS

I acknowledge, with gratitude, the advice and assistance of don Natale Ghiglione and monsignore Ernesto Moneta Caglio (the present and former directors of the Pontificio Istituto Ambrosiano di Musica Sacra), and of Kathryn Bailey, Alma Browne, Joseph Dyer, David Hiley, David Lenson and Paul Merkley. It will surprise no one to learn that I have not, in every instance, followed the advice that was so generously given, and it must not be supposed that my opinions conform in every respect to theirs. I am especially indebted to Joseph Dyer for encouraging me to develop the suggestion that the Tracts and Cantus entered the Mass as readings, although I cannot think he will entirely approve all of the consequences I have drawn from this hypothesis.

I
"CANTUS" AND "TRACTUS"

The Ambrosian chants commonly known as Cantus are the counterparts of the Gregorian, Old-Roman and Old-Beneventan Tracts. This is more than a general observation: in a number of cases it is the same chant – or an obviously related version – that was given one name in Milan and another elsewhere. The Milanese idiosyncrasy,[1] which was tenaciously preserved in Ambrosian books from the eleventh to the twentieth century, may be more than an example of the trivia that distinguish local ecclesiastical usages. The Ambrosian practice may indicate the correct etymology of the terms "cantus" and "tractus," about which there has been some disagreement.

The oldest appearances of "tractus," as the designation for the chant, seem to be in the earliest Gregorian Mass books, copied near the beginning of the ninth century.[2] However, the Roman basis of these

---

[1] The designation "TRACTUS CANTUS" does appear twice in the ninth-century Gregorian Cantatorium, *St Gall Ms 359*. See *Paléographie musicale* [PM], edited by the Monks of Solesmes (Tournai, 1899-) Series 2, vol. 2 (1924), 35, 90. In this context, it is perhaps the general, not the specific meaning of "cantus" that is intended. The Gregorian rubric should be read in the light of the discussion, below, of the medieval terminology.

[2] The six oldest have been published as *Antiphonale Missarum Sextuplex*, ed. René-Jean Hesbert (Rome, 1935).

ancient formularies, and the same usage in the Beneventan and Old-Roman manuscripts, suggest that the term had been employed earlier in Rome. The explanation of "tractus" is uncertain. It has a specific musical connotation, but it is also a common word apt to be used in ordinary circumstances (the case is rather like that of "modus"), and its common meanings are as varied as those of its many English derivatives and cognates, "tract," "track," "treck," "drag," "draw" and the rest.

A number of later medieval commentators interpreted "tractus" with reference to the supposed slow and mournful character of the chant. So Honorius of Autun, in the early twelfth century:

| Tractus a trahendo dicitur, quia trahendo id est tractim canitur. | We say "Tractus" from "drawing out," because to sing in the style of the Tracts is to sing in such a manner. |

and Hugh of St Victor (ca 1096-1141):

| Tractus autem quia gemitum et cantum lachrymabilem exprimit, lacrimas sanctorum . . . repraesentat. Unde tractus dicitur, quia sancti suspirantes ab imo pectoris gemitum trahunt.[3] | The Tract imitates the cry and the tearful modulation; it calls to mind the weeping of the saints. It is for this reason we say "tract," because the saints in their lamentations "draw forth" their cry from the depths of their heart. |

---

[3] These and other such references were cited by Charles (Dufresne, Sieur) Du Cange in his *Glossarium . . . mediae et infimae . . . latinitatis* (Paris, 1678, revised by Léopold Favre [Niort, 1883-87]), and (from Du Cange) by many subsequent authors, Jean-Louis D'Ortigue, Peter Wagner, Helmut Hucke, etc.

This explanation is plausible enough for the period represented by liturgical service books. By the beginning of the ninth century all of the occasions of the chant were, in some sense penitential.[4] However, the texts of the Cantus and Tracts are usually neutral, not mournful. Some, like LAUDATE DOMINUM[5] and *Jubilate domino* have even a festive character. And if the designation "tractus" is older than the restriction of the chant to occasions of penitence, which may well be the case, this interpretation is not very convincing – especially as earlier commentators give no indication that they were aware of it. Amalarius of Metz, a writer of the ninth century, is the earliest scholar to refer to the Tracts (Aurelian of Réôme, writing about the same time, does not mention them). And Amalarius would hardly – given his evident love of emotionally-charged metaphor and poetic interpretation – have missed such an opportunity to expatiate. He, however, remarks that:

tractus vero aliquando	sometimes the Tract
tribulationem, aliquando	expresses tribulation,

---

[4] Tracts and Cantus are assigned for some important feasts, but (except for Holy Innocents and Annunciation) (1) only when they were celebrated in the Lenten period, and then only if they did not fall on Sunday (when the Tract would be replaced by an Alleluia), or (2) for the Mass of the vigil. Although in later centuries the earlier character of vigils came to be obscured, they were originally conceived as preparations for the festivals that followed, and were thus occasions for penance. The Gregorian Feast of the Holy Innocents does not fall in the prohibited period, and the appearance of a Tract is a late anomaly not found in the earliest Gregorian books (in the Ambrosian the Alleluia was never replaced by a Cantus), and dates from a time when the "sorrowful" nature of the Tract seemed appropriate to the occasion. The Ambrosian "cantus" (actually, as we will see, a Psalmellus) on Annunciation might also appear to be an exception. But the celebration of the feast on the last Sunday of Advent was the result of a later revision of the calendar. Annunciation had earlier been celebrated in Milan, as elsewhere, on March 25 (that is, in Lent), and when the change was made, certain Lenten characteristics, including the singing of a Cantus, were retained. For a discussion of the circumstances, see P. Lejai, in *Dictionnaire d'archéologie chrétienne et de liturgie* [*DACL*], ed. F. Cabrol (1903-53), I, 1392, s.v. "Ambrosien (Rit)."

[5] Text incipits of the Cantus are given throughout in uppercase letters.

laetitiam sonat.[6]	sometimes joy.

The same writer also provides important information about the performance of the Tracts, drawing particular attention to the differences between them and the Respond-Graduals:

Hoc differtur inter responsorium, cui chorus repondet, et tractum cui nemo.[7]	Between the Responsory and the Tract, this is the difference: to the first the chorus answers, to the second, no one.

Amalarius does not, of course, wish to say that in the ninth century the lack of refrain was the only difference between the Tract and the Respond-Gradual, but he obviously thought the distinction was important. We will see later that the manner of performance of the Tract and Respond-Gradual is of great significance in distinguishing these chants, for the earliest references to them are susceptible to confusion. For the moment I want only to suggest that it was Amalarius's reference, which attests to the survival of the primitive practice, the chanting of the psalms *in directum* (that is, without choral refrain, neither antiphon nor respond), that led Giuseppe Tommasi and other liturgists[8] to suggest, more than two hundred years ago, that "Tractus" meant something like, "in one stretch," "uninterrupted." Although there is no reason to prefer it on etymological grounds, this too is a plausible explanation.

---

[6] *Liber officialis* 1, III, 14 (*Amalarii episcopi opera liturgica omnia*, ed. J. M. Hanssens in 3 vols. [Rome, 1948-50] II, 302).

[7] *Liber officialis* 1, III, 12 (Hanssens, *Amalarii II*, p. 299. The passage may owe something to Saint Isidore: "inter responsorios autem et antiphonas hoc differt, quod in responsoriis unus versum dicit, in antiphonis autem versibus alternant chori" [*Etymologiae* VI, XIX, 8 in *PL* LXXXII, 252].

[8] Cited by Peter Wagner in *Einführung in die gregorianischen Melodien* (third edition, Leipzig, 1911) I, 98.

About a hundred years ago, the Byzantinist Wilhelm Christ suggested another.[9] In Greek there is a word, "εἱρμός," that without being an obvious cognate, bears most of the same meanings as the Latin "tractus." Moreover, "heirmos" was a musical term employed by Byzantine musicians to designate a model hymn-stanza, a specimen setting (the Heirmologion provided one for each of the Odes of the Kanon sung in the morning Office) of the melody that was to be adapted to the other strophes.

I don't wish to suggest that the melodies of the Heirmoi are related in any significant way to those of the Tractus and Cantus. Neither do I wish to imply that there is anything (beyond the general principles that seem to govern nearly all early Christian chants) to connect the Byzantine and Latin musical procedures for adapting standard melodies to different texts. If, however, "heirmos" is understood to mean "the course" (one of the most common meanings of both "tractus" and its Greek equivalent), that is to say, the course the singer was to follow, "the way" he was to proceed – in effect, "the melody" – an analogy in the choice of the Ambrosian, Gregorian and Byzantine terms becomes apparent. I refer, of course, to the fact that "melody" is also a basic meaning – one of the most obvious – of "cantus."

In the context of the Byzantine usage it would seem that "melody-type" is a better interpretation of "heirmos" than the simple "melody." The Milanese context suggests that "melody-type" is also the correct interpretation of "cantus," for it is a striking musical feature of the Ambrosian Cantus that all are adaptations, variously elaborated, of the same tune.

---

[9] *Über die Bedeutung von Hirmos, Troparion und Kanon* . . . (1870), cited in Wagner, *Einführung* I, 99. See also M. Velimirovic, "The Byzantine Heirmos and Heirmologion," in *Gattungen der Musik in Einzeldarstellungen: Gedenkschrift Leo Schrade* (Berne and Munich, 1973), pp. 192-244.

II

"CANTUS" AND "TRACTUS"
IN THE AMBROSIAN BOOKS

It must be said at once that not all items referred to as "cantus" in the Ambrosian books belong properly to the type. Nor, as we shall see in a moment, is the term the only designation for the chants that do belong. The Milanese employed the title for pieces of other kinds when they were used in place of Cantus, and it would appear that they continued to use the word in its general sense. Just as in the case of "tractus" and "modus" mentioned above, there is an ordinary as well as a special meaning of "cantus," and the distinction is not always made clear (at least not to us) in the service books. These questions of medieval terminology must be considered in a broader context.

In the Ambrosian Ordinal[1] compiled about 1125 by Beroldus, a minor cleric in the Milanese archiepiscopal establishment, both "canticum" and "cantus" are found as references to the specific chant-type.[2] Marco Magistretti, the estimable editor of Beroldus, was inclined to

---

[1] *Beroldus sive ambrosianae mediolanensis kalendarium et ordines saec. XII*. ed. M. Magistretti (Milan, 1894).

[2] *Beroldus*, pp. 58, 59, 75, etc.; cf. 87, 101, 107, etc. (Here and subsequently, the page references to Beroldus's ordinal are those of Magistretti's edition of 1894.)

dismiss such appearances of "canticum" as simple slips,[3] but as the designation is found several times, and even repeated on the same page,[4] it would appear that, for those who later copied the ordinal if not for Beroldus himself, the usage was in some degree deliberate. The earliest Ambrosian antiphoners shed no light on the problem: they customarily abbreviate the title to the first three or four letters.[5]

It will be known to most of my readers that in some of the first Gregorian Mass books, "canticum" is similarly the designation for three Holy-Saturday chants that employ the standard Gregorian Tract-melody.[6] The explanation in these instances is that the three have texts drawn from the Biblical Canticles.[7] The Gregorian usage of "canticum" (for the Holy Saturday Tracts, at any rate) is clear enough. But (except, of course, where it is actually a canticle that is meant[8]) there is no explanation for the Ambrosian terminology – only the obvious one, that no distinction was intended.

"Cantus" and "Canticum" are synonymous in common Latin usage. If these terms can be understood in their general as well as their particular sense, then the appearance in the Beroldus ordinal of one word in place of another with the same meaning may (if indeed it was

---

[3] *Beroldus*, p. 202 (Magistretti's note 167).

[4] See, for example, *Beroldus*, p. 87.

[5] The editors of *PM* V and VI were not always careful. For example, "canticum" is transcribed from "cant" (on page 261 of the British Library manuscript) without any explanation. For the same chant, "cantus" is specified in the Manuale (*Manuale ambrosianum [Monumenta veteris liturgiae ambrosianae II]*, ed. M. Magistretti in 2 vols [Milan, 1905, reprinted 1971],) II, 168. All subsequent references to the Manuale, unless the *pars prima* is specified, are to the second volume.

[6] Hesbert, *Sextuplex*, pp. 97-99. The melodies are found, of course, only in later manuscripts.

[7] In the *Corbie Antiphoner* and in other early manuscripts (*St Gall 359*, for example; see above, page 11, note 1) the same title is repeated for a fourth Tract, but this is likely nothing more than a slip (Hesbert, *Sextuplex*, p. lx). This slip may, however, have influenced the compilers of the Ambrosian books. See below page 48, note 24.

[8] *Beroldus*, p. 105.

not considered a matter of complete indifference) be merely a question of literary style. In any case, a comparison of the usage of Beroldus and that of the Manuale (a much earlier Ambrosian service book containing the texts of the chants, but only a few rubrics, and no musical notation[9]) suggests that the terms could, in practice, be used interchangeably.[10]

A still more general use of "canticum," on this occasion with a meaning perhaps no more specific than "chant,"[11] may be the explanation for the designation of *Tenebrae factae*, the responsory (properly a Psalmellus[12]) that follows the reading from Isaiah after Tierce on Good Friday. The Ordinal refers to this chant as follows: "Canticum episcopale, aut sacerdotale, sive diaconile, iussu archiepiscopi: *Tenebrae factae sunt*, cum suo versu."[13] The Manuale directs: "presbyter aut diaconus cantet istud cant[icum]."[14] The British Library manuscript[15] specifies "cant[icum] primicerii"[16] the Metropolitano[17] specifies "cant[icum] archid[iaconile]."[18] In these instances the intent may simply be to indicate the singer (about which there was some evident uncertainty), not the liturgical type of the "chant." In the case of the analogous lessons on the other Fridays of Lent the responsories (these pieces will be discussed below) are titled "Tractus."[19]

---

[9] The Manuale is, roughly speaking, the Ambrosian equivalent of the *Sextuplex* manuscripts. In Gregorian regions such books were replaced relatively early by others in which the melodies were notated. The oral tradition of the melodies, and consequently the usefulness of service books containing only the words of the chants, persisted longer in Italy than in the north.

[10] Cf. the rubric for SICUT CERVUS in *Beroldus*, p. 11 and the *Manuale*, p. 204.

[11] Cf. the term "tractus cantus" referred to above, page 11, note 1.

[12] The Psalmelli are the Milanese counterparts of the Gregorian Respond-Graduals.

[13] *Beroldus*, p. 105.

[14] Pp. 86-87.

[15] London, British Library, add. Ms 34209 (the manuscript *L* in the Edition.)

[16] P. 247.

[17] Milan, Bibl. Capitolare del Duomo, Ms F 2.2 (manuscript *D* in the edition).

[18] Folio 128^v.

[19] Gregorio Suñol, in his *Antiphonale missarum*, perhaps following the usage of late manuscripts, perhaps only to avoid the issue, designates *Tenebrae* a "Responsorium."

At least four other chants that are properly Psalmelli (*Suscipiant domine*, for Annunciation, *Pacifice loquebantur*, for Palm Sunday, *Tamquam ad latronem*, for Holy Thursday, and *Occurrerunt Maria* for the Requiem[20]) were sung at Mass between the Epistle and Gospel, and are given the title Cantus (or Canticum) in the early Ambrosian books. These four are probably later assignments (some of the other reasons for thinking so will appear below), additions made when proper Cantus could, it seems, no longer be produced. In the modern Ambrosian books this same expedient has been used a number of times: *Timentes autem*, originally the Psalmellus at Tierce for the fifth Thursday of Lent, has been pressed into service as a Cantus for the late feast of St Joseph on March 19. The circumstances are similar in the case of *Afferentur regi* and *Dilexisti iustitiam*. These chants were originally Psalmelli "ad vigilias" for the Feasts of St Agnes and St Agatha, but in recent times have been sung at the vigil Mass of the Feast of the Nativity of the Virgin and the Feast of the Assumption,[21] respectively.

The substitution of "cantus" for "psalmellus" may be meant to indicate that the chant had a different mode of performance between the Epistle and Gospel than it would have in its normal position. (Unfortunately, the performance practice for the Psalmelli is not made entirely

---

[20] *Suscipiant* and *Pacifice loquebantur* have obvious points of similarity with other Psalmelli. (The second verse of *Suscipiant domine* can be found as the verse of the Psalmellus *Benedictus dominus*; the melody of *Pacifice* is very similar to that of the Gregorian Respond-Gradual with the same text). *Occurrerunt Maria* is normally the Psalmellus at Mass on the Sunday "de Lazaro," the fifth Sunday of Lent. The responsory *Tamquam ad latronem* for Holy Thursday is referred to in the Ordinal as "cantus lectorum," (*Beroldus*, p. 103) as "can[tus] lectori uni[us]" in the Metropolitano (f. 124) but (properly) as "ps[almellus]" in the British Library manuscript (p. 240). The assignment for the Requiem is given by Magistretti from a thirteenth-century source (see the *Manuale* I, 162). In Milan there was also a general Requiem (*Commemoratione omnium defunctorum*) sung on the Monday after the Dedication (later moved to November 2 to conform to the Gregorian usage); but for that occasion *Beroldus*, p. 128, assigns the Cantus DOMINE EXAUDI. See *Beroldus*, pp. 229-30, and Magistretti's note 269.

[21] Suñol, *Antiphonale*, pp. 454, 525, and 514.

clear in the early service books.) The use of the title "Cantus" is in any case understandable for chants found where Cantus were normally sung. Those acquainted with the Gregorian practice will recall a similar usage. Respond-Graduals (the equivalents of the Ambrosian Psalmelli) are assigned – usually with the title "Tractus" – in a number of cases where Tracts would be expected. Presumably these Gregorian assignments are also secondary.[22]

"Tractus" is never (as far as I am aware) found in Ambrosian books as the designation for the specific chant-type, but the Milanese did find other uses for the term. One of these was with reference to certain extended melismas. The "Tractus" *In tempore*, *Reges* and *Rex*, for example, in the British Library antiphoner,[23] are *neumae* – melodic tropes – provided for insertion ad libitum in the standard Mass and Office chants. "Tractus" is used similarly, from time to time (in place of the more usual term "melodiae"), to indicate an Alleluia melisma.[24]

I mentioned earlier that "Tractus" is also used as a designation for certain responsories of the Daily Office. In the first five weeks of Lent, except on Saturdays and Sundays, the Ambrosian liturgy required, after Tierce and similarly at Mass following None,[25] pairs of readings, the first from Genesis, the second from Proverbs – each followed by a responsory. For most days, the responsory for the second lesson after Tierce is not specified in the Manuale or the Antiphoner.[26] For the Proverbs lesson

---

[22] Wagner, *Einführung* I, 90; Hesbert, *Sextuplex*, p. lii; Paolo Ferretti, *Esthétique grégorienne* (Paris, 1938), p. 151. Helmut Hucke, in "Tractusstudien" (*Festschrift Bruno Stäblein* [Bärenreiter: Kassel and Basel, 1967], pp. 116-20) nevertheless argues that the second-mode Tracts are not simply Respond-Graduals.

[23] Pp. 182, 102, 36.

[24] Bedero, S. Vittore MS B, p. 306; Milan, Trivulziana MS A. 14, f. 2; Cannobio, S. Vittore MS (no number), f. 145^v; etc.

[25] *Beroldus*, pp. 86-87.

[26] *Manuale*, pp. 126, 128, 129, etc. The liturgy cannot be completely reconstructed from the Ordinal and the chant books. It might be supposed, at first sight, that no responsory followed the lesson from Proverbs. Although this remains a possibility, there are a few indications that make it unlikely. See *Beroldus*, p. 86: "Finito genesi et R[esponsorio], psalmello cum proverbio, presbyter ante altare . . . ." Two

at Mass, the Cantus of the Mass of the day was sung[27]; presumably the same chant served also for the second of the readings after Tierce.[28] On Fridays however, when there was no Mass,[29] the antiphoners do give responsories for the second reading, and these chants are called "Tractus." These five "Tractus," all employing more or less the same melody, are more properly Psalmelli.[30]

The most obvious explanation for the title – that these chants were sung *in directum*, and that the intended distinction between "Psalmellus" and "Tractus" is the one made by Amalarius in the passage given above – must be ruled out. The "Tractus" for the third Friday in Lent has a *repetendum*; and the Ordinal, referring to such pieces, mentions an alternation between soloist and chorus.[31]

It will be obvious from all that has been said above about the medieval terminology, that the Ambrosian repertory of Cantus is better defined by its musical characteristics than by rubrics. These characteristics we will consider in due course. For the moment, however, I want to continue with a few remarks about the liturgical position of the

---

responsories are specified in the analogous position on Holy Thursday (the first, a Psalmellus, the second the Cantus QUI EDEBAT). Moreover, the following rubric is found in the *Manuale* (p. 178) for the lessons after Tierce on the Wednesday of Holy Week: "Psalmell. de Iob et t[ractus?]" (followed, however, by the Psalmellus alone).

[27] *Beroldus*, p. 87.

[28] Cf. *Beroldus*, p. 102.

[29] As far as the lenten Fridays are concerned, the Ambrosian books seem to hold to a more ancient practice than the earliest Gregorian sources. Friday Masses are specified in the most of the Sextuplex Graduals (Hesbert, *Sextuplex*, pp. 58-59, 66-67, etc.

[30] *Beroldus*, p. 86. The "tractus" should be compared to the Psalmelli, *Deus manifeste*, *Speciosus forma*, etc. Although it may only be a slip, the Tractus for the fourth Friday of Lent is introduced as follows in the *Manuale*: "Psalmel. de Genesi Tract." It should also be noted that a quotation given above (note 26) refers to the responsory after the Proverbs lesson as a Psalmellus. The usage was not very strict in any case; Psalmelli are frequently referred to as Responsoria. See the *Manuale*, pp. 126 (notes to lines 6-7), 129, etc.; see also the British Library Antiphoner, p. 161.

[31] *Beroldus*, pp. 89-90.

chants, their function, their form and their performance – both before and after the appearance of the service books.

III

THE CANTUS IN THE LITURGY

To begin, on the following pages will be found a list of the Cantus in the earliest books, the chief liturgical assignments, and the scriptural source of the texts. It would appear that the proper association of the Cantus-Tract was with certain ancient lessons. It was principally a Mass chant, sung between the Epistle and the Gospel, the second and third of the readings required by the Ambrosian rite.

The Cantus shared the same circumstances as the other Ambrosian responsories (i.e. the Psalmellus at Mass and the Responsorium in the Office), that is to say, it was always sung in association with Scriptural readings; but it differed in important respects. These latter chants made use of a choral refrain and – almost certainly from the time they received their present elaborate musical form – only selected, appropriate, verses. The Cantus (and the early Tract, as Amalarius has made clear) was sung *in directum*, that is, without refrain, and without the participation of the chorus. Moreover, it would appear (from evidence that will now be presented) that the regular practice had been to sing, not selected verses, but whole psalms.

TABLE 1

THE CANTUS AND THEIR LITURGICAL ASSIGNMENTS[1]

THE CANTUS AT MASS

Christmas Vigil:	QUI REGIS ISRAEL	[Psalm lxxix, 1]
Epiphany Vigil:	SUPER FLUMINA BABYLONIS	[cxxxvi, 1]
Quadragesima 2:[2]	NISI QUOD DOMINUS	[cxxiii, 1]
	(ii) ANIMA NOSTRA EREPTA	[cxxiii, 6]
	(iii) ADIUTORIUM NOSTRUM	[cxxiii, 8]
Quadragesima 3:	AD DOMINUM CUM TRIBULARER	[cxix, 1]
	(ii) DOMINE LIBERA	[cxix, 2]
	(iii) HEU ME	[cxix, 5]
Quadragesima 4:	LEVAVI OCULOS MEOS	[cxx, 1]
	(ii) AUXILIUM MEUM	[cxx, 2]
	(iii) DOMINUS CUSTODIAT ANIMAM	[cxx, 8]
Quadragesima 5:	ECCE QUAM BONUM	[cxxxii, 1]
	(ii) SICUT UNGUENTUM	[cxxxii, 2]
	(iii) QUIA ILLIC MANDAVIT	[cxxxii, 4]
Lenten Mondays:	CONSERVA ME DOMINE	[xv, 1]
Tuesdays:	IN CONVERTENDO DOMINUS	[cxxv, 1]
Wednesdays:	DE PROFUNDIS CLAMAVI	[cxxix, 1]
Thursdays:	DOMINE EXAUDI ORATIONEM	[cxlii, 1]
Saturdays:	BENEDICAM DOMINUM QUI	[xv, 7]
Saturday in Quadragesima 5:	LAUDATE DOMINUM OMNES	[cxvi, 1]
	(ii) QUONIAM CONFIRMATA	[cxvi, 2]

Table 1 (continued)

THE CANTUS IN HOLY WEEK

Holy Thursday:	QUI EDEBAT PANES	[xl, 9]
Good Friday:	(TUNC HI TRES) BENEDICTUS ES DOMINE[3]	[Daniel iii, 51-52]
	(ii) ET BENEDICTUM NOMEN	[Daniel iii, 52]
	(iii) BENEDICTUS ES SUPER SEDEM	[54]
	(iv) BENEDICITE OMNIA OPERA	[57]
	(v) BENEDICITE CAELI DOMINO	[59]
	(vi) BENEDICITE ANGELI DOMINI	[58]
	(vii) BENEDICITE OMNES VIRTUTES	[61]
	(viii) BENEDICITE SACERDOTES DOMINI	[84]
	(ix) BENEDICITE SERVI DOMINI	[85]
	(x) BENEDICITE SPIRITUS ET ANIMAE	[86]
	(xi) BENEDICITE SANCTI ET HUMILES	[87]
	(xii) BENEDICITE ANANIA AZARIA	[88]
	(xiii) BENEDICAMUS PATREM ET FILIUM (QUONIAM ERIPUIT NOS AB INFERIS)	[88-89]
	SUPRA DORSUM MEUM	[cxxxviii, 3]
	(ii) DOMINUS JUSTUS	[cxxviii, 4]

Table 1 (continued)

Holy Saturday:
    (HYMNUM DANIELIS)
    BENEDICTUS ES DOMINE   [Daniel iii, 52]
    (ii) ET BENEDICTUM NOMEN   [52]
    (iii) BENEDICTUS ES SUPER SEDEM   [54]
    (iv) BENEDICITE OMNIA OPERA   [57]
    (v) BENEDICITE FONTES DOMINI   [77]
    (vi) BENEDICITE SERVI DOMINI   [85]
    (vii) BENEDICITE SPIRITUS ET ANIMAE   [86]
    (viii) BENEDICAMUS PATREM ET FILIUM

    (TUNC CANTABAT MOYSES)
    CANTEMUS DOMINO   [Exodus xv, 1]
    (ii) EQUUM ET ASCENSOREM   [1]
    (iii) ADIUTOR ET PROTECTOR   [2]
    (iv) HIC DEUS MEUS   [2]
    (v) DOMINUS CONTERENS BELLA   [3]
    (vi) DOMINUS REGNANS AETERNUM   [18]
    (vii) FILII AUTEM ISRAEL   [19]
    (SUMPSIT AUTEM MARIA)   [20]

    SICUT CERVUS DESIDERAT   [xli, 1]

---

[1] The numbering of the verses is according to the Ambrosian Psalter. There are, however, important differences between the Ambrosian version of the Psalms and the texts of the Cantus.

[2] For Quadragesima Sunday there was no Cantus in the early books. Lent, in Milan, began, not with the Wednesday before, but with the Monday following. For the Sunday "in capite quadragesimae" an Alleluia was sung.

[3] Because the Ambrosian versions of the canticles do not contain all the verses employed in the Chants, this Table gives the usual modern numbering. In some

Important indications that the Cantus had once involved whole psalms are provided by the choice of texts. These chants, whose place in the liturgy was fixed by the time of the earliest service books, are assigned only to penitential occasions. Yet the texts of the Mass chants (which are all taken from the Psalms) are not penitential but neutral in character. With perhaps one exception I will mention in a moment, an exception that is probably the result of a later revision of the liturgy, they are not obviously chosen to be appropriate to the occasions on which they are sung. Moreover, again almost invariably, the Mass Cantus with a single verse employ the opening of the poem;[4] those with more than one include the opening and the conclusion. Where the verses chosen have no special appropriateness for the occasions, such an arrangement, with the *incipit* and *explicit* of the poem, can be explained only as the remnant of a more luxuriant practice, the singing of the whole psalm.

I will consider at once the single exception to the first part of this last rule, and the one exception to the second. BENEDICAM DOMINUM QUI MIHI TRIBUIT is not the beginning of Psalm 15, but rather, Verse 7. However, in days when books were rare and much of the liturgy sung from memory, the divisions of Psalms into verses, and even the boundaries of the poems, admitted certain variations (I am not speaking here of the differences in wording that distinguish the Roman,

---

manuscripts (as in *MUh*, used for the Edition) the sixth verse appears before the fifth, doubtless to conform to the more usual order. The identification of the Latin translations used in the chants is far too complicated to be attempted here. It is worth mentioning, however, that the texts of the BENEDICTUS and the CANTEMUS, at least those verses that are found in the versions of the poems included at the end of the Ambrosian Psalter (see the *Manuale*, I, 164, 175, 176), are, with insignificant variants, those of the Ambrosian tradition. In the case of the other Cantus, the correspondence with the Ambrosian Psalter is not nearly as close.

[4] The psalmodic titles are not included in the Ambrosian psalter and have been ignored in the numbering. The Scriptural sources of all Cantus are given in Table 1. The so-called Psalter of Saint Ambrose ("secundum translationem sanctissimi ac venerabilis patris nostri Ambrosii") was published by Magistretti in *Manuale Ambrosianum I*.

Gallican, Milanese and other Latin translations of the Psalter).[5] In the Gregorian Office some of the longer psalms were customarily divided, and the parts – as though different poems – sung to different antiphons. At the Saturday vespers, for example, Psalm 143 is divided into two parts and Psalm 144 into three.

Although, as far as I am aware, none of the early Psalters divide Psalm 15 after the sixth verse, it may nevertheless be that the Milanese singers considered BENEDICAM DOMINUM to be a beginning. It does certainly introduce a section of the psalm that will stand alone,[6] and there is the analogy of Psalm 33 (*Benedicam dominum in omni tempore*), which has a similar incipit. This similarity between the seventh verse of Psalm 15 and the opening of Psalm 33 raises the interesting question whether the anomaly of the Cantus verse did not arise initially from a misreading of a cue "Benedicam dominum."

The conjecture that the Cantus psalm for Lenten Saturdays is irregular is considerably strengthened by the assignment of CONSERVA ME, the first verse of Psalm 15, as the text of the Cantus for the Mondays in Lent. If the texts of the Monday and Saturday Cantus were not meant to be from different psalms (Psalm 15 and Psalm 33), or were not at the time of the assignment considered to be independent poems, it must be accepted that the two Cantus were intentionally (and in the same week) drawn from the same source. That is not, perhaps, impossible. But there is nothing to explain the peculiarity, and if it does really represent the intentions of those who arranged the Ambrosian liturgy, it would be the single such instance in the repertory.

As for the second exception, the third verse of the Cantus AD DOMINUM is not the last verse of Psalm 119, but the second-last.

---

[5] See *The Oxford Dictionary of the Christian Church*, ed. F. Cross and E. Livingstone (Oxford, 1974), p. 1139, s.v. "Psalms." Concerning the various Latin Psalters in use in the West see Pierre-Patrick Verbraken, "Le psautier des tropistes," in *Research on Tropes*, ed. Gunilla Iversen (Stockholm, 1983), pp. 65-75.

[6] A modern Latin translation of the Psalms published by the Pontifical Biblical Institute divides Psalm 15 into two sections, the second beginning, as in the Saturday Cantus, with the seventh verse. See *Biblia sacra iuxta vulgatem clementinam* (Desclée, 1947), p. 8*.

Once again, it may be a simple slip. It seems likely, however, that this verse was preferred for the opportunity it provided, on the word "heu," for the (obviously) added melisma. (The musical structure of this chant will be considered later.)

Other internal indications that the Cantus were intended to provide for the recitation of whole psalms are furnished by the musical analysis of the chants. As we shall see presently, all Cantus conform to a pattern that was evidently suggested by the structure of the psalms. The Cantus melodies are, at the most fundamental level, simple recitation formulae.

LAUDATE DOMINUM, the chant for the fifth Saturday of Lent, may be the one exception to the general rule that the Cantus sung in the Ambrosian Mass have neutral psalm-texts. LAUDATE is a proper Cantus, both musically and textually (the whole of the brief Psalm 116), but it is probably a later assignment. Palm Sunday, although, of course, it falls in Lent, commemorates the triumphal entry of Jesus into Jerusalem a few days before his crucifixion. And the liturgy of the day developed, in the course of the Middle Ages, many of the characteristics of a festival (including, very often, processions and even dramatic re-enactments of the historical events of Scripture), features that came, in certain striking respects, to outweigh the penitential character of the season.

The fifth Saturday of Lent is – as it were – the vigil of Palm Sunday, and I would like to suggest that LAUDATE DOMINUM, because its text seemed appropriate to the joy of Palm Sunday, was substituted for the usual Lenten-Saturday Cantus. This hypothesis is supported by the singularity of the assignment (the fifth is the only Lenten Saturday distinguished by its own Cantus) and by the appropriately "joyful" character of the psalm verse. (LAUDATE is, however, used in Gregorian books for other occasions, the Saturday of the lenten Ember Days, for example, where its text cannot be thought especially appropriate.) There is also the consideration that LAUDATE – alone of the lenten ferial chants – has two verses. And finally, although this will not be presented until later, there is musical evidence that this Cantus is a late Ambrosian adaptation.

The Ambrosian liturgy for Palm Sunday exhibits a number of other signs of retouching,[7] and even instability. It is not, in fact, the principal Mass "ad sanctum Laurentium"[8] that survives, but the lesser one celebrated when the clergy returned to the (Winter) Cathedral; and for this lesser Mass (which itself is probably a later addition[9]) there is no proper Cantus. Instead, one finds *Pacifice loquebantur* (properly classified as a Psalmellus, if it is Ambrosian at all), whose text is a psalmodic pastiche[10] evidently compiled to be appropriate to the occasion, and whose melody is very similar to that of the fifth-mode Respond-Gradual with the same text assigned in Gregorian books for the previous Friday. One of the manuscripts of the Manuale contains a note[11] that identifies LEVAVI OCULOS (no other verse is specified) as the Cantus for the lost stational Mass, but this seems a very unlikely assignment, since LEVAVI is the chant for the fourth Sunday in Lent, and the importance of Palm Sunday suggests that its principal Mass would receive a proper Cantus.

It should be said that the neutral character of the Cantus psalmody is an important indication of its antiquity, for the ancient Mass and Office referred much less to the specific events of the Christian calendar than the liturgy of the later Middle Ages. When we add to this observation another, namely the unlikelihood that the Cantus and Tracts – among the longest and most florid of the Ambrosian and Gregorian melodies – would be special embellishments added as extra features on penitential occasions, we are led to conclude that these chants must have been an ordinary, not exceptional, feature of the Mass, and, that before the introduction of the Alleluias they had been sung more generally throughout the year.

---

[7] Some details of the Milanese ceremonies not described in the Ordinal have survived. See Magistretti's notes 197, 203 in *Beroldus*, pp. 210-213.

[8] See Magistretti's note 200 in *Beroldus*, p. 212.

[9] Such extra Masses, which were a regular feature of the Milanese liturgy, exhibit many signs of late composition. See T. Bailey, *The Ambrosian Alleluias* (The Plainsong and Mediaeval Music Society: Englefield Green, 1983), p. 36.

[10] Cf. Psalm XXXIV, 20 and Psalm LIV, 4.

[11] *Manuale*, p. 172; cf. British Library Ms add. 34209 (p. 223): "Ad mis[sam] olivar[um] can[tus] Levavi oculos."

IV

THE EARLY USAGE

The singing of psalms by a solo singer at Mass is certainly very ancient. It is described, and not as a novelty, in the Apostolic Tradition of St Hippolytus, a Roman document of the first part of the third century:

| Et postea [quam] episcopus obtulit calicem, [eorum] qui conveniunt calici psalmum dicet, omnem cum alleluia, dum dicent omnes. Cum recitabunt psalmos, dicent omnes alleluia.[1] | After the bishop has offered the chalice, he shall recite a psalm, one of those suitable for the chalice, [that is,] with an "alleluia," all joining in [at this word]. Whenever [such] psalms are sung, all shall sing the "alleluia." |

The opening words of a sermon delivered in Africa by St Augustine towards the end of the fourth century refer to a whole psalm (perhaps a relative of the Cantus-Tract, as I will explain) sung at Mass between

---

[1] Bernard Botte (ed.), *La tradition apostolique de saint Hippolyte* (Münster, 1963), p. 67. The passage is difficult, but the general sense is not at issue. I have preferred not to follow Botte's (French) translation.

the Epistle and Gospel,[2] that is, in the usual position of the Cantus in the Ambrosian liturgy:

Apostolum audivimus, psalmum audivimus, Evangelium audivimus; consonant omnes divinae lectiones ut spem non in nobis sed in Domino collocemus . . . .[3]	We have heard the Apostle [the Epistle], we have heard the Psalm [the Cantus-Tract?], we have heard the Gospel; the divine readings are all agreed that we must place our hope, not in ourselves, but in the Lord.

That a whole psalm was sung is suggested by the context. Augustine would hardly have used the word "psalmum," nor is he likely to have included it among the "divinae lectiones," if what was sung was a single verse.

---

[2] In the East, the singing of psalms between the Mass lessons is attested to in a number of the oldest accounts of the Christian liturgy. (See the *Apostolic Constitutions* II, 57, 6 [ed., J. Quasten in *Monumenta eucharistica et liturgica vetustissima* (Bonn, 1935), 182]). The arrangement survived in both the Armenian and Coptic Churches. (See J. Hanssens, *Institutiones liturgicae de ritibus orientalibus* [Rome, 1930] II, 344-45; *DCA*, 1789, s.v. "Responsoria"; Duchesnes, *Origines*, 178.) Psalms between lessons may be older than Christianity. Louis Duchesne (*Origines*, 179) remarks: "les chants de psaumes intercalés parmi les lectures de la messe remontent à la même antiquité que ces lectures elles-mêmes et . . . ils nous viennent en droite ligne du service religieux des synagogues juives. Dans la liturgie chrétienne ces chants sont la plus ancienne et la plus solenelle représentation du Psautier davidique." (See also, Martimort, *L'église*, p. 344, n. 2; *DCA* I, 740, s.v. "Gospel, the liturgical.") Eric Werner reminds us, however, that witnesses to the practice of the synagogue are rather late. See "The Origin of Psalmody," in *Hebrew Union College Annual*, XXV (1954), 327-45.

[3] Sermo clxv, cap. 1, *Patrologia latina* [*PL*], ed. J. Migne in 221 volumes (Paris, 1857-1866), XXXVIII, col. 902.

There are a number of other similar references in the writings of St Augustine:

Primum lectionem audivimus Apostoli . . . deinde . . . cantavimus Psalmum exhortantes nos invicem, una voce, uno corde dicentes, *Venite adoremus, et prosternamur ei, et fleamus coram Domino qui fecit nos,* et ibi: *Praeveniamus faciem ejus in confessione, et in psalmis jubilemus ei.* Post haec, evangelica lectio . . . . Has tres lectiones . . . .[4]	We have heard the first lesson, from the Apostle, . . . then we sang a psalm, exhorting one another, singing with one voice and one heart, *Venite adoremus, et prosternamur ei, et fleamus coram Domino qui fecit nos,* and then: *Praeveniamus faciem ejus in confessione, et in psalmis jubilemus ei.* Afterwards, the Gospel lesson . . . . These three lessons . . . .
Et ad hoc pertinet quod etiam apostolica lectio ante psalmi canticum praesignavit dicens, *Exulte vos veterem* . . . .[5]	To this belongs what the apostolic lesson before the singing of the psalm referred to in saying, *Exulte vos veterem* . . . .

(In the following, it is clear from the context that Augustine is referring backwards.)

Hoc ergo psalmum audivimus, hoc apostolum audivimus . . . .[6]	We have heard the psalm, we have heard the Epistle.

---

[4] Sermo clxxvi, cap. 1 (*PL*, XXXVIII, 90).

[5] Sermo xxxii, cap. 4 (*PL*, XXXVIII, 197).

[6] Sermo 170, cap. 7 (*PL*, XXXVIII, 930).

There is a reference to the Roman practice, a reference very similar in circumstance to those of St Augustine, in a sermon delivered at Mass by Leo I, Pope in the years 440 to 467:

Unde et Davidicum psalmum, dilectissimi, non ad nostrum elationem, sed ad Christi Domini gloriam consona voce cantavimus.[7]	Dearly beloved, we have sung with one voice the psalm of David, not for our own edification, but to the glory of the Lord.

No one, as far as I am aware, has made the suggestion, but it seems obvious that we must at least consider whether the psalm sung at Mass – in Africa, at any rate, between the Epistle and the Gospel – was not some form of the Cantus-Tract. This is, by no means, an implausible inference. I hasten to add, however, that there is little likelihood that the melodies sung in the fourth and fifth centuries would have survived intact in the Ambrosian, Beneventan and Gregorian service-books five, six, or seven hundred years later.

Although I will attempt to show later that it is nonetheless reasonable to infer that Augustine and Leo were speaking of the chant that became the Cantus and the Tract, there are what appear to be contrary indications. The use of the first-person plural by Augustine and Leo (particularly in the light of the description, given above, from the Apostolic Tradition[8]) might suggest the participation of the congregation. The *prima facie* interpretation of these passages might lead to the conclusion that the psalms at Mass were sung responsorially, that is to say that they were early versions, not of the Cantus and Tracts, but of the Psalmelli and Respond-Graduals.

This in fact, was Peter Wagner's view. He would have us see the two complete verses of Psalm 94 cited by Augustine in the second ex-

---

[7] Sermo iii (*De natali ipsius*, cap. 1) PL LIV, 145.

[8] It should be noted, however, that Apostolic Tradition refers not to the psalm sung between the Epistle and Gospel, but to another sung later in the Mass, after the Communion.

cerpt above (from Sermon 176) as the actual congregational responses.[9] This interpretation is not impossible, although the reference is far from explicit.[10] It must be said, however, that Wagner's two "responses" are quite opposite in mood, and even one of them would be rather ponderous as a congregational refrain for a psalm with only nine other verses. In the absence of specific references, one must be wary of concluding that the performance of the psalm at Mass was invariably responsorial. Augustine and Leo do indeed say, "we have sung," but the plural verb-form may be nothing more than a rhetorical reference to psalms sung by the soloist on behalf of all those present. "Cantavimus" (even "cantavimus consona voce") may be no more indicative of vocal congregational participation at Mass than the ubiquitous "oremus."

In any case, I would like to suggest that there is no need, in the circumstances, to insist on an absolute distinction between a "psalmus responsorius" and a "psalmus tractus." It is entirely possible that the form of the Mass psalm referred to by Augustine and Leo was altered in deference to the great popularity of responsorial singing in the late fourth and early fifth century. It would be a matter of little moment to incorporate a refrain. It would involve (as far as the soloist is concerned) no change whatever in what was usually sung.[11] It is, of course, also possible that the "psalmus tractus" had involved congregational refrains

---

[9] Wagner, *Einführung*, I, 81.

[10] Explicit descriptions of responsorial psalmody do appear in the writings of Augustine, for example, "Legenti respondentes cantavimus" (*Ennaratio in psalmum 40*, in *PL*, XXXVI, 453); but one would need to be quite sure that the references are to Mass. There is similar evidence for the East. In the Apostolic Constitutions (edited by J. Quasten, *Monumenta eucharistica et liturgica vetustissima* (Bonn, 1935), one reads (page 182) that the people were to join in with the responses ($\chi\alpha\grave{\iota}$ $\overset{c}{o}$ $\lambda\alpha\grave{o}\varsigma$ $\tau\grave{\alpha}$ $\overset{,}{\alpha}\chi\rho o\sigma\tau\acute{\iota}\chi\iota\alpha$ $\overset{c}{\upsilon}\pi o\psi\alpha\lambda\lambda\acute{\epsilon}\tau\omega$). In the later sixth century, explicit references to Mass do appear. Cf. Gregory of Tours: "ut diaconum nostrum qui ante diem ad missas psalmum responsorium decantavit . . . " (*Historia Francorum*, VIII, 3, edited by Bruno Krusch and Wilhelm Levison in *Monumenta Germaniae historica: Scriptores rerum Merovingicarum*, I (1951), 1, 328.)

[11] Consider the case of the Ambrosian canticle BENEDICTUS ES, which is sung to the cantus melody, and has a refrain, "amen" sung after each verse.

from the beginning, and that it was only later (perhaps when the psalm was abbreviated) that these were abandoned. And finally, it is possible that some of the psalms read at Mass were sung responsorially, others in directum.[12]

Amalarius's remarks and many other indications make clear that, from the beginning of its recorded history in the ninth century, the abbreviated psalm known as the Cantus-Tract was seen, not as an independent item, but, like the Respond-Gradual, as a dependent complement of the Mass lessons. But Cantus-Tracts involving whole psalms sung by a soloist are not essentially different from lessons, and the question naturally arises whether the Cantus had originally been conceived as one of them.[13] It seems unlikely that such a hypothesis can ever be proved, although I will later return to some of its interesting consequences. For the moment, there is the matter of the abbreviation to consider.

Whether it was a lesson, or a chant associated with lessons, the Cantus (as the evidence we have seen indicates) was severely curtailed. The most likely reason for such an abridgement is that the musical setting became so elaborate that it became impractical (in a Mass that was becoming more and more complex in other respects as well) to continue to sing whole psalms. St Augustine in a well-known passage, mentions a simple style of psalm singing insisted upon by Athanasius (ca 296-373), Bishop of Alexandria, a style that was "closer to speaking than singing" (*tam modico flexu vocis faciebat sonare lectorem psalmi ut pronuntianti vicinior esset quam canenti*).[14] In the same passage Augustine also mentions (and here he may have in mind the practice

---

[12] Michel Huglo has suggested just this in his interesting study of the sixth-century Psalter of St Germain. See "Le répons-graduel de la messe, évolution de la forme, permanence de la fonction," in the *Schweitzer Jahrbuch für Musikwissenschaft* (new series II, 1982), 63.

[13] See, above, the reference by St Augustine to the Cantus-Tract as one of the "divinae lectiones."

[14] *Confessiones*, X, 33 (PL, XXXII, 800). This passage was quoted by St Isidore in the seventh century, but he would have us see the practice as that of the "primitiva ecclesia" (ibid., note 2 [PL, LXXXIII, 742]), not only of Athanasius.

of Milan[15]) "the sweet singing" of the psalms that was "usual in his day" (*melos omne cantilenarum suavium, quibus Davidicum psalterium frequentatur auribus meis removeri velim*), a style that was probably more ornate, and certainly more seductive, whose effect he distrusted.

There is at least one difficulty with assuming that the Cantus-Tract functioned as a responsory. In the Gregorian usage, the Tract did not follow the Epistle; it followed the Respond-Gradual (as all who read this will know), without an intervening lesson. This apparent anomaly, two responsories and one lesson, has been variously explained. It is sometimes suggested that the Tract is what remains of the original Gradual psalmody, even that "the Tract was nothing more than the Gradual as it was chanted in seasons of humiliation . . . a third verse . . . added to the anthem."[16] This hypothesis does not account for the psalmody presently associated with the Respond-Gradual, nor does it explain why a Tract that originated in this way would have survived as an independent chant. These questions will be taken up again later, but, as far as the number of responsories in the Gregorian Mass is concerned, the arrangement in the Ambrosian books suggests another explanation.

There are indications that the Roman Mass, on which the Gregorian was based, might originally have been more like the Ambrosian, with two lessons, regularly, before the Gospel.[17] Such an early correspondence is actually found, in rare instances,[18] in Gregorian books. If such vestiges

---

[15] See Enrico Cattaneo, *Note storiche sul canto ambrosiano* (Milan, 1950), p. 12.

[16] W. Scudamore in *Dictionary of Christian Antiquities* [*DCA*], ed. W. Smith and S. Cheetham (in two vols., Toronto, 1880), I, 747, s.v. "Gradual": R. Hoppin, *Medieval Music* (New York, 1978), p. 129. Cf. Wagner, *Einführung, I, 99*.

[17] See J. A. Jungmann, *Missarum Solemnia* (5th edition, in 2 vols., Vienna, 1962), I, 507. Evidence for three readings in the seventh-century Roman Mass is found in the Comes of Würzburg (see G. Morin, "Le plus ancien Comes ou lectionnaire de l'église romaine," *Revue bénédictine*, XXVII (1910), 46ff.). There are similar indications in a fragmentary Beneventan missal (no. 421 in K. Gamber, *Codices liturgici latini antiquores* [Freiburg, second edition, 1968]).

[18] "Dans les rares messes [i.e., Gregorian Masses] ou la leçon prophétique s'est conservée, on exécute le graduel entre cette leçon et l'epître et l'alleluia ou le trait entre l'epître et l'évangile" (Duchesne, *Origines, p. 178*). See also Jungmann, *Missarum*, I, 543.

represent the general early-Roman practice, this is a virtually certain indication that the Cantus-Tract had never been part of the Gradual psalmody, that – whether as a lesson in its own right or as a responsory – the chant stands in its proper place in the Mass.

But to return to the question of the purpose of the Cantus-Tract, if it had not originally been considered a *cantus responsorius*, it is easy enough to see how it might come to be so perceived. The analogy of the Respond-Gradual and Psalmellus would have suggested this new function for the abbreviated remnant.

I want now to put forward a theory of the evolution of the Cantus-Tract, a hypothesis that, to be sure, cannot be proven from the documents presently available, but one that seems to explain the circumstances better than any now current. I would like to propose that the (whole) psalms referred to by Augustine and Leo were Mass lessons, not responsories. This, I would suggest, is the first stage. For Africa we have a number of references to the Epistle, to the Psalm (perhaps sung with responses) and to the Gospel, but no references to a chant that corresponds to the Respond-Gradual and Psalmellus as we know them. I am suggesting that such chants were not yet customary.[19] In the second stage, two responsorial chants were introduced into the Mass, not necessarily at the same time: the *Responsorium graduale* after the Epistle, and – except for penitential occasions – the Alleluia between the Psalm and the Gospel. I say not necessarily at the same time, since the symmetry of lessons separated by chants was quite obviously not a concern: in the Gregorian Mass there are regularly two responsories (the Respond-Gradual and the Alleluia) between the Epistle and Gospel.

If, as it appears, the Cantus-Tract of the service books is only what remains of a whole psalm sung at Mass, and if (as we assume) the reason for this abbreviation was that the manner of its performance had become elaborate and "musical," "closer to singing than speaking" (to

---

[19] Helmut Hucke has concluded that the *responsorium*, the relatively short chant, began to replace the *psalmus responsorius* only in the second half of the fifth century. See his articles, "Gradual (i)" in *The New Grove*, VII, 599; and "Das Responsorium," pp. 153-55.

invert Augustine's phrase) – if, in effect, the Cantus-Tract had come to be regarded as a chant and not one of the lessons, it is easy to understand why it might have seemed inadvisable to retain it when the Alleluia was introduced. In the Gregorian usage, had the Tract kept its place in all Masses, there would have been, for most of the year, three solo-chants in succession. The Tract and Alleluia are both long and ornate, and such a concentration of elaborate solo singing might well have aroused the kind of scruples that troubled Augustine and many other Fathers of the Church.[20] The old Tracts and Cantus, no longer lessons, but not needed as responsories, might well have seemed expendable after the introduction of the Alleluia, whose great popularity in the West led to its rapid proliferation in the sixth and seventh centuries.

As for the Ambrosian Mass (with its extra reading), the abbreviated Cantus, presumably no longer recognized as the remnant of a lesson, assumed another role and served as the responsory when the Alleluia was not sung; and the final arrangement of chants alternating with lessons (i.e. Prophecy, Psalmellus, Epistle, Cantus (or Alleluia), Gospel) was achieved.

---

[20] Saint Jerome warns those entrusted with the singing of the psalms in church (*quibus psallendi in ecclesia officium est*) against "theatrical melodies" (*theatrales moduli*). See his *Epistolas ad Ephesios*, III, 19 (*PL*, XXVI, 528).

V

THE CANTUS OUTSIDE MASS

Although the Cantus have no regular place outside Mass (the same may be said for the Tracts in the Gregorian usage), there are a few appearances in the morning Office and at Vespers that require explanation. The question is, why were Cantus assigned on these occasions and not Responsoria, the usual responsorial chants of the Ambrosian Office?

I will begin with those easiest to explain: the Cantus sung (as I have suggested above) as responsories following the second of the two lessons read after Tierce on weekdays of Lent. There is, unfortunately, no way of determining when these extra lessons were introduced, but if the second responsory is borrowed from the Mass of the day (where a similar pair of lessons was read), and the prayers and chants of the subsequent processions were borrowed from the ceremonies of the Major Litany,[1] it may be supposed that the whole arrangement is secondary, from a time when the principles that originally governed the assignment of chants to the Mass and Office were no longer understood, or were no longer in force. If any Cantus sung after Tierce on lenten weekdays were

---

[1] *Beroldus*, pp. 86-87; see also Magistretti's note 165 on page 202. In the Ambrosian rite the observances of the Major Litany were held on the three days following Ascension.

simply borrowed from the Mass of the day, their use on these occasions can be explained as a later expedient, and need not concern us further.

All the other Cantus used outside of Mass are to be found in Holy Week. The liturgy of Holy Week is in a great many respects a special case, for it includes a number of ceremonies that do not occur regularly, and among them, observances of diverse age and provenance. Some of these observances are of great antiquity, preserving features of the Mass and Office that have not survived elsewhere. Others are obviously of much more recent addition, borrowed or developed from practices that are foreign in origin, and on that account offering exceptions to any general principles that may govern the choice of chants for the rest of the year. Holy Week is a time of "almost Masses," of "not quite Vespers," when the usual clear division of the liturgy into Mass and Office is not always possible. It is not to be hoped, therefore, that the practice for the Holy Week Cantus can be fully explained, especially in the narrow context of this study. There are, nevertheless, a few observations to be made.

The Cantus for Holy Week, although they belong without question to the same musical class as the Mass chants, were not sung at Mass, at least not at the time of the earliest Ambrosian service books. Moreover, three of them are exceptional in another respect as well. It is clear that their texts, the first two of which are not the beginnings of psalms, have been chosen because they are appropriate to the occasions. QUI EDEBAT PANES MEOS is the very psalm-text cited by Jesus (John XIII, 18) at the institution of the eucharist on Holy Thursday, the day before his crucifixion; SUPRA DORSUM MEUM FABRICAVERUNT PECCATORES is meant, evidently, to refer to the sacrifice of Christ on the Cross on Good Friday; SICUT CERVUS DESIDERAT AD FONTES AQUARUM refers to the baptismal font, blessed at Vespers on Holy Saturday.

The position of the Holy Thursday Cantus is not perhaps as anomalous as it first appears. I have mentioned, now more than once, that on Monday to Friday of the first five weeks of lent, pairs of lessons (from Genesis and Proverbs) were read at an extra office after Tierce and also at the Vespers Mass; and I have suggested that for the readings in the morning the second responsory, which is not usually specified, was the same Cantus that is assigned for the second lesson at Mass.[2] On Holy Thursday the Cantus QUI EDEBAT is assigned as the second responsory at a similar extra office. It seems likely that this office, which is otherwise unexplained, stood in place of Mass on a day that was originally aliturgical. In such circumstances, the assignment of QUI EDEBAT seems much less irregular.[3]

The circumstances on Holy Thursday and on the ordinary lenten weekdays are not exactly parallel. At the Holy Thursay Mass it is not QUI EDEBAT that is assigned, but *Tamquam ad latronem*. This chant, however, and indeed the Vespers Mass itself, give every indication of being late additions.

As we have already seen, *Tamquam ad latronem*, the present Mass "Cantus" for Holy Thursday, is not properly a Cantus at all, but a Psalmellus – a piece evidently chosen for the appropriateness of its text, which refers to the arrest of Christ in the Garden. It must be said that the hypothesis that would have us see QUI EDEBAT as the original "Mass" chant leaves unexplained the choice of this particular verse, since the text of a Mass Cantus would not normally (the one possible exception I have already mentioned) be appropriate to the occasion. I can only offer the general observation that the use of specifically appropriate

---

[2] Only on Fridays, when there was no Mass, is the second responsory specified.

[3] It may seem surprising that the Mass for the Thursday in Holy Week, an occasion that might seem ideal to commemorate the institution of the Eucharist, should not be ancient; but there is Gregorian evidence as well as Ambrosian to suggest this. The earliest Roman sources also indicate an incomplete Mass on Holy Thursday. See H. Schmidt, *Hebdomeda sancta* (2 vols, 1957), II, 736 ff. It must be said, however, that the circumstances in the two liturgies are not otherwise parallel: the Milanese is, as it were, a Mass without the eucharist; the Roman, which begins with the Offertory, is on the contrary a Mass without lessons. It is interesting to note that the Gregorian Holy Week liturgy exhibits other signs of late revision. The Tract *Eripe me*, for the Good Friday Mass, was described near the year 900 as "nuperrime compilatum." This reference is found in the *Liber de divinis officiis* (*PL*, CI, 1209), sometimes attributed to Amalarius, although earlier it had been assigned to Alcuin. See Hanssen, *Amalarii*, I, 53-55; Hesbert, *Sextuplex*, lix. See also Apel, *Gregorian Chant*, 511.

texts appears to be a later feature. For those occasions when Psalmelli are substituted (when, presumably, genuine Cantus could no longer be provided), the texts of the Psalmelli are invariably chosen for their specific references to the occasions. The extra office after Tierce on Holy Thursday (and in any case, the chant QUI EDEBAT) may date from an intermediate period, after the Cantus psalmody had been curtailed, but when, nevertheless, a proper musical setting for such an appropriate verse could still be provided. The melody of QUI EDEBAT is in some respects irregular (this will be shown later), and the irregularities are of a kind that indicate a later date.

If QUI EDEBAT is not to be explained as a Mass chant, there is another circumstance that might also account for the use of a Cantus instead of one of the usual Office responsories. The chants generally known as Responsories are described in a number of ways: sometimes as occupying a position between lessons,[4] sometimes as "answering" the preceding reading.[5] The first explanation is merely neutral; the second – even if in some instances a relationship between the lesson and the preceding responsory can be demonstrated – is probably owing to a specious etymology: "responsorium" more properly refers to the chant's manner of performance (that is, with a choral refrain, the "response"[6]) than to any function as an "answer" to the reading that preceded. Examples of responsories that are obviously appropriate in this latter respect are rare, and some of the correspondences may be fortuitous, or the result of later contrivance.

There are, in fact, indications that some responsories were thought of as introducing lessons, that is to say that they were meant to refer forwards, not backwards.[7] One reads that in the Armenian rite psalms

---

[4] *DCA*, "Responsoria," p. 1789; etc.

[5] See, for example, M. Huglo, "Le réponse-graduel de la messe," p. 53: "les lectures de l'Ancien et du Nouveau Testament étaient suivies d'un psaume destiné à souligner le texte sacré"; see also W. Apel, ed., *The Harvard Dictionary of Music* (2nd ed., Cambridge, 1969), p. 727, s.v. "Responsory"; etc.

[6] Duchesne, *Origines*, p. 118, etc.

[7] See Jungmann, *Missarum*, I, 545.

were sung before the first Mass lesson.[8] I have suggested elsewhere that the Alleluia – which replaced the Cantus and Tract on most occasions – was thought of as a preparation for the Gospel.[9] Perhaps the Cantus-Tract, sung in this position when the Alleluia was not, came to have the same association. (It is interesting, in speculating on the proper association of responsories, to note that the Gospel lesson is not followed by a responsory: the Milanese *post evangelium* is a processional antiphon.) On Holy Thursday in the morning Office, a Responsorium might otherwise have followed the reading from the Book of Wisdom, but it may be that a Cantus was considered more appropriate when there was to be – as at Mass – a subsequent lesson from the Gospel.[10]

On Good Friday, exactly the same arrangement is found: the Cantus SUPRA DORSUM is sung as the responsory after the reading from Daniel at Vespers. But once again the lesson that follows is from the Gospel.[11] This explanation for the assignment of these two Cantus is all the more convincing when it is observed that there are (leaving aside the late borrowings from Mass discussed above) only four occasions in the Ambrosian liturgy – and for these four I hope to provide other plausible explanations – when the Cantus is not found in association with the Gospel.[12]

The few Cantus neither sung at Mass nor followed by Gospel lessons all occur in the ancient vigils of Good Friday and Holy Saturday. Although these appearances seem to present exceptions to the normal usage (the possibility that these Cantus were considered to belong to the same category as the Mass chants will, however, be considered in a moment), there can be no doubt that some at least of these exceptional Holy Week assignments are ancient. What is more, two of these chants

---

[8] *DCA*, p. 784.

[9] Bailey, *Ambrosian Alleluias*, pp. 11-12; Ewald Jammers, in *Das Alleluia in der gregorianischen Messe* (Münster, 1973), refers to the chant as the "Heraldruf."

[10] *Beroldus*, p. 102.

[11] *Beroldus*, pp. 107-108.

[12] I am aware, of course, that Psalmelli are also found before the Gospel, but I am assuming that these chants were assigned at a later time, when authentic Cantus could no longer be provided.

will be seen to be rare survivors (if somewhat curtailed) of the earliest practice: they are employed for the recitation of long psalmodic texts – in both cases, canticles.

The rubrics of the Ambrosian books specify two lessons at Vespers on Good Friday, each followed by a responsory. I have already mentioned that the second responsory, SUPRA DORSUM, is followed by a Gospel lesson, and I have suggested that this circumstance is the explanation for the assignment of a Cantus instead of the Responsorium that would normally be expected. The "canticum" BENEDICTUS ES, the chant following the first lesson, is also a Cantus, standing apart in some respects from the others, but belonging without doubt to the same musical class. It is not followed by a Gospel lesson, and must be explained differently.

The first Vespers lesson (Daniel, III, 3 ff.), the Cantus (Daniel, III, 51 ff.) and the second lesson (Daniel III, 91 ff.) appear at first sight to be three separate items. But they can also be construed as a continuous narrative, a narrative in which BENEDICTUS ES, the Canticle of Daniel, is sung, not by the lector continuing with the lesson-tone and the simple recitation style of prose readings, but to a more elaborate musical formula, one more appropriate to poetry.

The suggestion arises, in such a circumstance (where the "responsory" is in fact an integral part of the lesson), that the portion now identified as a Cantus was not originally conceived as an independent chant. What appear to be two lessons, each followed by a responsory, can be interpreted as a single lesson, its poetic portions distinguished by a changed mode of performance.

This arrangement, which we will see again, is not unique to Milan. The earliest Gregorian Mass books assign Tracts (these are the chants designated *cantica* that we have already noted) in similar circumstances on Holy Saturday. The first three of the four responsories are related to their lessons in such a way that the reading and the following chant form a continuous narration. Such an arrangement for Holy Saturday (with lessons and their responsories directly related) is not the only one to be found in the early Gregorian books.[13] But it may be assumed that

---

[13] The prayers and Tracts that follow are provided for only four lessons in some

the disposition in which the Canticles are introduced by the preceding lesson is older; in other cases, although some of the same lessons and responsories are found, this necessary relationship between the parts has been lost. I mention the Gregorian arrangement on Holy Saturday not only to show that the kind of relationship between lesson and responsory found on Good Friday and Holy Saturday in the Ambrosian books was more widely known, but also to suggest the priority and influence in these respects of the Roman customs.

To return to the Ambrosian Good Friday vespers and to what I have suggested should properly be thought of as a single long reading from Daniel, the musical formula that provides the changed mode of performance is, of course, the standard Cantus melody.[14] And in these circumstances, the assignment of a Cantus is perfectly understandable, for it was the original function of this chant to provide for the recitation *in directum* of just such poems. The Canticle of Daniel, which is very long, has been considerably abbreviated on this occasion[15]; only thirteen verses are sung, including, as usual, the opening of the poem and its conclusion.[16] But even though the complete canticle is not sung,[17] the

---

early Gregorian sources (see *Sextuplex*, pp. 97-98 and *The Gregorian Sacramentary*, ed. H. A. Wilson [London, 1915], pp. 54-55); in other sources, for six lessons and twelve (ibid., pp. 154-157, the so-called Supplement to the Gregorianum). Twelve lessons are called for in the very ancient Murbach Lectionary (see Hesbert, *Sextuplex*, lxi).

[14] This is the practice of Milan. In similar circumstances elsewhere the lector did sometimes continue, but the reciting-tone, and the style, changed (one encounters directions such as, "hic mutes sonum." See *PM*, XIV (1931-34), 271-72. Cf. Hesbert, *Sextuplex*, lx; Jungmann, *Missarum*, I, 435.

[15] Perhaps also the lessons.

[16] The conclusion of the thirteen-verse version of the canticle is a special doxology composed in the same style as that which precedes. Appended after this doxology are two concluding verses – *versus ad repetendum*, as it were. This conclusion, set to the same reciting tone as the introduction to the canticle (i.e., *Tunc hi tres*), is musically quite different and is clearly an added feature. It is not found in the Holy Saturday version of the BENEDICTUS.

[17] It is difficult to imagine that the entire BENEDICTUS ES was ever sung in Milan, at least not to the elaborate melody known to us.

Good Friday chant furnishes a revealing and rare example of the Cantus psalmody as it was before it was so severely curtailed.

On Holy Saturday, the Ambrosian vigil required six lessons. For three, Psalmelli are assigned as responsories. For the others, "cantica" are given. These are, of course, Cantus.

The text of the responsory following the third lesson, from Exodus, is taken from the same canticle (the Hymn of Daniel) as that of the first Vespers responsory on Good Friday. The Holy Saturday chant employs even less of the poem: only seven[18] verses (including one that is not found in the chant sung the previous day), and the same special doxology.[19] But the beginning, end and most of the verses of the second BENEDICTUS ES are the same on both occasions – as is, of course, the musical setting – so that the responsory for the third lesson on the Saturday is little more, in effect, than a shortened repetition of the Good Friday chant. It is as though the Holy Saturday responsory were simply borrowed, this impression strengthened by the observation that the Canticum lacks, in its second appearance, any connection with its lesson. This borrowing presumably occurred at a time when the special circumstances that had called for the use of the Cantus melody were forgotten.

The arrangements for the fourth reading at Vespers on Holy Saturday[20] are similar to those of the *Canticum Danielis* of Good Friday. A direct relationship between lesson and responsory (the Cantus *Tunc cantabat Moyses . . . CANTEMUS*) is again evident. The reading (Exodus XIII, 18ff.[21]) introduces the canticle, seven verses of which

---

[18] In the *Codex Metropolitano* (f. 133ᵛ) cues are provided for only three verses: BENEDICITE FONTES, BENEDICITE SERVI, BENEDICAMUS PATREM. The other four may, of course, have been sung nonetheless.

[19] In this case, the doxology does conclude the chant. There is no added concluding verse as there was on Good Friday.

[20] There is a difference of opinion between *Beroldus* (pp. 110-11) and the *Manuale* pp. 202-204) about the order of the lessons. The arrangement in *Beroldus*, where the lessons (from Genesis, Exodus and Isaiah) are given in pairs, seems more likely to be correct.

[21] This is the lesson specified in *Beroldus* (p. 110). In the *Manuale* (p. 203) the cue is "Haec est haereditas servorum."

(including the first and last) are sung. The kinship of the Gregorian and Milanese assignment for Holy Saturday is evident, for some of the lessons – and two of the responsories are shared. And moreover, these Cantus-responsories of the Easter vigil, although obviously of the same class of chants as the other Cantus, stand apart in some respects from the other Ambrosian examples. They seem to stand closer to the early Roman tradition that must be the common ancestor of the Gregorian, the Old-Beneventan, the Old-Roman[22] and the Ambrosian versions that we know.[23] It is interesting to note that, of the Tracts and Cantus that share texts, only those of Holy Saturday have the same liturgical assignment.

The last Ambrosian lesson of the Holy Saturday vigil is followed by the Cantus, SICUT CERVUS. The text of this chant, although appropriate enough for its lesson (Isaiah I, 16 ff), has no necessary connection with what precedes. But in any case its appearance, and (in this instance) the designation "canticum," is very likely owing to Roman influence: SICUT CERVUS is the chant generally given last for this occasion in the Gregorian books.[24] It is clear from these sources that SICUT CERVUS (no doubt originally followed by the continuation of Psalm XLI) was meant to accompany the procession to the baptismal font.

The use of psalms to accompany Christian processions is unquestionably ancient,[25] and the choice of a Cantus as the musical setting has obviously been made because this chant was considered appropriate in these circumstances. The assignment of SICUT CERVUS for the

---

[22] To avoid confusion, I should mention that "Old-Roman" is used here in its special sense, that is, with reference to the chants found in certain Roman books of the eleventh and twelfth centuries.

[23] The musical evidence will be given later.

[24] Where, as I have already mentioned, the designation "canticum," rather than "tractus," seems to be nothing more than the unthinking repetition of the title used (correctly) for the preceding chants.

[25] See T. Bailey, *The Processions of Sarum and the Western Church* (Toronto, 1971), pp. 93-101.

processional psalm is yet another indication that the Tracts and Cantus were proper for the chanting of whole psalms, and not merely selected verses. In Milan, SICUT CERVUS was obviously intended to serve as a responsory; it is another chant that is assigned for the procession to the site of the baptisms.[26] It is clear, however, from the earlier evidence of the Roman practice, that the assignment of the Cantus in this instance is secondary, from a time when the original relationship of type and function were no longer understood.

If the suggestions I have made are accepted, it will be seen that the assignment of all four Cantus not followed by Gospel lessons can be explained in the same way: whatever their latest employment, all had originally involved the recitation of extensive psalmodic texts.

I want now to return to a suggestion I made earlier: that the Cantus and Tracts are properly Mass chants. There are two types of responsories found at Mass. One involves relatively brief texts, and only rarely more than one psalm-verse. To this type belong the Ambrosian Psalmellus, the Gregorian Respond-Gradual and the Alleluias. It has been suggested that the Respond-Gradual had originally involved whole psalms. This is by no means proven and, in any case, it seems to me can only be argued in a narrow sense, that the chant we now know perhaps replaces a *psalmus responsorius* of quite different musical character. What does seem certain is that the present elaborate style of the Respond-Graduals and Psalmelli can only have been intended for brief texts.

The other Mass responsory (in keeping with all that has been said, it might be better to say, chant later treated as a responsory) is the Cantus-Tract. This type originally involved whole psalms, and although it may be supposed that the melodies had been somewhat simpler, their structure (as we will see) is such as to suggest that they were intended for the recitation of extensive texts, that the chants as they are known to us preserve at least the essential features of the original melodies.

The first type of responsory, represented by the Responsorium, was multiplied outside of the Mass; the Cantus and Tracts were not. One may speculate that the latter chants had been employed more exten-

---

[26] *Beroldus*, p. 111.

sively in the Office, and that they were replaced later, when the large number of lessons made it impractical to sing whole psalms as responsories. It may be that later liturgical ideals were better served by Responsoria that involved the participation of the choir than by Cantus and Tracts sung by a solo singer, even Cantus and Tracts reduced to a single verse. It seems more likely, however, that these chants had never been a regular part of the Office; that they belong to an earlier stratum in the development of the liturgy; that at the time of their vogue there were no regular occasions for them outside Mass.

Although the lessons and responsories of the western Office are very numerous, far outnumbering those of the Mass, the Scriptural lessons of the Mass and ancient Vigils seem to be much older. In the Greek Church, it would appear that the earlier practice prevailed: there are, in the Eastern Daily Offices, no (regular) lections from Scripture.[27] It has been suggested that in Rome, regular Office lessons – and their Responsoria – were introduced relatively late, perhaps only towards the seventh century.[28]

As for the few Cantus found outside Mass, some, as we have seen, are obviously late assignments; and those that are ancient – all found in Holy Week – need not, perhaps, be considered absolute exceptions. I have already suggested that the Cantus QUI EDEBAT of Holy Thursday is sung at an office that stands in place of Mass. I want to make the same case for the others. The Ambrosian Vigils of Good Friday and Holy Saturday included certain items – the *Orationes solemnes*, the blessing of the Font – that were elsewhere considered part of the fore-Mass (to use a liturgist's term). In the earliest Gregorian books (and doubtless also in the Roman books on which they were based), these observances

---

[27] In thus restricting the readings, the early Church may have been following the Jewish practice, which confined Scriptural lessons to the Sabbath. See F. Cabrol, in *DACL*, XV, 2232, s.v. "Leçons." See also Duchesne, *Origines*, pp. 48-49.

[28] Duchesne writes (*Origines*, p. 473.): "A Rome . . . les lectures, réservées d'abord aux antiques services de la vigile et de la messe, ne s'introduisent dans l'office qu'au bout d'un certain temps, vers le septième siècle." See also *DCA*, I, 951, s.v. "Lection"; G. Dix, *The Shape of the Liturgy* (2nd ed., 1945), p. 470; *DACL*, XV, 2232.

were usually included with the Mass pieces.[29]

The early Gregorian and Milanese books contain no regularly constituted Masses for Good Friday or Holy Saturday. On these occasions the ancient Vigils were retained (although, of course, they had come to include some items added only later). In the early centuries, these Vigils provided a focus for public worship on important days (when, nevertheless, the eucharist was not to be consecrated). That is to say that they served, in this respect, as substitutes for Mass. And in keeping with this, they included certain forms and observances normally confined to the Mass: lessons, and, whether as readings in their own right or as responsories, the Cantus and Tracts.

---

[29] See Hesbert, *Sextuplex*, lxi: "ces cantiques du Samedi-Saint doivent être considérés comme compris dans l'organisation primitive de l'Antiphonale Missarum."

VI

THE SINGERS OF THE CANTUS

Before we turn to the somewhat lengthy examination of the musical characteristics of the Cantus, something should be said about the performance of the chant. Unfortunately, the Ordinal and the Manuale are not very complete in this respect. It may be inferred from what indications there are that the Cantus was normally sung by the principal boy, the *puer magistri scholarum*,[1] presumably in the ambo.[2] The assignment of the *puer* associates the Cantus with the other elaborate chants of the Mass, the Psalmellus and the Alleluia: in these too, it is the boy soloist that was featured – the difference being that in their performance the choir had also a part. The *puer magistri scholarum* did

---

[1] *Beroldus*, pp. 75, 87, 101, 102, 111. There seems little doubt that (except for the cases specified below) only one boy sang. The remark, "pueri magistri scholarum canunt cantus et psalmellos" (*Beroldus*, p. 75), might be interpreted differently, but it is probably only an indication that two different boys sang these chants. Presumably, the Psalmelli sung in place of Cantus at Mass were also sung by the *puer magistri scholarum* (see *Beroldus*, pp. 49-50). There were, however exceptions. At the evening Mass on Holy Thursday, *Tamquam ad latronem* is described as a "cantus lectorum" (*Beroldus*, p. 103).

[2] See *Beroldus*, p. 110 (see also the instructions for the Psalmellus, p. 50).

not, however, sing all the Cantus. At the Mass (the evening Mass at Vespers) for the vigil of festivals, the *clavicularius ebdomadarius* (the *clavicularii* were drawn from the ranks of the *Lectores*) was to sing,[3] and from this may perhaps be inferred a general rule, that boys sang the Cantus in the morning liturgy, lectors in the evening.[4]

This "rule" nevertheless admitted exceptions. At the evening vigils of Christmas[5] and Epiphany,[6] a boy was assigned to sing the Cantus (perhaps in deference to the Christ-child?). On Good Friday evening, for obvious reason, "pueri" (presumably three) joined the *magister* in the ambo[7] for the singing of the Hymn of the Three Children in the Fiery Furnace. This *magister* is presumably the "ebdomadarius magister scholarum" who was assigned the responses ("amen") sung at the conclusion of the verses; it is unlikely that he joined the boys in the singing of the canticle itself. The introductory verse (*Tunc hi tres*) was sung by a lector alone. The long verse (*Quoniam eripuit*) sung at the conclusion of the canticle was begun by the *magister*, who was joined (at the words "Confitemini domino") by the "chorus." (These enframing verses, as I have already mentioned, appear to be a later addition. They employ quite different music. See the Edition, below.) The Cantus, SUPRA DORSUM, that closes this complex of two lessons and a canticle from Daniel was sung, as would be expected in the evening, by a lector.

The other version of the *Canticum Trium Puerorum* on Holy Saturday was also sung by boys (again, one may assume, three), in the

---

[3] *Beroldus*, p. 58.

[4] The same rule seems to apply to the Psalmelli. See above, page 52, note 1.

[5] *Beroldus*, p. 75.

[6] One of the manuscripts of the Manuale (*Manuale*, p. 86) contains one note: "cantus pueri Super" (i.e., SUPER FLUMINA).

[7] *Beroldus*, p. 107. The Manuale gives few directions about the singers, but in the case of this canticle remarks: "infantes cantent simul in pulpito cum magistro scolario" (*Manuale*, p 189).

ambo, the first verse, solo.[8] There is no mention of the participation of the *magister* in the shorter version of the BENEDICTUS, although one may perhaps assume that he sang "amen" at the ends of the verses, as on Good Friday. The canticle of Moses (*Tunc cantabat Moyses*) of Holy Saturday was assigned to four of the *clavicularii*.[9]

---

[8] *Beroldus*, p. 110. Cf. *Manuale*, p. 203: "Benedictio cum [in]fant[ibus]." In the *Codex Metropolitano* (f. 133), before the introduction, "Hymnum Danielis," is the rubric, "infans solus dicat."

[9] *Beroldus*, p. 110.

VII

THE MELODIES

In the pages that precede, there has been occasion to anticipate some of the results of the analysis of the Cantus melodies that now follows. Mention has been made of a "pattern that was evidently suggested by the structure of the psalms." It has already been announced that the "Cantus melodies, at the most fundamental level, are simple recitation formulae." Of course, such clarifications become apparent only gradually, after detailed study. But since it would be pointless to pretend to be entirely ignorant of conclusions already revealed in the course of previous arguments, and since to be generally aware of the conclusions is in any case helpful in the understanding of the rather complicated charts and comparisons that follow, it seems best to present these conclusions at once, trusting that support for them will not be wanting in the arguments and musical examples.

The Cantus melody is merely one form – one of the most elaborate – of a tonal structure found very widely in ecclesiastical chant, Latin and Greek, a melody whose simplest version is, in fact, the most common Ambrosian psalm-tone.[1]

---

[1] See T. Bailey, "Ambrosian Choral Psalmody: The Formulae," *Rivista internazionale di musica sacra*, I/3 (1980), 316. The form (with *initium*) given in Example

Example 1

The Most Common Ambrosian Reciting-tone
and a Frequently-Found Alternate Termination.

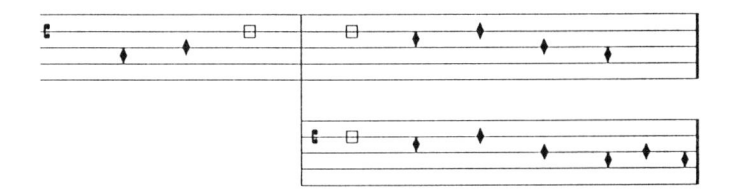

In the plainest Ambrosian psalmody this formula accommodated a complete psalm-verse. There was no mediant inflection, nor a second *initium*: the first semiverse concluded, and the second semiverse began, simply, on the reciting tone. The verses were treated, musically, as units. In Gregorian simple-psalmody, a mediant inflection was employed to articulate the psalm verses, so that the bipartite structure characteristic of most of them was paralleled in the musical structure of the recitation tone. In the case of the Cantus, which was not a simple psalmodic form but an elaborated one, the reciting tone was quadripartite: the semiverses of the psalms were themselves divided (often rather artificially), and the reciting formula – an embellished form (although not necessarily a derivative) of that given in Example 1 – was normally employed for each of the four parts.

It must be said at once that this simple explanation of the Cantus melodies does not take into account a complication, namely that the cadence at the caesura is always extended to conclude on the note f, and that the following *initium* begins consistently on that same f – so consistently that it might appear to be a structural tone, not (as is obviously the case at the beginnings of other phrases in the Cantus, where openings on f are also to be found) a prosthetic. It is proper to speak of a single complication, not two, for it is evident that these features are related – although it cannot now be ascertained whether the extension

---

1 is that of the Milanese *antiphona in laudate*. In the recitation of the Psalter the *initium* may have been absent.

to f of the phrase before the caesura was an added detail intended as a preparation for the idiosyncratic opening figure that follows, whether, on the contrary, it was this closing that influenced the following *initium*, or whether they were conceived together to mark the caesura.

The first of the three seems the most likely, for it can easily be shown that the cadence on f is not an indispensable feature of the Cantus. When there are too few syllables in the first semiverse to require both parts of the standard melody (the structures of all the Cantus are compared in Tables 2, 3 and 4 below), it is normally the second part, that ending on f, that is omitted. And in such cases, the second half of the melody, although following a musical phrase that terminates on g, begins as usual on f. That phrases beginning on f do not depend on a previous cadence on the same note is in any case obvious, for such phrases occur initially.

Although this is not the place to consider the precise relationship between the Gregorian and Ambrosian versions of the chants, it is significant, with respect to our understanding of the features under discussion, that in the case of the Tracts, the phrase-ending on f is not invariably associated with the caesura (there is no obvious reason for its occurrence; it may simply be a matter of musical variety). Nor is such an f-cadence, in the Gregorian versions, always followed by a phrase beginning on the same note.

There is no question that these irregular features are important in the development of the Cantus, but when all the variants of the basic formula have been compared and studied (the reader will not be spared), it will be seen that the complication is appropriately characterized as a detail.

The tonal skeletons of the four divisions of the standard Cantus melody, that is, the notes that provide (as I hope to show) the underlying musical structure of the (normally) quadripartite Cantus psalmody, are given in Example 2. Such simplifications of elaborate melodies are usually difficult to defend, and are very easily abused. In the present instance, however, the basic tonal structure I have identified is not a mere abstraction. It is an actual melody (as we have seen, the principal Ambrosian formula for psalmodic recitation) and, further, a melody that has a plausible association with the Cantus, which is, of course, a psalmodic form. Moreover, the relationship between the elaborated and simple forms of this melody (that is, between the Cantus and the psalm tone) will be seen, in almost every case, to be clear and uncontentious.

Example 2

The Structural Tones of the Ambrosian Cantus Melody.

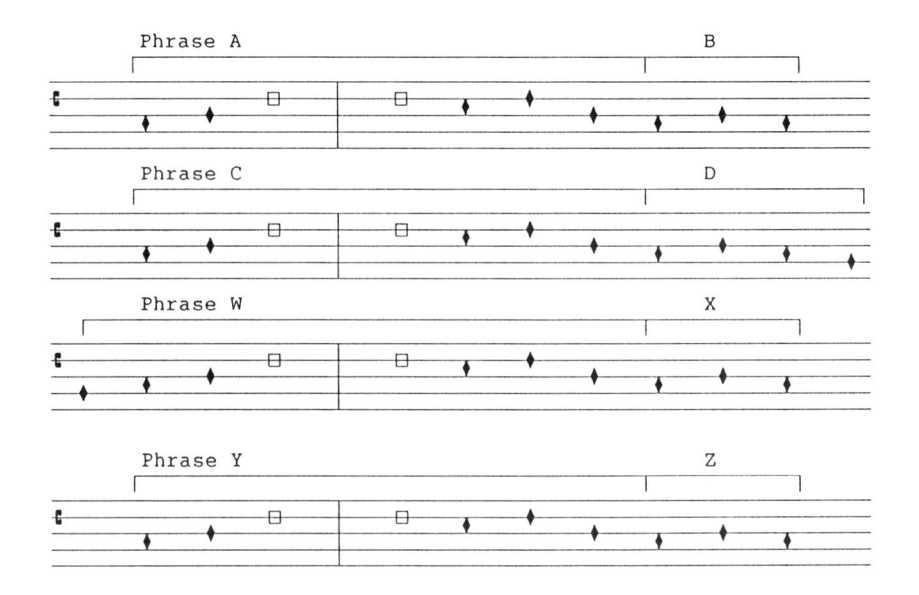

If the hypothesis underlying these analyses is correct, the music — I'm speaking, of course, of the essential structure of the musical phrases, not the melodic details — for the text-phrases of each subdivided verse ought to be syntactically interchangeable. This is actually the case, or very nearly, for the Old-Beneventan Tracts,[2] and for all but the initial and final phrases of the Gregorian versions. It may once have been the case for the Ambrosian. But while the earlier musical form of the Cantus may have been simpler — fluid, improvised by the singer for each verse of the psalm, closer to the psalm tone of Example 1 — the subsequent

---

[2] See *PM*, XIV, 371.

elaboration of the chant produced musical characteristics, inessential but stable, that now distinguish the music of the Cantus from other versions of the basic melody-type, and also differentiate, one from the other, the four sections of the elaborated formula.

In Example 2 (and in the various charts and examples that now follow), letters, whether upper or lower case, stand for related musical passages: A and C refer to the musical settings of the first and second parts of the semiverse before the caesura, W and Y refer to the music for the parts of the second half of the psalm-verse. The letters B, D, X and Z stand for very stable cadential prolongations – usually textless, and probably later features. Support for these assumptions about phrases B, D, X and Z will be given presently, but the reader may already have observed that such prolongations of the concluding note of the Cantus formula have their counterparts in simple psalmody. I am referring, of course, to the alternate termination for the simple formula given in Example 1.

In Tables 2 to 4 will be found charted the structure of all of the Ambrosian Cantus. The distinctions (indicated by means of upper- and lower-case letters), between exact, less exact, and incomplete correspondences, apply only within each table. However, all phrases identified by the same letters, whether in the Mass chants or the Cantus of Holy Week, are related. These charts contain the simplest representation of the structure of the chants, and it will obviously be necessary to demonstrate the correspondence of these schemata to the actual melodies. But before that is undertaken, it will be useful for the reader to observe the remarkable regularity of their formation.

The repetitions that will be noticed, in Tables 2 and 3, of the A phrase (with or without the cadential prolongation, the B phrase) require a word of explanation. Most psalm verses divide naturally into two parts, these parts usually related by parallelism or opposition of syntax and ideas – most psalm verses, but not all. There are not a few that could more naturally be divided differently. In simple psalmody, such irregular psalms are adapted, sometimes awkwardly, to the regular psalm-tone.

In the later Gregorian practice, psalm verses whose sense or extraordinary length call for more than one division are accommodated by the flex. Earlier, however, it had been the practice, when a three-member verse was encountered, to repeat the first part of the psalm tone.[3] A similar procedure was employed for the Cantus. Although a few cases must be explained differently, the repetition of the first part of the formula, the A phrase (or the A and B together) usually accommodates verses with a very long first-member, or verses whose sense (it would seem) called for more than one division.

In the Tables, some of the chants will appear to lack elements of the standard melody. Such gaps need not, in every instance, indicate damage, and the reader is alerted to two other explanations. Firstly, some of the Cantus are settings of verses whose first half is too short to be divided (DOMINE EXAUDI, BENEDICAM DOMINUM, DOMINUS JUSTUS), and in such circumstances it seems to have been the normal practice to omit the phrases C and D. In the case of the canticle CANTEMUS, the gaps in the alphabetic series are perhaps misleading. It is convenient, since it corresponds to the structure of the latest form of the Cantus melody (the form of most of the chants) to employ A B C D and W X Y Z to represent the musical divisions of the two halves of the psalm verse. But the melody employed for the verses of CANTEMUS may well preserve characteristics of a different and earlier form of the Cantus: elements B and X are perhaps properly absent.

While the structure of the cantus is fairly represented in Tables 2 to 4, these, of course, simplify things greatly. The details of the melodies present a good many more relationships than can be shown conveniently. This kind of deficiency is only to be expected in such representations (the more important of the relationships that are not indicated with letters will be pointed out later when the actual melodies are compared).

The charts demonstrate that some parts of the chants (the phrases represented by capital letters in Tables 2, 3 and 4) are melodically very stable, other parts (represented by lower-case letters) less so. The divergence occurs where one would expect it: in those portions of the melody that had to be adapted to different texts. Much of the stability of the melodies is owing to the recurrence of melismas.

---

[3] See *Commemoratio Brevis de Tonis et Psalmis Modulandis*, ed. T. Bailey (Ottawa, 1979), 16 *et passim*.

The melismas that I consider to be cadential prolongations occur so regularly in the Cantus that it is appropriate to assign them letters (B, D, X, Z). Since these insertions occur between the text-bearing phrases, the appearance of these letters does not obscure the structure of the chants the Tables are intended to clarify. But there are other melismas that are less regularly used, and as they have been inserted within phrases – not without a certain logic, as I will attempt to show – to have indicated them with letters or other signs would have rendered the Tables nearly useless. The reader must therefore be cautioned that the stability suggested for certain of the texted portions is slightly misleading. The close correspondence of melodic phrases identified with capital letters, A, C, W and Y, is partly owing to the appearance of recurring melismas that are probably later features.

Finally, before the Tables are presented, the reader should be made aware that much of the exact repetition of musical phrases in the canticle settings, especially in the settings for the second part of the verses, accompanies the literal repetition of phrases of text, these repetitions having, essentially, the effect of fixed "responses."

In Table 2 and in those following, capital letters indicate a close or exact melodic correspondence, lower-case letters, a less exact correspondence, parentheses, an incomplete melodic correspondence, and an asterisk, an extraneous insertion. The arabic numbers (as in A1, B2 and the rest) are used to distinguish stable variants.

TABLE 2.
THE STRUCTURE OF THE MASS CANTUS[4]

FIRST VERSES

Qui regis Israel		a	B2	c	D	w	X	Y Z
Super flumina Babylonis		a	B	c	D	w	X	Y Z
Nisi quod dominus		a	B	c	D1	w	x	y Z1
Ad dominum cum tribularer		a	B	c	D2	(W1)		
Levavi oculos meos	a B	A1	B1			w	X	Y1 Z
Ecce quam bonum		a	B1	c *	D2	W1	X1	Y1 Z
Conserva me domine		a	B	c	D	w	X	(Y) Z
In convertendo dominus		a	B2 *	c	D1	w		Z1
De profundis clamavi		a	B	c	D1	w		Z1
Domine exaudi orationem		a	B			w	X	Y Z
Benedicam dominum qui		a	B			w	X	Y Z
Laudate dominum omnes		a	b	c	D	w	X	(y) (Z1)
Qui edebat panes				c	D1	w	X	Y Z
Supra dorsum meum		a	B	c	D	w	X	Y Z
Sicut cervus desiderat		a	b	c	d	w		Z1

SECOND VERSES

Quoniam confirmata	a B a B	A2	B1	c	D	w	X	Y Z2
Dominus justus concidet		A2	B1			w	X	Y Z2
Anima nostra erepta	a B	A1	B1	C1	D2	(W1)		Y1 Z
Domine libera animam		A1	B1	C1	D2	W1	X1	Y1 Z
Auxilium meum a domino		A2	B1	C1	D2	W1	X1	Y1 Z
Sicut unguentum in capite		A2	B1	C1	D2	W1	X1	Y1 Z

THIRD VERSES

Adjutorium nostrum		A2	B1	C2	D2	W1	X1	Y1 Z2
Heu me quod incolatus	a B2	A1	B1	C2	D2	W1	X1	Y1 Z2
Dominus custodiat animam		A2	B1	C2	D2	W1	X1	Y1 Z2
Quia illic mandavit		A2	B1	C2	D2	W1	X1	Y1 Z2

---

[4] For reasons I have already given, I include QUI EDEBAT, SUPRA DORSUM, and SICUT CERVUS among the Mass pieces.

TABLE 3.
THE STRUCTURE OF THE BENEDICTUS CANTICLES

(Good Friday Version)

	Tunc hi tres[5]							M			N	
(i)	Benedictus es domine	A	B	A	B	A	B	C	D	W	X	Y1	Z
(ii)	Et benedictum nomen					a		C	D	W	X	Y1	Z
(iii)	Benedictus es super sedem					A	B	C1	D	W	X	Y1	Z
(iv)	Benedicite omnia opera	A	B	A	B	A	B	C	D	W	X	Y	Z
(v)	Benedicite caeli domino					A	B	C	D	W	X	Y	Z
(vi)	Benedicite angeli domini			A	B	A	B	C	D	W	X	Y	Z
(vii)	Benedicite omnes virtutes	A	B	A	B	A	B	C	D	W	X	Y	Z
(viii)	Benedicite sacerdotes					A	B	C1		W	X	Y	Z
(ix)	Benedicite servi domini			A	B	A	B	C	D	W	X	Y	Z
(x)	Benedicite spiritus	A	B	A	B	A	B	C	D	W	X	Y	Z
(xi)	Benedicite sancti	A	B	A	B	A	B	C	D	W	X	Y	Z
(xii)	Benedicite Anania Azaria					A	B	C1	D	W	X	Y	Z
(xiii)	Benedicamus patrem	A	B	A	B	A	B	C	D	W	X	Y	Z
	Quoniam eripuit nos	M		M		M		M			N		

(Holy Saturday Version)

(i)	Benedictus es domine	A	B	A	B	A	B	C	D	W	X	Y	Z
(ii)	Et benedictum nomen					a		C	D	W	X	Y	Z
(iii)	Benedictus es super sedem					A	B	C1	D	W	X	Y	Z
(iv)	Benedicite omnia opera	A	B	A	B	A	B	C	D	W	X	Y	Z
(v)	Benedicite fontes domini			A	B	A	B	C	D	W	X	Y	Z
(vi)	Benedicite servi domini			A	B	A	B	C	D	W	X	Y	Z
(vii)	Benedicite spiritus	A	B	A	B	A	B	C	D	W	X	Y	Z
(viii)	Benedicamus patrem	A	B	A	B	A	B	C	D	W	X	Y	Z

---

[5] The Good Friday version of the BENEDICTUS is framed by verses musically unrelated to the Cantus melody. They are set to an ornamented reciting tone, the two parts of which are indicated by M and N in this chart.

TABLE 4

THE STRUCTURE OF THE CANTEMUS CANTICLE

	Tunc cantabat Moyses[6]					M			N		
(i)	... Cantemus domino					n			W	Y1	Z
(ii)	Equum et ascensorem	A							W	Y	Z
(iii)	Adiutor et protector	A			c	D			W	Y	Z
(iv)	Hic deus meus	O				D		*	W	Y	Z
(v)	Dominus conterens bella	A1	B	C	D				W	Y	Z
(vi)	Dominus regnans aeternum	A1	B	C	D				W	Y	Z
(vii)	Filii autem Israel	O				D			W	Y	Z
	Sumpsit autem Maria					M	M	M M	N		
	... Cantemus domino					n	D		W	Y1	Z

In the following pages, in Examples 3 through 18, will be found comparisons of all the phrases identified by letters in Tables 2, 3 and 4. I want to be begin with some general remarks about the relationship of these phrases to the basic melody given in Examples 1 and 2, and about the arrangement of the comparisons. The structural notes of the phrases that are compared (the notes that form the simple psalm-tone of Example 1) are indicated in the musical examples by means of the wedge-shaped signs below the musical staves – these signs serving as well to align the melodies and make clear certain affinities obscured by damage. Although I have confidence that the relationship of the suggested melodic skeleton to the Cantus phrases will be seen without difficulty, the reader must expect to find in the developed melodies more than the bare reciting formula of simple psalmody. The Cantus *initium*

---

[6] The CANTEMUS is framed by introductory and concluding verses not properly part of the canticle. The melody employed for the words not found in the canticle is an ornamented reciting tone (the two parts of which are indicated by M and N in the chart), essentially the same as that for the framing verses of the Good Friday version of the BENEDICTUS.

is frequently introduced by prosthetic notes, the termination is almost always extended by the characteristic melismatic prolongation. Both *initium* and termination are variously elaborated: their structural intervals are often bridged by passing tones, and their structural notes, in the course of the elaboration, are often touched more than once.

All parts of the formula have been elaborated, but the elaboration is not uniform. Most, of course, is centred on the reciting note, and arose (in the first instance, at least) from the need to accommodate the formula to however many syllables the psalm verse presented. This prolongation is by no means confined (as it would be in the case of simple psalmody) to mere recitation on c', but it is clearly centred around that note

There is more to be said about the way the reciting tone is prolonged, but for the moment I want only to mention that the elaboration takes place in two ranges. One is situated mostly below c' (although d' is occasionally touched). This appears represent an older procedure. Sometimes, probably as the result of later elaboration, there is a further prolongation of the reciting-tone, a prolongation that seems not, since it is usually melismatic, to arise from exigencies of the text. This has a higher tessitura, reaching to e' and even f'.

Most of my readers will know that in simple psalmody, when there were too few syllables for the reciting formula, the *initium* and termination were regularly preserved, even if the reciting tone had to be omitted. In the Cantus phrases too, the reciting tone is occasionally absent. Some of these phrases appear to have suffered damage (by which I mean they are lacking some of the structural tones of the suggested type-melody, or have lost other melodic features found more or less consistently in related chants). Such damage is indicated in the comparisons by means of empty brackets. But other Cantus phrases in which the reciting tone is absent (the A phrases of BENEDICAM and QUI REGIS, for example) are perhaps to be explained – as in simple psalmody – by the circumstance of too few syllables. (Although the elaboration of the melodies has provided, in every case, enough notes for the syllables of the Cantus phrases, this elaboration may be presumed to be secondary, and to have occurred after the structure of these Cantus had been established.)

The text of the psalms is not included with the phrases compared in the following musical examples. Practical considerations make it impossible. But even if that were not the case, to include the text would reveal little beyond the fact that there was a tendency (doubtless the result of later conflation of the melodies) to repeat melodic details when words are repeated.

No one acquainted with early ecclesiastical chant will expect the meaning of the words to affect the course of the melody. (The treatment of the words "heu" and "jucundum" will appear as striking exceptions to this dictum, but there are other circumstances to suggest that this is the result of a later retouching.) No one would wish to deny that there is often in liturgical chants a connection between text and music, but it is normally a technical relationship rather than a semantic one. It has to do, not with the appearance of words like "up," "down," "fast," "slow," and their representation in music, but with the occurrence of accented and unaccented syllables at certain important structural points in the melodies.

The importance in the Cantus of this kind of relationship will need to be assessed, and therefore – although the words themselves cannot be included – I have indicated the position of the syllables, distinguishing those that are accented (these are marked with a small v-like trait), those unaccented (a dot) and monosyllables (the two signs superposed). In poetry with regular prosody, the accent (or length) of a monosyllable is generally determined by its position. Although the Latin versions of the psalms have some prosodic features and, of course, an obvious poetic character, they belong to the literary class of cadenced prose; the monosyllables, therefore, must be read as neutral, either accented or unaccented.

I must draw to the attention of the reader that the musical phrases (A, B, C, and so on) in the following comparisons are identified by the text incipits of the verses *in which the phrases are found*; these incipits are not, in most cases, the opening words of the Cantus (the words that usually identify the Chants). It should especially be noted that the words used to identify the musical phrases are not – except in the case of (most) A phrases – those that are represented by the signs that show the position and accent of the syllables.

The four versions of the Cantus given in the Edition do not, of course, agree in all details. And as none of the four has any claim to special authority, I have felt free to choose (in the relatively few instances where the versions differ significantly) the one that offers the most points of comparison.[7] This is not to ignore such differences (the versions of the British Library manuscript are particularly interesting, and may, in certain of their details, represent an earlier stage in the elaboration of the chants), but in keeping with the purpose of these tables, which is to show the operation of standard themes and secondary conflation.

There has been no rigid principle applied in the ordering of the musical phrases that are compared in the following pages. In general the melodies are arranged from simple to complex, and so as to bring together, as often as is practical, those that are most similar.

A number of the important conclusions that are to be drawn from these examples will emerge only after all parts of the melodies have been examined, and after the reconsideration of Tables 2, 3 and 4 in the light of the understanding that only a close examination of the melodies will provide. There are, however, some observations that are best made after each phrase is presented, while the musical examples are still at hand.

In the case of the more complicated examples that for practical reasons must be arranged over a number of pages, I have provided, in addition to the corresponding musical examples, tables that display the musical relationship by means of an alphabetic notation. No musician will prefer this kind of presentation, but it has the advantage that the relationship of a large number of phrases can be comprehended at a glance.

---

[7] Not wishing to complicate the examples any more than necessary, I have not indicated the sources of excerpts, which can be determined readily by reference to the edition.

TABLE 5

Phrases "a," "B," "B1," and "B2" in the Mass Cantus.[8]

```
Qui regis      :                   G            g A  [ ]                                                       BC   bA                              Ga     g
Quoniam        :                   G              A   C                                                        BC c Aggag                           Gab    g
Quoniam (2)    :                   G              A   C                                                        BC c Aggag                           Gab    g
De profundis   :                   G             gg A  C                                              b    a   BC   bA                     ba       Gab    a g
Super flumina  :                   G             gg A  C                                              b    a   BC   bA                     ba       Gab    gg
Levavi         : ddf       gf      C             gg Ab C                                              b    a   BC   bA    gf                aba     Gab    gg
In convertendo:       ag   Ga                    gg A  C                                              b    a   BC   Ag    a                 ba      Ga     g
Laudate        :           Ga                    gggA  C                                              b    a   BC c A     agf                       Gabc   ba g
Supra dorsum   :      g    G           bc              Ab  Cc                                         b        BC   A                                Gab    ba g
Sicut cervus   : g  g Ga   bc baa                gggAbaagCcb      c   ab    ag   bag  ababc aBC  bA                                                  Gabc   ba(g)
Domine libera  :           [ ]                   [ ]   C          dc             ab cb BC    A                                                       Gab    ba g
Nisi quod      :           gfe G                   g Ab Cc       cdc       b          ababcb BCdc A                                         ba       Gab    a g
Ad dominum     :      f    G                       g Ab Cc       cdc       b          ababcb BCdc A                                         ba       Gab    a g
Heu me         :           dGaba bcab            ccbgg Ab C  b   abcc           ba eab cbaBC  bAg agf                                       gaba     Ga     g
Anima          :      g    dGab  bc ba                 Ab  C     dcc            ba eab cbaBC  bAg agf              abagabaagf Gab    gg
Ecce quam      :           gfe G  cbc                  Ab  Cc                   ba eab cbaBC  bA                   baagfaGabcbaba g
Benedicam      :faabagag f aagf  G                     gg A [ ]                                BC   A     gfgg                     abaagf  Gab    gg
Conserva       :           ga gf [ ]                     A  C bab c babcaagfgabcbagg a      cbaBC  bA                                        ba     Gab    gg
```

[8] The quotation marks require explanation. The letters used to designate parts of the Cantus melodies refer to specific phrases only when they are given as "A" or "b," and so on. When such letters are given without quotation marks, it is the corresponding phrase of all the Cantus that is meant.

Example 3

Phrases "a," "B," "b," and "B2" in the Mass Cantus.

Example 3 (continued)

Example 3 (continued)

The phrases compared in Example 3 (except "B1") are proper to the first verses of the Mass Cantus. However, phrases "a," "B" and "B2" do appear, exceptionally, in some second and third verses – not in place of their typical A and B phrases, but introduced before them. This will be made clear by reference to the structure of QUONIAM CONFIRMATA, ANIMA NOSTRA and HEU ME in Table 2. These exceptional appearances are to be explained, in the case of the first two chants, by the extraordinary length of the psalm verses. It was apparently thought more appropriate, when the standard second- or third-verse formula was not sufficiently long, to borrow phrases from the first-verse melodies than to repeat the elaborated forms "A1," "A2" and "B1." An explanation for HEU ME will be offered later.[9]

In Example 3 the reader will have noticed that the A phrase of ECCE QUAM is followed, not by "B," the expected cadential prolongation, but by "B1," the more elaborate version proper to second and third verses. We will see later that ECCE QUAM has been elaborated in a number of other ways as well. There are no obvious liturgical reasons that would explain this special treatment.

Although the note g does occur among the prostheses, I have suggested by the arrangement in Example 3 that CONSERVA is lacking the first note of the underlying *initium*. The A phrases of QUI REGIS and BENEDICAM will be seen to lack the reciting tone. This, as I have already suggested, is probably to be understood as a normal psalmodic practice when the texts were very brief: in the first case there are only three syllables, in the second, only four. The A phrase of DOMINE EXAUDI has also only three syllables, but in this instance the adaptation is irregular: it is the *initium* that is omitted. It must be said that it is not unknown in simple psalmody to omit the *initium*, and the absence of the figure need not be considered certain evidence of damage. On the other hand, to omit the *initium* for the opening verse does seem unusual, especially in ornate psalmody, and in view of this, one should perhaps look for some explanation.

It may be, quite simply, that the original opening of DOMINE EXAUDI was lost (in an oral tradition, a not unlikely occurrence), and

---

[9] See page 79.

that its music was reconstituted by reference to the other melodies. The first phrase of DOMINE EXAUDI is quite similar to the corresponding part of NISI QUOD. (The similarity of DOMINE EXAUDI and NISI QUOD extends to the second half of the melody as well; see Example 11, below.) But if the singers did reconstruct DOMINE EXAUDI in this manner, it would appear that the formulaic basis of the Cantus had been forgotten, for the model has been adapted quite irregularly: only the latter part of the phrase is used, and only as much as needed for three syllables.

The reader will have observed, in making the comparisons just mentioned, that AD DOMINUM also resembles NISI QUOD. It may be, in this case as well, that the similarity is the result of an attempt to reconstruct AD DOMINUM after a momentary failure of the oral tradition, a failure made obvious in this case by the damage apparent in the latter part of the melody (see Table 2).

One is inclined to see similarities such as those between DOMINE EXAUDI, NISI QUOD and AD DOMINUM as significant because the opening phrases of the Cantus are normally differentiated. (In this they are unlike the Tracts, where – although perhaps through later revision – the initial musical phrases are almost perfectly regular). There are other similarities that should also be noted. The beginnings of DE PROFUNDIS and SUPER FLUMINA are identical, and the melody used is exactly that of the "A" and "B" of the BENEDICTUS canticle (see Example 5). I can offer no explanation for this correspondence, except to suggest that it is the result of a later conflation, and that the influence of the canticle melody, sung forty-three times on Good Friday and Holy Saturday, has prevailed.

The melodic details of ECCE QUAM, ANIMA NOSTRA and HEU ME are also very similar. The specific circumstances that led to this similarity cannot now be ascertained, although I will return later to the case of HEU ME, which does offer some opportunity for speculation in this respect. In any case, the conflation of the Cantus melodies, which perhaps ought to be understood as part of the process of elaboration, is only to be expected in chants so closely related, both melodically and liturgically.

In Example 3, the A phrase of BENEDICAM will be seen to stand apart from the other melodies. A comparison of Examples 3 and 12 will suggest that the beginning of this chant has been influenced by the distinctive opening figure of the phrase "W1." This brief melodic figure, as the study of these examples will gradually make clear, has been particularly pervasive in the conflation and elaboration of the Cantus.

The musical figure designated "B2" in QUI REGIS, IN CONVERTENDO and HEU ME, especially in view of the regularity of the other Mass Cantus in this respect, may appear to be nothing more than an incomplete form of the usual B phrase. There are, however, a number of indications that what has been preserved in these three instances is an earlier stage of the characteristic elaboration of the last note of the Cantus type-melody. First, the brief form appears several times; second, it is common in simple psalmody (see Example 1); third, the figure (as we will see later in Example 19) seems to form a recognizable constituent in some of the elaborated forms of the D and Z phrases (all the cadential prolongations are versions of the same figure); and finally, it is a normal form of what corresponds to the B phrase in the Gregorian and Old-Roman versions of the melodies (see Example 20). This matter will be taken up again.

I have already had occasion to mention that much of the variety encountered in the Cantus is owing to differing elaborations of the reciting-tone of the type-melody. Such diversity (inessential embellishments aside) is made necessary by the varying number of syllables in the psalm text. In the phrases compared in Example 3 it will be noticed that this elaboration takes place below the reciting tone; the d' above is reached only occasionally. In most of the phrases compared in the example there is a further prolongation of the basic formula between its penultimate note and the *finalis*. This feature, probably a secondary development, is not particularly striking in the melodies of Example 3. But I want to bring it to the reader's attention, since in other phrases yet to be examined, an elaboration at the corresponding point of the formula will be seen to be very important.

In simple psalmody, the adaptation of the text to the reciting formula is straightforward. In the case of the psalm tone given in Example 1, for instance, the melody is adapted cursively, that is, without regard for the accent of the words; the reciting tone is reached by the third syllable; the termination is begun on the fourth-to-last. The adaptation of the text to the A phrases of the first verses of the Cantus (although it may at one time have been more regular) is entirely casual. The form of B that concludes the first phrase of BENEDICAM DOMINUM, CONSERVA ME, ANIMA NOSTRA and SUPER FLUMINA might seem to have been intended to accommodate the proparoxytone of their final syllables. But if so, the accommodation is not very consistently carried out. A similar proparoxytone is found at the conclusion of the first phrase of DOMINE EXAUDI, NISI QUOD and HEU ME, and in these cases the "accentual" form of B (with an extra note at the end) is not used.

The accentual treatment of psalm formulae is a later development in simple psalmody, and it seems obvious that the "accentual" form (if such was the intention) of the B phrase is the result of a similar late retouching in the Cantus. The phrase B is not properly the termination figure of the type-melody; it is an ornamental elaboration of the *finalis* of the formula, an elaboration that has retained, in most cases, its original melismatic form.

TABLE 6

Phrases "A1," "A2," and "B1" of the Mass Cantus.

Levavi oculos	:	f G	A g	ccccc		Accdedcdbcbcdca Gabcbabag
Domine libera	:	G cc c	ggA	bccccc		A (etc.)
Anima nostra	:f aba ag f G		ggA g	cccccc		A (etc.)
Heu me	:fffaba ag f G		g A g	ccccc		A (etc.)
Quoniam confirmata:		G	A	bC	ba	BCbbAccdedcdbcbcdca Gabcbabag
Domine iustus	:	G c bcba	Abag ababC		ba	BCbbA (etc.)
Dominus custodiat	:	G c bcba	AbaggababC		ba	BCbbA (etc.)
Auxilium meum	:	Gab c ba	Abag ababC		ba	BCbbA (etc.)
Adiutorium nostrum:		dGab c ba	Abag ababC		ba	BCbbA (etc.)
Sicut unguentum	:	gagaef Gab c abcba	Abag ababC		babcbaBCbbA (etc.)	
Quia illic	:	gagae Gabbc abcba	Abag ababC		babcbaBCbbA (etc.)	

76

Example 4

Phrases "A1," "A2" and "B1" of the Mass Chants.

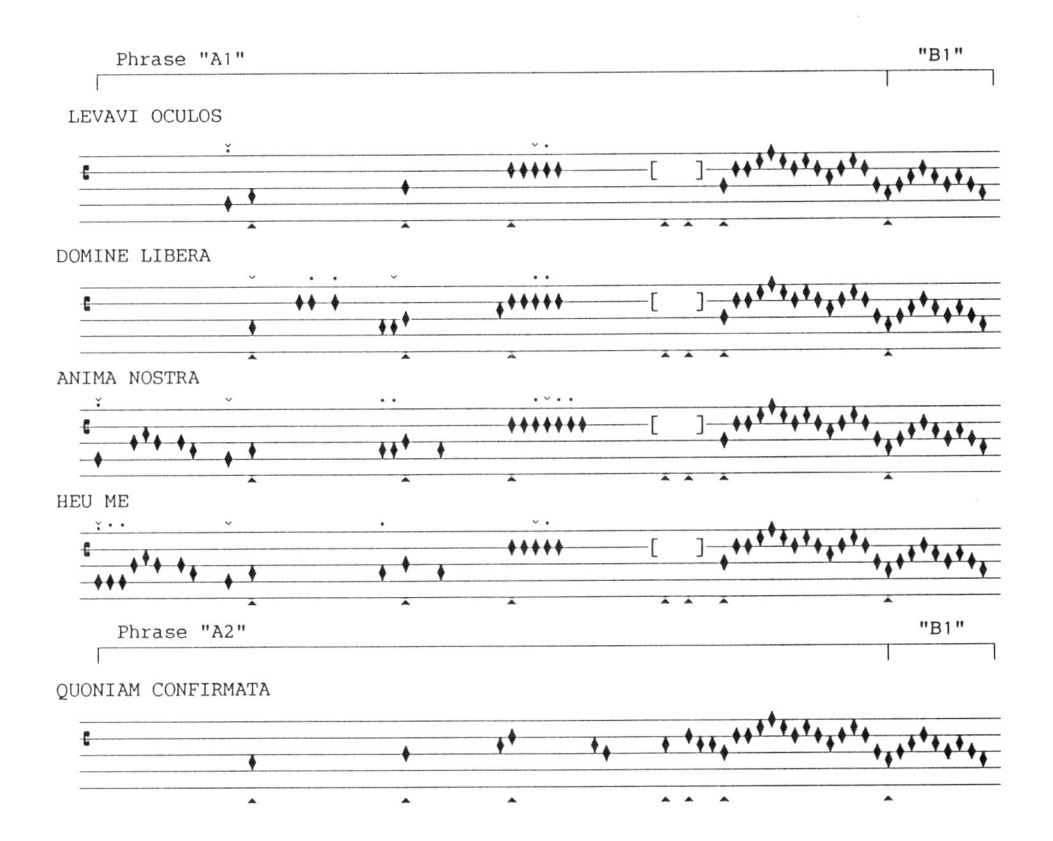

Phrase "A1"   "B1"

LEVAVI OCULOS

DOMINE LIBERA

ANIMA NOSTRA

HEU ME

Phrase "A2"   "B1"

QUONIAM CONFIRMATA

Example 4 (continued)

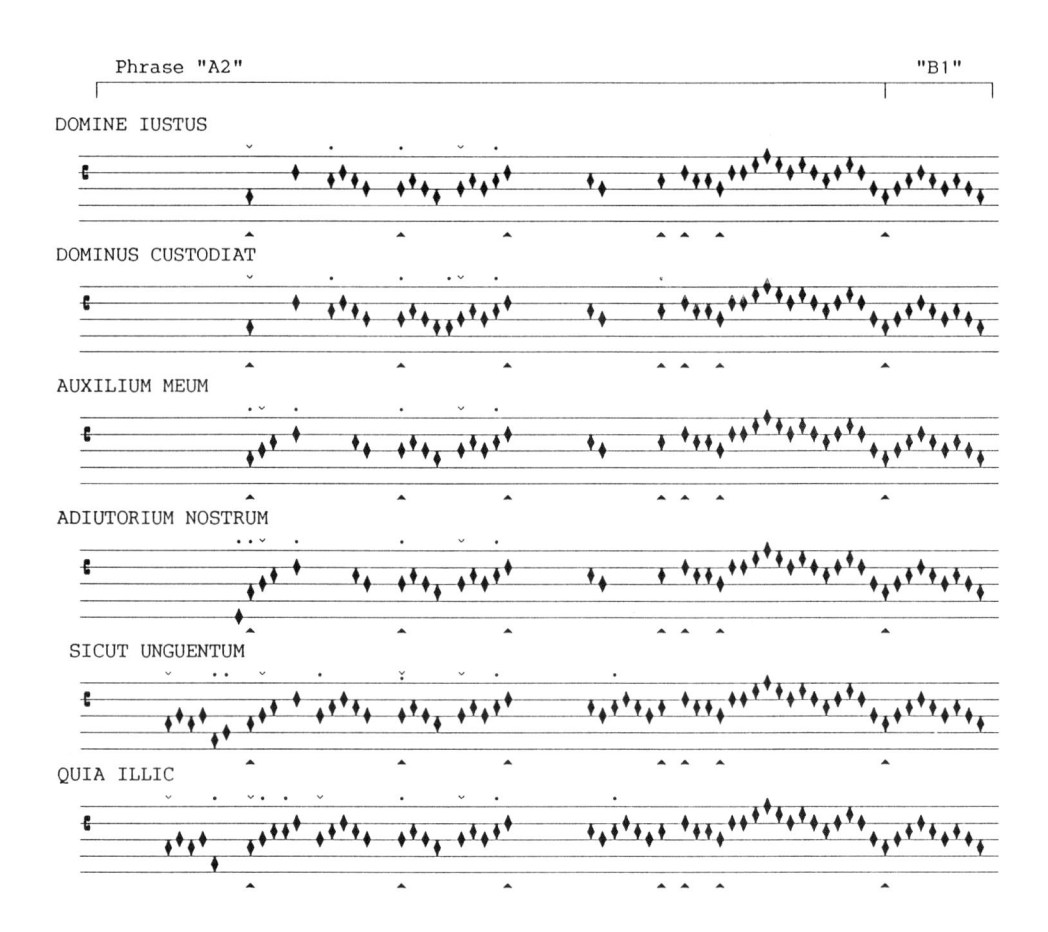

The phrases compared in Example 4 are proper to second and third verses of the Mass Cantus. The appearance of "A1" and "B1" in LEVAVI OCULOS and the occurrence (mentioned above) of "B1" in ECCE QUAM (LEVAVI OCULOS and ECCE QUAM are both first verses) should be regarded as exceptional.

"A1" and "A2" are much more stable than the A phrases of the first verses of the Mass Cantus, and are invariably concluded with the phrase "B1." It would appear that "A2" is the characteristic third-verse form. HEU ME presents an exception to this proposition, but one that can easily be explained. This chant begins with a long melisma on the word "heu," a melisma that is evidently a late addition (the reasons that lead to this conclusion will be given later). The melisma has been borrowed from the opening of ANIMA NOSTRA, or in any case closely resembles the beginning of this second verse. And the similarity (which we have already noted) has obviously led the singers of HEU ME to finish the melisma with the continuation of the ANIMA NOSTRA melody, i.e. "A1," instead of with "A2," the proper third-verse form.

The circumstances of AUXILIUM MEUM and SICUT UNGUENTUM can be explained similarly. The opening of these second verses might be expected to employ phrase "A1." Instead one finds the usual third-verse opening. But it will be noticed that the beginnings of these chants employ, quite exactly, the melodies of ADIUTORIUM NOSTRUM and QUIA ILLIC, respectively (both of these, third verses). And it may be supposed that the melodies presently employed for the beginnings of AUXILIUM and SICUT UNGUENTUM have come to replace (for reasons that cannot now be ascertained) those originally used for these chants. Such exact correspondences between text-bearing phrases of different Cantus are exceptional and are probably always the result of late conflation.

The reader will notice in Example 4 that the termination figure of the phrase "A1" does not correspond exactly to type. Missing are two of the "essential" notes of the psalm tone that forms, as I hope to show, the structural basis of each of the four phrases of the Cantus. These structural notes are not missing in "A2," which is very closely related, and it seems likely that their absence in "A1" is merely an accident to be attributed to a momentary failure in the oral transmission of the melodies. Although there are four appearances of "A1," they are all so similar that it is probably better to consider the "deficient" phrase as a single variant repeated, than as a confirmation of an independent tradition. However, the simpler outline of "A1," and the use in this phrase of bald recitation – which is not found elsewhere in the Cantus, but is a frequent feature of the corresponding phrases of the Tracts – should alert us to the possibility of Gregorian influence.

The beginning of "A1" in ANIMA NOSTRA and HEU ME has obviously been influenced by the characteristic opening of the phrase "W1." We have already noted a similar influence on the phrase "a" of BENEDICAM. That this kind of conflation was acceptable to the singers is perhaps further support for the suggestion made earlier, that the four musical phrases of the Cantus melody are fundamentally interchangeable.

The regularity of the second- and third-verse melodies aside, the principal difference between the phrases "A1" and "A2" and the opening phrases of the first verses of the Cantus (those marked in Table 2 with a lower-case "a") is that the former have been extended by means of a melisma. This melisma, always the same, is inserted following the last syllable, after the penultimate note of the termination figure. (An analogous elaboration, although not nearly so pronounced, has already been noted in the melodies presented in Example 3.)

We have already observed that the essential elaboration of the formula, that which was required to accommodate the varying number of syllables of the text, lies mainly below the reciting tone. The melisma inserted in "A1" and "A2" is purely decorative, and exploits a higher tessitura, between the reciting-tone and the e' a third higher. It is interesting, as a demonstration that there are certain persistent tendencies in the development of melody (in the West at least), to note that in "A1" and "A2" the added melisma – the cadenza, as it were – occupies the same relative position, just before the *finalis* of the formula, as the cadenzas featured in later European music.

The melodies used for the beginnings of second and third verses display much less diversity than the A phrases of first verses, but there is another important difference between the phrases marked "a" and those marked "A1" and "A2'." Whereas the placement of the syllables is completely unsystematic in the case of the former, in the latter (although an element of doubt must remain when there are so few cases to consider) there is some evidence of order. The position of the last three syllables in the phrase "A1" appears to be regular in three of the four cases. (The phrase "A1" of LEVAVI is set to only three syllables, and conforms as far as possible to the pattern.) There is no convincing evidence of accentual treatment. As for "A2," the last three syllables are placed regularly in all cases (all, that is, with text: the phrase "A2" is entirely melismatic in QUONIAM), and there is persuasive evidence that this placement has been made with reference to the position of the final accented syllable. The question whether this accentual treatment was an original feature of these phrases, or is owing to late retouching, will be considered later.

Example 5

Phrases "A," "a" and "B" of the BENEDICTUS Canticles.

```
                              Phrase "A"                        Phrase "B"

        CANTICLE VERSE

        1, 3-12, "fontes"    :   · ·  ˇ ·           ˇ              —
        1(2), 4(2), 4(3),
            6(2), 10(2)      :   — ˇ    —           ·              —    ·
        1(3), 7(2), 9(2),
            11(2), 13(2)     :   — ˇ    —           ·              —
        7(3)                 :   · ˇ    —           ·              —
        10(3), 11(3), 13(3)  :   · ˇ    —           ·              —    ·
        13                   :   · ·   · ˇ          ·              —
```

VERSE 2

The phrase "A" of the canticle BENEDICTUS is so regular that its twenty-nine adaptations can be represented with only two lines of music. In Example 5, the numbers 1 to 13 in the left-hand column are the verse-numbers of the longer, Good Friday, version of the canticle; "fontes" refers to "Benedicite fontes," the only additional verse found in the second version. The numbers in parentheses indicate whether it is the first, second or third appearance of the motive that is referred to. Otherwise the arrangement in the example is obvious enough. Notes not found in all cases are given in parentheses (in the columns above, a dash shows where the extra note is not required); the accent of the syllables is indicated in the usual way.

The phrase "A" in the BENEDICTUS is very simple, and conforms closely to the suggested type (the structural notes are indicated, as in Examples 3 and 4, with wedge-like signs). The phrase "a," although it bears an obvious relationship to the "A" used for the twelve other verses (and, of course, to the A phrases of all the Cantus melodies), sets the beginning of the second verse of the BENEDICTUS apart from the rest of the canticle.

There is nothing to explain this singular treatment. The sense of the first text-phrase of Verse 2 does not allow its twelve syllables to be divided naturally, but the same can be said of many other long first-phrases that have been, nevertheless, divided and adapted to "A" in the usual way. The source of the irregular melody for the opening of the second verse is easily found: the BENEDICTUS phrase "a" bears an unmistakeable likeness to the "A" melody of CANTEMUS DOMINO, the other canticle. This relationship is confirmed by the absence, in both cases, of the the B phrase, an absence that would appear to be normal in the CANTEMUS, but exceptional (and otherwise unexplained) in the BENEDICTUS.

There is clear evidence of accentual treatment in the adaptation of the phrase "A" of the BENEDICTUS; however, it is interesting to observe that the procedure is not consistent. A close study of the examples will reveal, for one thing, that the prosthetic g is sometimes used where it is not strictly necessary. There is also another more obvious inconsistency: a proparoxytone in the last syllables is on eight occasions accompanied by the "accentual" form of the B phrase. But far more often (in the case of the proparoxytone presented by the last three syllables of "Benedictus es" and "Benedicite," for example, which are so often repeated) the same pattern is accommodated by the (second) epenthetic note a, and the usual form of the B phrase.

The reader will have observed in Table 3 that the Good Friday version of the BENEDICTUS is framed by verses musically unrelated to the Cantus melody. They are set to an ornamented reciting tone (the two parts of which are indicated by M and N in the table).[10] This reciting tone is essentially the same as that used for the verses that frame the CANTEMUS on Holy Saturday, although, curiously, a different pitch-level is chosen for the second occasion. (The special verses that introduce and conclude the BENEDICTUS and the CANTEMUS can be compared in the Edition.)

Example 6

The A and B Phrases of the CANTEMUS.

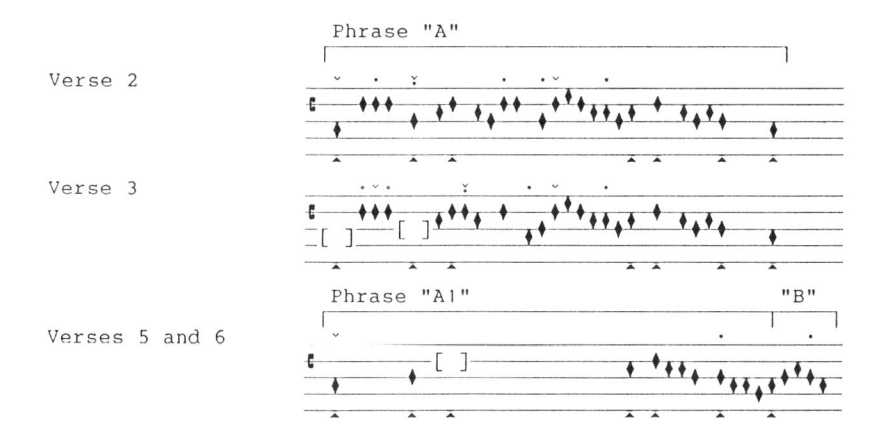

---

[10] Suñol, in the *Antiphonale missarum* of 1935, lists the introductory verse *Tunc hi tres* among the Psalmelli (to which it has certain similarities). However, the related introduction to the CANTEMUS DOMINO (i.e., *Tunc cantabat Moyses*) he lists only under "Varia."

As we have noted just above, the CANTEMUS (like the BENEDICTUS) is framed by a pair of verses that were evidently later additions. The introductory verse (*Tunc cantabat Moyses*), although musically unrelated to the Cantus, has intruded upon the structure of the Chant. The first syllables of the canticle proper (i.e. "cantemus") are not set to motive "A," as would be expected, but to a phrase that is obviously related to the melody of the added introduction.[11] (The comparison can be made by referring to the Edition.)

The melody used for the concluding verse is similar to that of the introduction and foreign to the Cantus. The text (*Sumpsit autem Maria*) is not properly part of the canticle, even though some of the words are repeated (the second "cantemus domino," etc., is spoken by the prophetess Miriam – i.e., Maria – not by Moses). However, the words of Moses repeated by Miriam are given the same music the second time – an obvious procedure, but one that tends to confuse the form by returning to the authentic melody of the Cantus at the close of the "foreign" setting of the added conclusion.

The A phrase of the third verse of CANTEMUS may have lost its *initium*. If the beginning is explained as a prosthetic recitation, the melody can be made to conform easily enough to the suggested type, since all the notes of the basic reciting formula do actually appear. There is, however, no need to force this issue. The phrase is perhaps better explained by reference to the A phrase of Verse 2, in which the operation of the standard formula is clear and uncontentious. (The melody of the second verse should also be compared to the beginnings of the Mass chants SUPRA DORSUM, SICUT CERVUS, ECCE QUAM, etc.) When the A phrases of the second and third verses are compared, they will be seen to have so much else in common that some of the notes

---

[11] It is interesting to observe that in *MUh* (see, below, the Edition) the melody for the last three syllables of the introductory verse and for the first four syllables of the Canticle has been revised, obviously in the interest of tonal consistency. *MUh*, written in 1387, is considerably later than the other sources used for the edition, but unease about the irregular beginning of the CANTEMUS is perhaps also the explanation for a variant in *D*, a manuscript of the twelfth century, where (as also in *MUh*) the melody of the fourth syllable, (Cantemus *domino*), reaches c'.

missing in Verse 3 (these suggested "defects" are indicated by means of brackets in the comparison) might plausibly be repaired. It is, however, common practice in simple psalmody to omit the *initium* after the first verse, and the absence of the figure is not certain evidence of damage.

The fifth and sixth verses are somewhat irregular. The absence of the reciting-tone is probably to be explained (as before) by the shortness of the text: in each there are only three syllables. The B phrase, not otherwise found in the CANTEMUS canticle, may have been added as a makeweight by later singers accustomed to the figure in the other Cantus.

Although I have not included it in Example 6, the elaborate melody (designated "O" in Table 4) for the first part of the fourth and seventh verses requires some comment. This phrase exploits the high range in a way that might suggest a relationship with the similar elaboration of the A and C phrases of the second and third verses of the Mass Cantus. But the irregular melody for the two canticle verses, although one cannot rule out the possibility that it has developed from some version of the A phrase, can now only be treated as extraneous. In some respects at least the phrase is congruent with the others: it centres around the same c' (the reciting tone of the underlying psalmodic formula of the Cantus), and it seems to conclude with the usual termination figure. The two appearances of the phrase "O" can be compared in the Edition.

"O" would seem to replace some combination of A and C phrases of an earlier version. There is nothing (it might be safer to say, nothing obvious) about the texts that would explain this special treatment. The additional musical phrase inserted after "O" in Verse 4 (this is represented in Table 4 by the asterisk, and occurs with the words "Deus patris mei") is extraneous, although it employs familiar motives. Since this extra phrase has been required by the very long text of the verse, it would appear to be part of the same late revision that resulted in the substitution of "O" for the standard melodic phrases employed in the other verses of the canticle. It is clear that at the time the canticle was revised the adaptation of text to a standard melody was no longer understood.

It will be noticed that there is some regularity in the adaptation of the melody to the text in the CANTEMUS, although only with respect to the last three or four syllables. There is perhaps too little evidence to really decide the question, but there is also some indication of concern for the text accent in the placement of the last two (three, in the case of a proparoxytone).

TABLE 7

Phrases "c," "D," "d," "D1," and "D2" in the Mass Cantus.

```
Laudate         :            (G)b A b C ba    B  C         Agf                       G a  gbcbabagagf
Conserva        : g       G     A b Cc a a B  C         Agfg                      G a  gbcbabagagf
Qui regis       : g     g G     A b C ba      B  C  cbcb A                        G a  gbcbabagagf
Quoniam         : gaf   g G     A b C ba  a[ ][ ]dc     Agf                       G a  gbcbabagagf
Supra dorsum    : g   d   G     A b[ ]        B  C  dc  Agfg                      G a  gbcbabagagf
Ad Dominum      : g   e   G     A b[ ]b       B  Cddc   b A                       G abagbcbabagagf
Ecce quam       : g fe    G  bgA b C ba       B  C      bbA *          bag        eG abagbcbabagagf
Sicut cervus    : g     gaG  [ ]b C babagB    C         b A            bag        Gfa  g   abag   f
Nisi quod       :         G     A b C ba   [ ][ ]       A   a bababagagb          G a  g   abagagf
In convertendo  : g   dg G      A b[ ] a a B  C         b Ag   abba    agag       G a  g   abagagf
Super flumina   : g       G b A b[ ]       [ ][ ]       Ag ga bab baga bbag  G a  gbcbabagagf
De profundis    : g       G     A b[ ] a   [ ][ ]       Ag   abbaba    agagb      G a  g   abagagf
Qui edebat      : g     g G     A b[ ] a a[ ][ ]        A   a bababagagb          G a  g   abagagf
```

87

Example 7

The Phrases "c," "D," "D1," "D2" and "d" in the Mass Cantus.

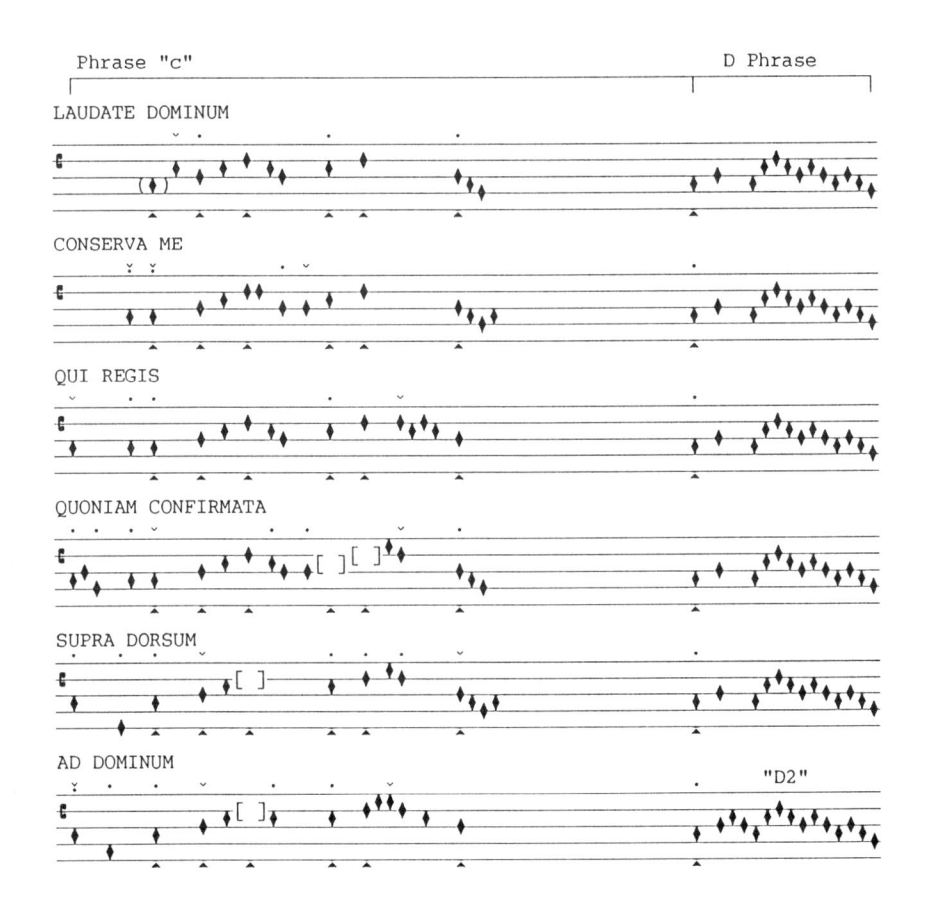

Example 7 (continued)

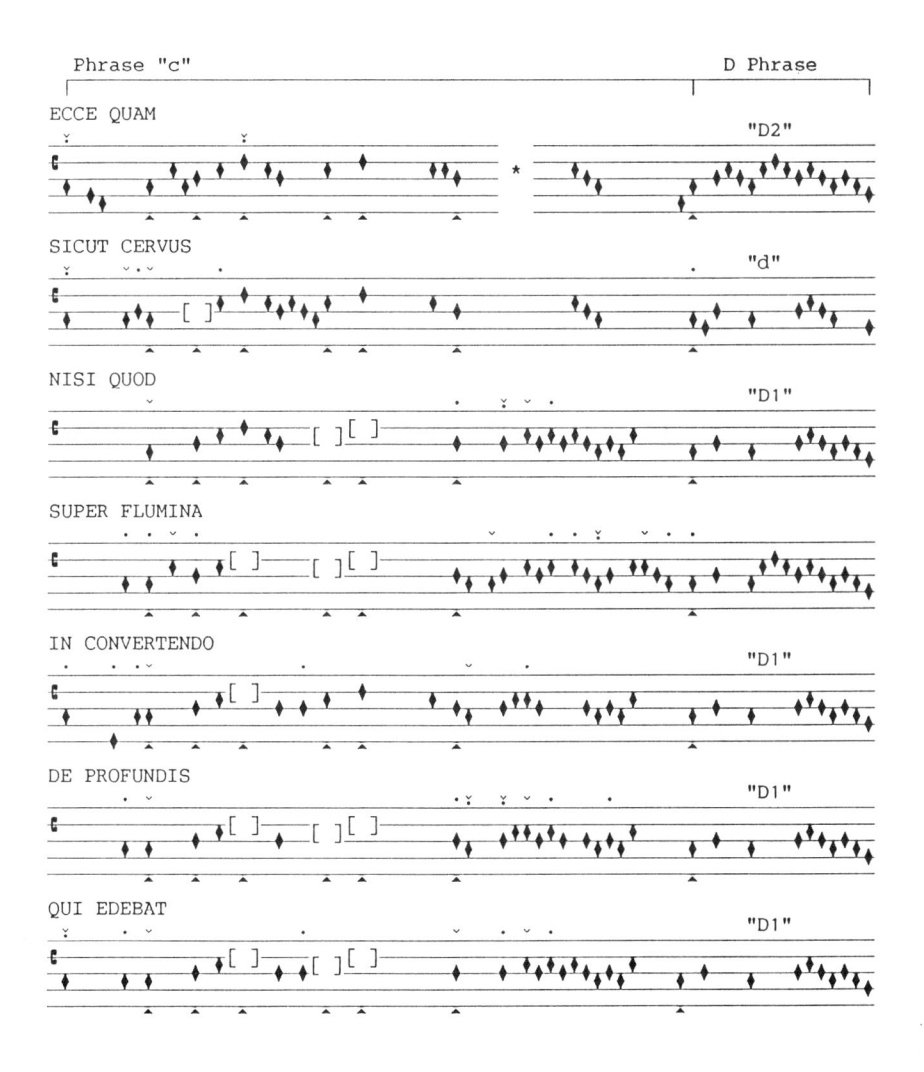

The phrases "c," "D" and "D1" are proper to the first verses of Mass Cantus. It is impossible to decide whether the "c" found in QUONIAM CONFIRMATA, which is a second verse, should be considered regular or irregular: the indications are contradictory. The appearance in the same chant and in DOMINUS IUSTUS of "A2" and "Z2," phrases proper to last verses, suggests that "C2" would have been a more consistent choice than "c." But it is also possible that "c" was used intentionally, and would be found in any more such verses, (were there any[12]) that required this phrase. That the two second-verses under consideration do not employ the "X1" and "Y1" used for second and third verses of the Sunday chants, but rather the "X" and "Y" of the first verses, seems to support this view. The lack of consistency in the choice of the components of these two second-verses (and other evidence, as well) seems to indicate that these chants are late additions to the repertory.

I have suggested by means of gaps in the melodies, and by the alignment of Example 7, that a number of the "c" phrases have suffered damage. The first thing to be noticed is that what corresponds to the reciting-tone is missing in six of the thirteen melodies compared. That the reciting tone should be absent is not unheard-of in psalmody (as we have already observed), although in the six cases under discussion it cannot be explained as owing to any lack of syllables.

Also lacking in five of the melodies compared in Example 7 are two notes of the underlying termination figure, i.e., the fourth and fifth of what I have suggested are the structural elements of the psalmodic formula. The justification for considering such melodies (and the above-mentioned larger number of "c" phrases in which the reciting tone of the formula is absent) to be "damaged" – belonging nevertheless to type – is found by comparing them with other clearly related phrases in which all the basic elements are present.

The damage with respect to the notes of the termination figure in DE PROFUNDIS, QUI EDEBAT, NISI QUOD, QUONIAM and SUPER FLUMINA is confirmed by reference to closely related chants such as IN CONVERTENDO and SUPRA DORSUM, which are undamaged

---

[12] LAUDATE DOMINUM and SUPRA DORSUM are the only Cantus with two verses.

in this regard. It is significant that in the corresponding (and obviously related) parts of the Gregorian and Old-Roman versions of DE PROFUNDIS, the operation of the underlying termination figure is easily seen.[13] In any case, if the operation of the type-melody seems somewhat uncertain in these particular phrases of the Mass Cantus, we are justified in looking beyond the immediate comparisons for confirmation that these damaged melodies did originally conform more closely to type. One must look also at the C phrases of the second and third verses, at those of the canticles, and (since the same formula is the basis of all four parts of the Cantus melody) even to the other text-bearing phrases of the Cantus.

Although all text-bearing phrases – those assigned the letters A, C, W and Y (whether upper or lower case) in Tables 2, 3 and 4 – are indeed constructed around the same notes of a formula, the melodies have developed certain idiosyncrasies that distinguish them. I refer to characteristic forms of the decorative flourish that concludes each of the four phrases and to certain other inessential but stable melodic details. It is idiosyncratic features such as these that clearly identify the opening of QUI EDEBAT (when it is compared to the C phrases of NISI QUOD, DE PROFUNDIS and IN CONVERTENDO) as a "c." Such a beginning is found only this once (the Cantus properly begin with some form of the A phrase), and the irregularity is only one of a number of indications that this chant may be, like the Gregorian Tract for Good Friday, "nuperrime compilatum."

The reader will not be surprised to notice that all of the D phrases compared in Example 7 (in fact, the D phrases of all the Cantus) conclude on f. Five of the D phrases of the Mass Cantus first-verses stand apart in being somewhat briefer than the others. I have suggested, by the designation "D1" in the musical examples and in the tables, that four of these are complete, and represent an independent tradition (and perhaps an earlier stage of elaboration). But it remains also possible that they are defective, that they should properly have the same form as that used to conclude all the other C melodies, and that they should be designated "(D)." In support of the first hypothesis, I might draw

---

[13] See Example 20 (a).

attention to Examples 8 and 9, below, where the D phrase of the BENEDICTUS and CANTEMUS canticles will be seen to be very similar to the "D1" of the Mass chants. Although the implications of this will not be considered until later, I want also to point out that this "D1" is associated (in three of four appearances) with "Z1," a version of the final cadential prolongation with a similarly restricted range.

In AD DOMINUM and ECCE QUAM, "D2" replaces the expected "D." AD DOMINUM, as we have already observed, has somehow lost the latter part of its melody, and this defect has been repaired without regard for the structure proper to Cantus first-verses. ECCE QUAM (we will see even more of this later) has been very extensively elaborated, for reasons that are not now apparent, and the substitution of the more florid second- and third-verse cadential flourish must be seen as part of this deliberate elaboration.

As might be expected from what we have already observed in the A phrases, the extension of the reciting tone (to accommodate the varying number of syllables to be set to the C phrase) lies mostly below c'. A number of the C phrases in Example 7 (see NISI QUOD, DE PROFUNDIS, IN CONVERTENDO, QUI EDEBAT and SUPER FLUMINA) have – like most of the A phrases in Example 3 and all those of Example 4 – been further elaborated after the penultimate note of the termination figure. Although this elaboration is not as pronounced as in the phrases "A1" and "A2" and in some the other phrases that will be studied shortly, I want once again to draw attention to this consistent feature. I should perhaps mention that this development after the penultimate note of the termination figure is not to be considered part of the "D1" phrase, whose exact boundaries can be determined by comparing the phrases "c" and "D" of SUPER FLUMINA with the "c" and "D1" of NISI QUOD, DE PROFUNDIS, IN CONVERTENDO and QUI EDEBAT.

The first semiverse of SICUT CERVUS was perhaps meant to conclude with "D" or "D1." It will be noticed that the phrase that does appear (it has been designated "d" in Table 2) is exactly the same as the conclusion of the corresponding part of the standard melody in all fourteen verses of the BENEDICTUS canticles. This particular correspondence is to be explained by liturgical circumstances: SICUT CERVUS and the shorter version of this canticle are both sung at Vespers on Holy Saturday, and a conflation of two closely related melodies sung in such proximity is only to be expected.

The adaptation of the psalm-text to the thirteen C and D phrases found in the first verses of Mass Cantus seems to be casual with respect to the placement of the syllables and their accent. However, in about half of the cases, the final syllable is placed at the beginning of the D phrase, and this tendency may be evidence of an earlier stage of the Cantus, surviving from a time when the adaptation of text to the melody was more methodical.

Example 8

The Phrases "C1," "C2" and "D2" in the Mass Cantus.

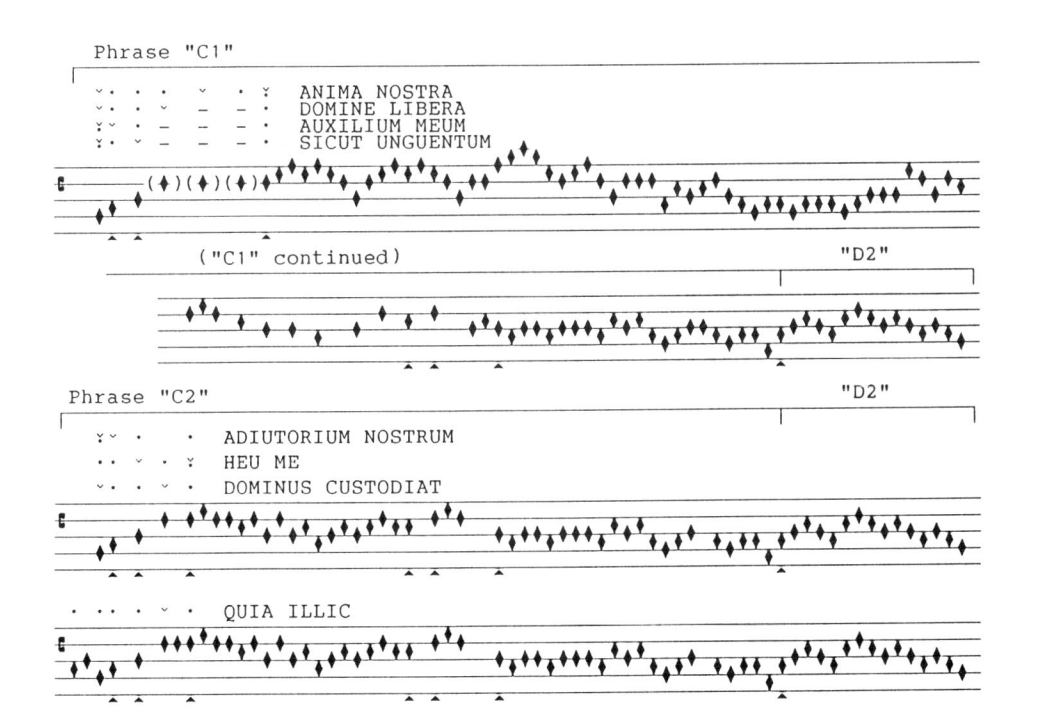

The Phrases "C1" and "C2" are proper to the second and third verses, respectively, of the Mass Cantus; "D2" is proper to both. The appearances of this last phrase in AD DOMINUM and ECCE QUAM (see Example 7 and Table 2), both first-verses, must be considered exceptional. It is, however, these occurrences that allow us to determine the exact boundaries of "D2," which might otherwise be construed to include the preceding melisma, a melisma that is characteristic (as we will see) of second and third verses.

The C and D phrases of the second and third verses are very stable. The melodies have been greatly developed, and in this development it is possible to distinguish certain elements, and perhaps even stages.

The main features of the elaboration of "C1" and "C2" are the inserted melismas. One of these, exactly the same in "C1" and "C2," will be seen to have been introduced – if we refer to the basic structure of the type-melody – after the penultimate note of the termination figure. This melisma corresponds, in position and function (that is, as a pre-cadential flourish or cadenza) with the insertion we have already observed in the phrases "A1" and "A2" in Example 4. The melodies, however, are quite different. The melisma of "C1" and "C2" is reminiscent of (and was perhaps suggested by) the similar elaboration found in five of the C phrases employed for first verses of Mass Cantus. See Example 5, IN CONVERTENDO, NISI QUOD, DE PROFUNDIS, QUI EDEBAT and SUPER FLUMINA.

"C1" and "C2" have been further elaborated by means of other melismas inserted earlier in the melodies, on the last syllable, before the commencement of the termination figure. The melisma is longer in "C1," the second-verse phrase, than in "C2," the characteristic phrase of third verses. The longer melisma displays the kind of (late) development by means of successive repetition that is so characteristic of the Ambrosian Alleluia *melodiae*, and exploits both the high range and the low. The corresponding melisma of "C2," probably earlier, lies mostly below the reciting-tone.

Although the C melody used for seven of the eight second- and third-verses begins on f (as did also a number of the A phrases of the Mass chants), it is important not to be misled by this statistic. The C phrases of the second and third verses are so similar that it might be fairer to describe the situation in different terms: not seven melodies beginning on f, but rather one, used seven times. The eighth melody (that of QUIA ILLIC) begins, more regularly, on g – as do almost all of the rest of the C phrases of the Cantus verses. Since the C phrase of the Cantus melody invariably concludes on f (I have already suggested that this is in anticipation of the idiosynchratic opening of the W phrase), one must at least consider whether the opening on f might not be a late retouching in the interest of symmetry and tonal consistency. Unfortunately, this interesting question must remain undecided.

The texts sung to the C phrases of the second and third verses are assigned mechanically, without regard for accent, to the opening notes of the melody; the last syllable is always placed at the beginning of the first of the added melismas. When there are more syllables than can be accommodated by the opening figure, except in the case of QUIA ILLIC, they are chanted, simply, on the reciting-tone. The procedure is fairly consistent, but, characteristically, not completely rigorous. The extra syllables of QUIA ILLIC are sung to prosthetic notes; the third syllable of the C phrase of AUXILIUM MEUM is set to a podatus, even though it might seem more consistent to have adapted the *initium* to four syllables by omitting the first c'.

Example 9

The Phrases "C," "C1" and "D" of the BENEDICTUS Canticles.

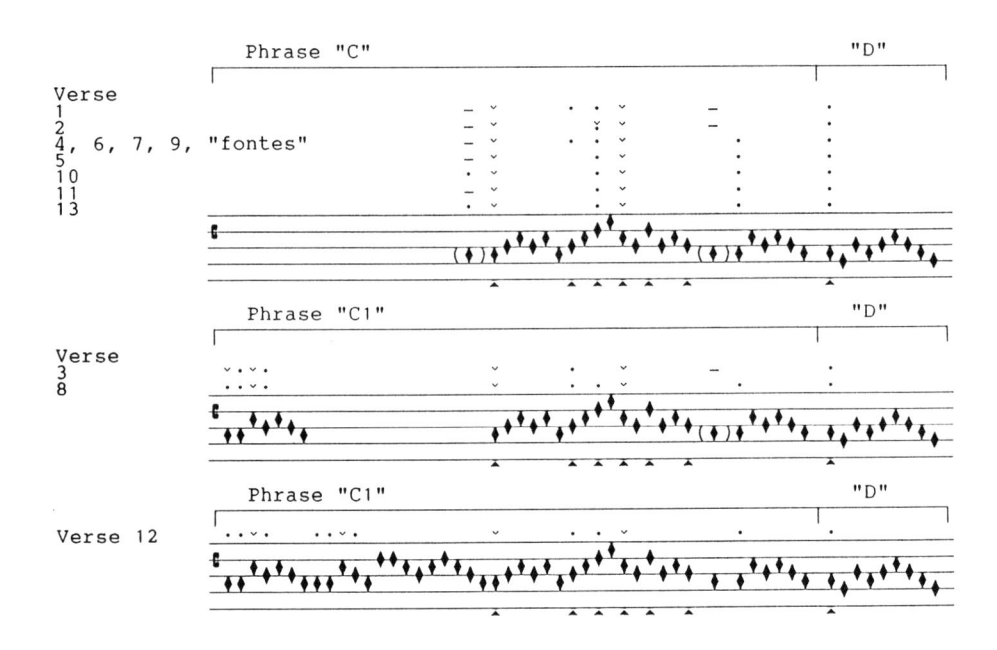

The fourteen verses of the BENEDICTUS canticles employ the same D-phrase and (except for insignificant details) only two versions of the C melody: one, when there are six or fewer syllables, the second (otherwise the same), with an introductory phrase to accommodate up to eight syllables more. These introductory phrases aside, the melody conforms closely to the suggested type, although, as is so often the case, there has been some elaboration after the penultimate note of the underlying structural formula.

In both "C" and "C1" the last two of the accented syllables and the two or three that are unaccented are assigned with almost perfect regularity. In "C1" the extra syllables are set regularly, but cursively, to the introductory motive. The D phrase is always sung to the last syllable (it is this feature that has determined the boundary between the C and D phrases). In the case of the phrase "C1" of the twelfth verse, there are enough syllables that the introductory motive has had to be repeated (in some sources[14] a short melisma is appended the second time).

Example 10

The Phrases "C," "c" and "D"
of the CANTEMUS Canticle.

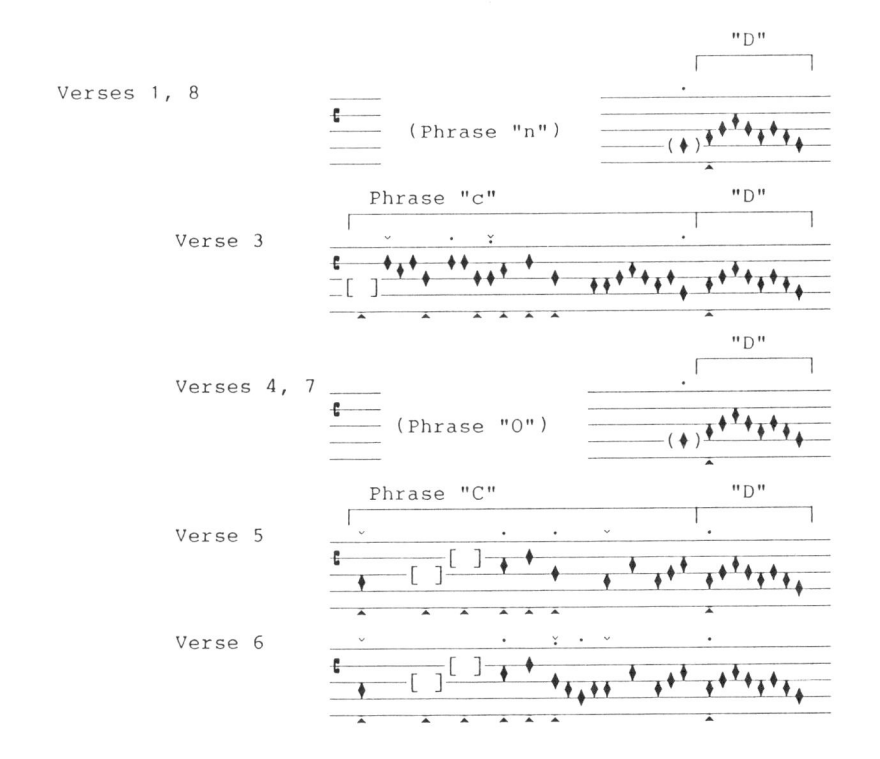

---

[14] See the Edition.

In neither of the C phrases of the CANTEMUS is the *initium* of the underlying (hypothetical) reciting formula found complete. The melodies of Example 10 consist almost entirely of an elaboration of the termination figure of this formula, with an extension (like the others we have seen before, centering around the note a) between its penultimate note and the beginning of the cadential prolongation, the phrase "D." This "incompleteness" suggests damage in the CANTEMUS, and a momentary failure of the oral transmission – an impression that is strengthened, not only by the substitution of two foreign phrases ("n" in verses 1 and 8, "O" in verses 4 and 7) for standard material[15], but as we will see shortly, by the awkward adaptation of the text in some of the later phrases of the canticle.

The boundary between the C and D phrases has been decided by reference to the corresponding parts of the BENEDICTUS, which are similar in melodic detail, and by the position of the final syllable in Phrase "C" of the CANTEMUS. The extraneous passage marked with an asterisk in Table 4 will be discussed later.

In verses 5 and 6 there is a similarity in the disposition of four of the five syllables. But with the exception of phrase "C" (which appears, in this respect and in its closer conformance to melodic type, to represent an earlier, more systematic practice that has been obscured or lost in the other verses) the present adaptation of the text to the melody is casual.

---

[15] See Table 4.

TABLE 8

The Phrases "w" and "X" of the Mass Cantus.

Nisi quod	:	f abf g bagaa f	Ga		A b	C		dc			B	[ ]bA	Gabcbaba	g
Qui edebat	:	f a g f	G	ggggA		C b		cdc		agg	c bc	Bcd C	A	gGa	b gg
Conserva	:	f a g f	G		Ag	C		dc	bcd	agg	c bc	Bcd C	A	Ga	aba g
Benedicam	:	f a g f	G	g	Ag	C		dc	bcd	agg	c bc	Bcd C	A	Ga	aba g
De profundis	:	f [ ]			A	Cc	c	cbaab cc babcdc			Ba	C	bAba	G	
Sicut cervus	:	fgabf gabag f	fGa	ggggA	b	Ccab	gac	c abg cdbabcdc			Ba	C	bAba	G	
In convertendo	:	f	G		A	Cc bc	acdcdc	cdbabcdcbacbabaggabccabcbaB			C	bAba	G		
Dominus iustus	:	f ab a ag	fgfG	bbg	A b	C b	ac	c	bcdc		abcb B	C	A	Gab	ba g
Domine exaudi	:	f ab a ag	fgfG	b g	A b	C b	ac	g	bcdc		abcb B	C	A	Gab	ba g
Laudate	:	ff a g	f	g	A b	C					abcb B	C	A	Gab	ba g
Levavi	:	f	G	g	A b	C		dcba b			abcb Bcd	C	Aba	Ga	bagg
Quoniam	:	ffgab gg ga gf	fGab	ggg	A b	C		dc			abcb B	C	A	Gab	ba g
Qui regis	:	f a g	fgfG	b g	A b	C b	a				ccabcb B	C	A	Gab	ba g
Supra dorsum	:	f a g	f G		A b	C b	a				ccabcb B	C	A	Gab	ba g
Super flumina	:	ff a g	f G	g	A b	C b	a				ccabcb B	C	A	Gab	ba g

Example 11

The Phrases "w" and "X" of the Mass Cantus.

Example 11 (continued)

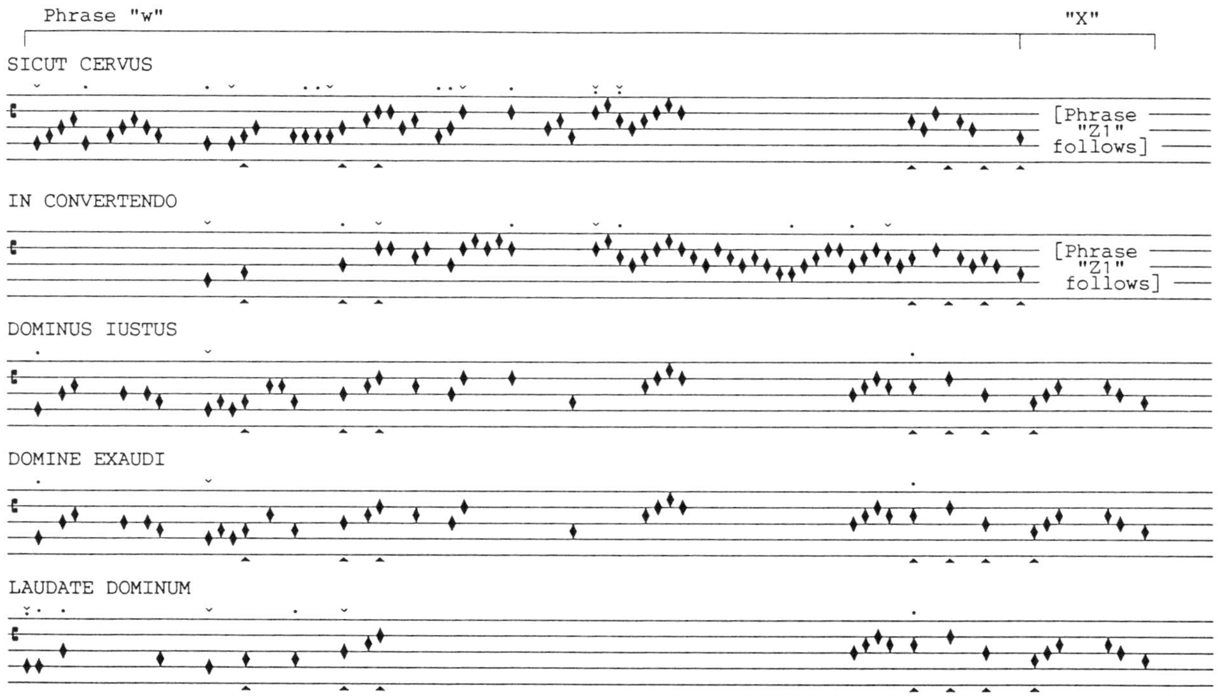

Example 11 (continued)

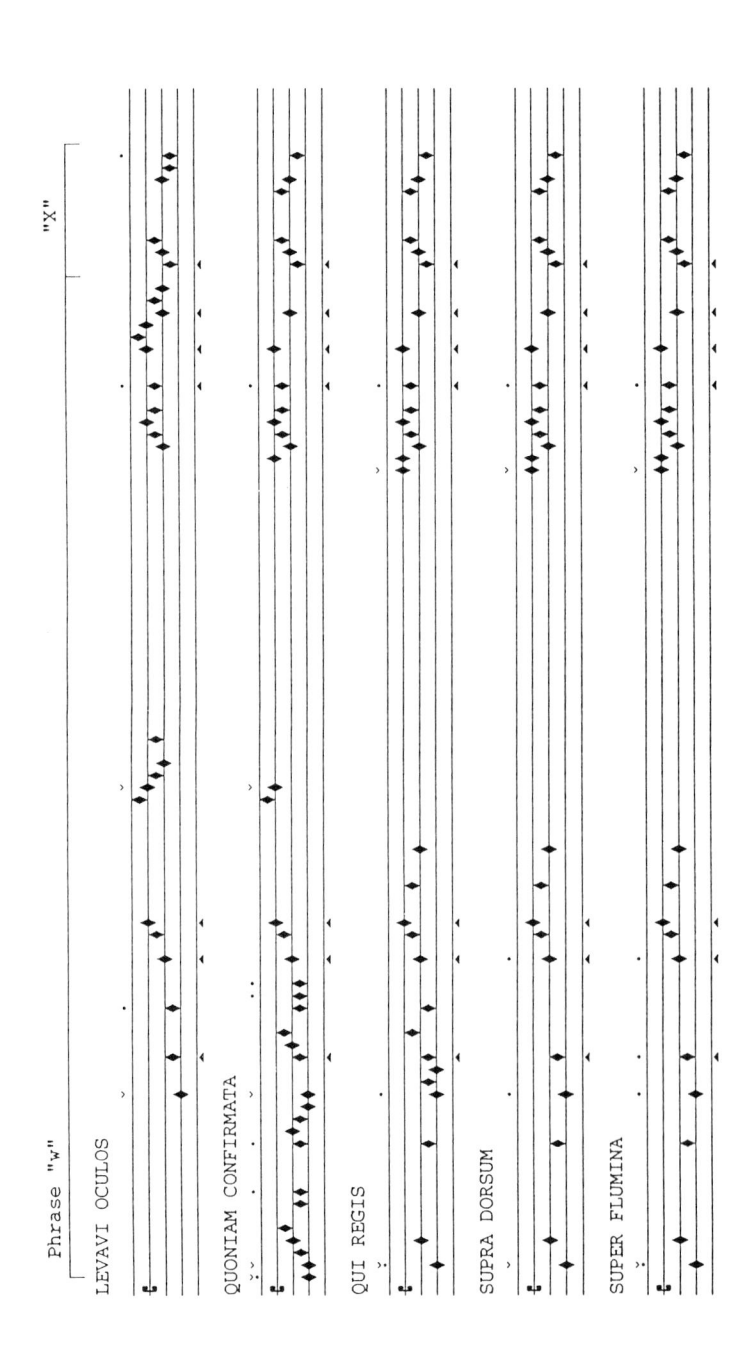

The phrases "w" and "X" are proper to all first verses of the Mass Cantus, and also to the second verses of the ferial chants. The "x" of NISI QUOD is, it will be noticed, the "B1" of the second and third verses, but it is obviously best explained in the circumstances of Example 11 as a simple elaboration of the usual "X." NISI, as we have seen, is quite extensively elaborated (see also below, the commentary to the Y phrases).

Perhaps the first thing to be noticed in the comparison of the "w" phrases in Example 11 is that all presently begin on the note f.[16] It is the consistency of the opening of the W phrases that is striking, not its nature. Beginnings on f are frequently encountered among the A and C melodies. And although none of the W phrases now begin with the first note of the *initium* that we have assumed to be basic to all four parts of the Cantus melody, all but one of the W phrases of Example 11 do feature the note g in their opening figures. There is no need, therefore, to see the idiosyncratic opening of the melodies given in Example 11 as anything more than a prosthesis prefixed to the standard formula, that is to say, a later and inessential embellishment. In the Gregorian Tracts (whose melodies are, as we will see, closely related), the conclusion of the first semiverse on f and an *initium* beginning on the same note after the caesura are not consistent features.

Nevertheless, after the caesura, the Cantus begin so consistently with an f that one wonders whether later singers did not lose sight of the basic structure – whether they did not later come to conceive the opening as an embellishment of the figure f a c′ (perhaps the only other authentic Milanese *initium*[17]). The bare triadic opening of the W melody of DE PROFUNDIS might appear to be evidence of this

---

[16] The W phrases of all Cantus have this feature, which, as I have already suggested, is probably the explanation for the extension to f of the cadential flourish that closes the first half of the psalm verses.

[17] The earliest Ambrosian books contain only two figures: g a c′ (d e g) and f a c′. See T. Bailey, "Ambrosian Psalmody: An Introduction," in *Rivista internazionale di musica sacra*, I/1 (1980), 89.

new conception. But the end of this phrase is so like that of IN CONVERTENDO that it seems safer to suppose that DE PROFUNDIS has suffered some damage or alteration, and that the beginning of its W phrase had originally, like that of IN CONVERTENDO (and those of almost all the other Cantus), included the note g. The Gregorian version of what corresponds to the W phrase of DE PROFUNDIS does begin on g. (Please see Example 20 (a); see also the commentary to the "W" phrases of the CANTEMUS, where the structural ambivalence of the first notes following the caesura is again evident).

The X phrase will be seen to be missing in a number of the melodies compared in Example 11. Table 2 shows that the expected cadential prolongation does not follow the W phrase in five of the Mass Cantus. In all of these cases the second half of the psalm verse was too short to be divided, or in any case, treated as one unbroken phrase. In such an event, the proper procedure seems to have been to set the text to the W phrase, and (omitting X and Y) append the Z phrase directly. This has been done for IN CONVERTENDO, DE PROFUNDIS and SICUT CERVUS; and presumably would have been done for AD DOMINUM (whose melody breaks off abruptly).

There is an exception to this "proper procedure" for semiverses that were too short to be divided, and although it is not found in Example 11, it is best mentioned here. In ANIMA NOSTRA (whose fragmentary W phrase is given in Example 12 with those of the other second verses), the first syllables of the text after the caesura are set, as usual, to the beginning of the W Phrase. But (as though the singer realized only at this point that there were not sufficient syllables) the W phrase breaks off, and the rest of the text is set to the characteristic Y and Z phrases – which, it would appear, were considered indispensable. One may speculate that before second and third verses received their present elaborate settings, the second semiverse of ANIMA NOSTRA would have been treated in the fashion of IN CONVERTENDO and the others.

The distinctive embellishment of the termination figure in IN CONVERTENDO, DE PROFUNDIS and SICUT CERVUS is noteworthy. This figure (I refer to the last eight notes of the W phrases of these three chants in Example 11) seems to be associated particularly with the phrase "Z1" (see below, the commentary to Example 15).

The W and X phrases of the Mass Cantus first-verses demonstrate the casual attitude of the singers with respect to the placement of the text, although the two occurrences of the "accentual" form of the "X" are associated with a proparoxytone. Something of an earlier, more systematic approach to text setting (from a time when the melodies were less elaborate?) is perhaps still to be seen in the coincidence, in more than half of the examples, of the last syllable with the first note of the termination figure. Some method is also to be seen in the assignment of the first two syllables to the opening notes of the phrase. But the regularity in the placement of the opening syllables is more likely owing to the later influence of "W1" (obvious in the case of QUI REGIS, DOMINUS IUSTUS and DOMINE EXAUDI, but discernible also in one or two of the other melodies), the phrase that is characteristic of the second and third verses.

The influence of the phrase "W1" is particularly strong in QUI REGIS, DOMINUS IUSTUS and DOMINE EXAUDI; indeed, the only significant difference between the "w" phrases of these chants and the phrase "W1" is that in the former a melisma is lacking. We will see later that "W1" – entirely fortuitously, as it happens – is adapted to either three of four syllables in seven of its eight complete appearances. It seems likely that the virtual adoption of this phrase in the three first-verses (replacing, it may be supposed, earlier versions of "w" that displayed the usual melodic diversity) was suggested by the simple circumstance that the text to be set in the case of QUI REGIS, DOMINUS IUSTUS and DOMINE EXAUDI presented the requisite number of syllables.

I would like to propose that in this tendency to re-employ a favourite phrase (a phrase whose influence we have also observed in a number of the "a" melodies of Examples 3 and 4) we see the operation of the process of "normalization," a term I will use to describe the later substitution of uniformity for diversity. We will see later (normalization will be discussed further below) that this process was more completely carried out in the case of the "Y" of the Mass Cantus. One may well suspect that a similar development accounts for the uniformity of the initial phrases of the Gregorian Tracts.

Example 12

The Phrases "W1" and "X1" in the Mass Cantus.

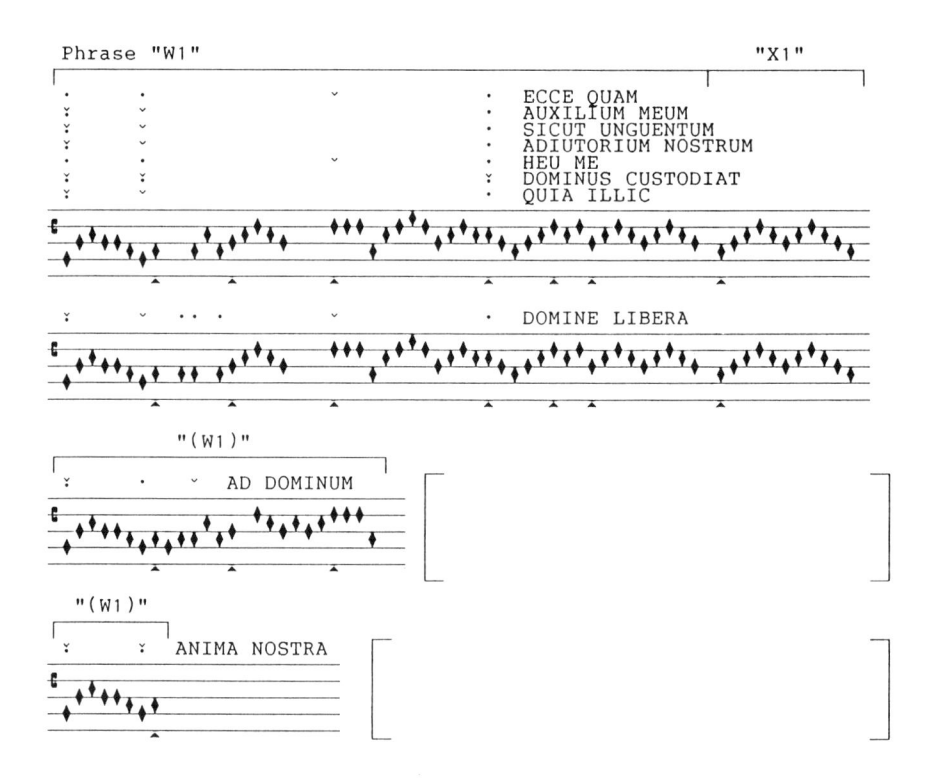

[musical notation: Phrase "W1" ... "X1" with texts ECCE QUAM, AUXILIUM MEUM, SICUT UNGUENTUM, ADIUTORIUM NOSTRUM, HEU ME, DOMINUS CUSTODIAT, QUIA ILLIC]

[musical notation with text: DOMINE LIBERA]

[musical notation "(W1)" with text: AD DOMINUM]

[musical notation "(W1)" with text: ANIMA NOSTRA]

The phrases "W1" and "X1" are proper to second and third verses of the Sunday Cantus. The appearances of these phrases in ECCE QUAM, a first verse, must be regarded as exceptional.

The melody "W1"-"X1" (which is adapted to the text-phrase following the caesura) is exactly the same in seven of its eight complete appearances; the two fragments are the same as far as they go, and the eighth is only very slightly different. The note-for-note exactness of the W phrase (unusual for text-bearing parts of the Cantus) is probably explained by the circumstance – as I mentioned earlier, entirely accidental

– that the texts set to the seven identical melodies of Example 12 all have either three or four syllables. It was perhaps this feature (as in the similar case of QUI REGIS, DOMINUS IUSTUS and DOMINE EXAUDI, discussed just above) that led singers to employ the "W1"-"X1" melody for ECCE QUAM, although it may only have been the simple desire to elaborate a Cantus that has, as we have seen, been singled out for special treatment.

The termination figure has been considerably elaborated. It may be presumed that the beginning of this part of the formula (which would otherwise be difficult to decide) is marked, as in most of the W phrases of the Mass Cantus first-verses, by the position of the last syllable. This determination is confirmed by reference to the analogous parts of DOMINUS JUSTUS and DOMINE EXAUDI. In these two chants (as we have seen in Example 11), the W phrases, although somewhat less developed and without the melisma, are very like those of the second and third verses. When these similar "w" phrases are also taken into consideration, the boundary between "W1" and "X1" cannot be in doubt.

The melisma just referred to is the counterpart of the others we have discussed in the phrases "A1" and "C1," and is inserted in "W1," as usual, between the penultimate note of the underlying recitation formula and its *finalis*.

Although the (complete) "W1"-"X1" melodies offer only three configurations of text and music, it may reasonably be inferred, especially when the behaviour of the similar first-verse forms of the W phrases is considered, that the position of the first two syllables and that of the last (the last two syllables when there are more than three) was fixed by rule. There are too few examples to decide whether this rule took into account the position of the accent.

Example 13

The Phrases "W" and "X"
of the BENEDICTUS Canticles.

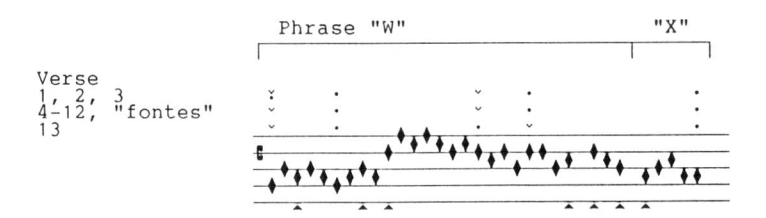

The "W" and "X" phrases of the BENEDICTUS conform closely to the suggested type, although the elaboration of the reciting tone in the high range (reaching to the e′) is probably an indication of later development.

The fourteen appearances of the W phrase in the BENEDICTUS canticles include only three different text phrases ("et laudabilis," "hymnum dicite" and "hymnum dicamus"), each with five syllables, and adapted to the melody with perfect regularity. In spite of the appearance of the "accentual" form of the X phrase, which in two of the three cases is associated with a proparoxytone, conflicting indications in the thirteenth verse make it impossible to decide whether the settings have been made with regard for the accent.

Example 14

The Phrase "W" of the CANTEMUS.

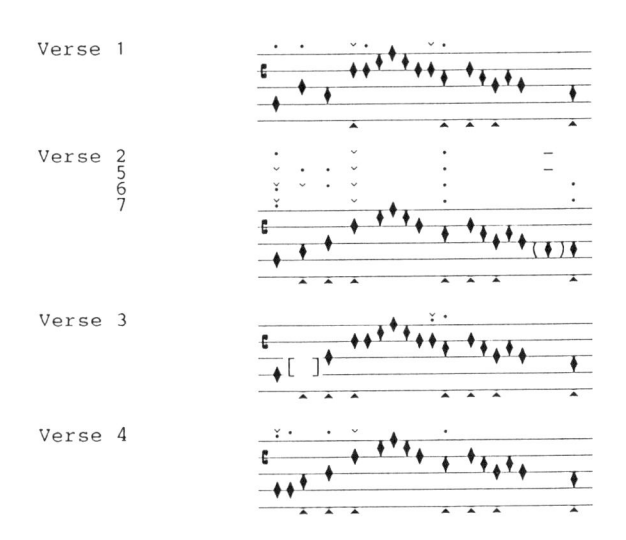

Verse 1

Verse 2
5
6
7

Verse 3

Verse 4

The W phrase is (virtually) the same melody in all appearances. It conforms closely to the suggested type, except for the interchanging of the second and third notes in the first verse and the omission of the g in verse 3, both of which variants can be attributed to the ambivalence of the opening figure (the uncertainty as to whether it derives from the g a c', the *initium* of the suggested type-melody, or an alternate, f a c').

In Verses 1, 2, 4, 5 and 6, the syllables are placed regularly, with concern (as can be seen by comparing the fourth and sixth verse to the others) for the position of the last accent. All of these phrases have five syllables, except in the sixth verse of the canticle, where an extra syllable is accommodated by an additional note at the conclusion.

The adaptation of the standard melody to three of the verses of the CANTEMUS has been done irregularly. One is tempted to say, badly. In Verse 3, the present placement of the text forces the singer to run together the musical phrases "D," "W" and "Y" (which, nevertheless, retain their proper form). The two syllables marked in Example 14 for the third verse belong to two different text-phrases. Phrases "W" and "Y" are similarly run together in Verses 4 and 7.

In verse 3, the awkward expedient has obviously been prompted by the lack of syllables. I don't wish to suggest that the melodies ought to be corrected, but it is easy enough to say what the proper procedure should have been: Verse 3 has no need of the phrase "c." The five syllables "factus es mihi" ought to have been set to the W phrase (as we have noted, most of the other W phrases in the CANTEMUS are set to five syllables). There seems to be no reason why the four remaining syllables of the verse could not have been adapted to phrases "Y" and "Z." In verse 4, the irregularity is removed if the melisma on the second "eum" is begun five notes earlier. As for Verse 7, the fourth syllable of the phrase "in medio" ought to have been accommodated by an extra note at the end of the W phrase, as in verse 6, and the two remaining syllables set to "Y" and "Z" as in the ("corrected") verse 4 (see Example 18).

Example 15

The Phrases "Y," "(Y)," "y," "(y)" and "Y1" in the Mass Cantus.

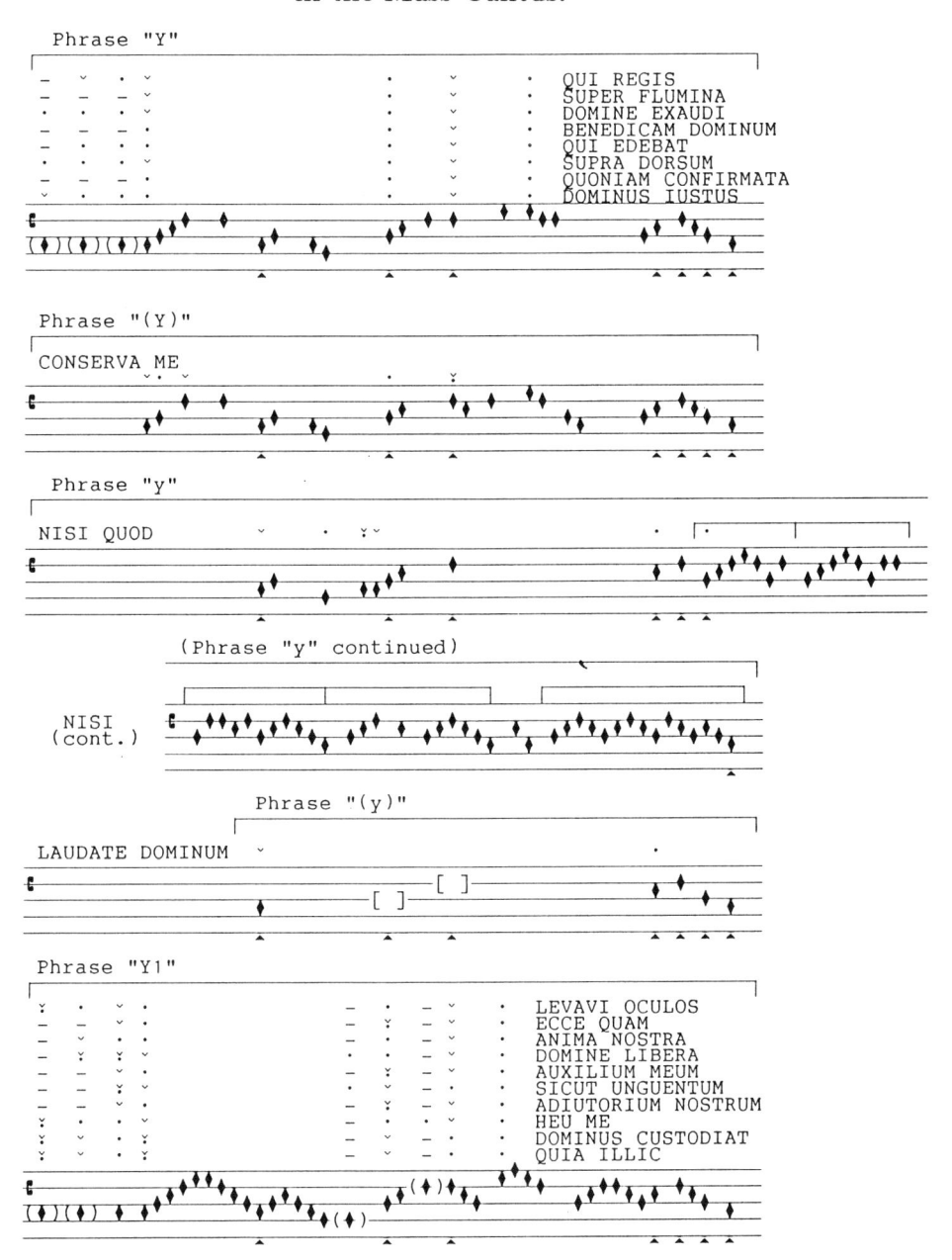

Phrase "Y" is proper to the first verses of Mass Cantus, and also to the second verses of ferial chants; "Y1" is proper to all other second and third verses. The appearance of "Y1" in LEVAVI and in ECCE QUAM must be regarded as exceptional.

The phrase "Y," except for prosthetics, is identical in all eight appearances. In these, the text is adapted with perfect regularity. It might appear that in the adaptation of the text to the melody, attention has been paid to the last accent; but it should be noted that in the eight examples there happen to be no occurrences of the proparoxytone in the concluding syllables. It may be significant, with respect to this question, that a proparoxytone does occur in "Y1" (a more elaborate, but obviously directly related phrase), and there the syllables have been set cursively.

CONSERVA ME stands somewhat apart. The Y phrase has been fitted to the text differently, although an adaptation like that of the eight other "regular" Y phrases in Example 15 would obviously present no difficulties. The Y phrase of CONSERVA, like that of NISI QUOD, which is to be considered just below, may survive from an earlier stage in the development of the Cantus, from a time before the process I call "normalization" took place.

The striking melodic uniformity of the phrases "Y," a uniformity that is by no means entirely owing to the appearance of standard melismas, is more characteristic of second and third verses, and appears rather out-of-keeping with the rest of the text-bearing phrases in first verses. NISI QUOD, which, like CONSERVA, stands apart from the others in this respect, may represent a different[18] and earlier tradition, a tradition in which the Y phrases exhibited the same melodic variety as the other text-bearing parts of the first verse melodies.

That NISI QUOD does represent an independent and authentic tradition seems all the more likely when it is observed that the "y" of this verse is followed by "Z1." This simpler (and presumably earlier) version of the concluding cadential flourish (see Example 16), is sung

---

[18] Local differences must have been considerable in an orally transmitted repertory, before the codification of the twelfth century established the official versions of the melodies.

on all occasions when "Y" is not found. The present unvarying form of "Y" and its inevitable continuation by "Z" would appear to belong to a later stage in the development of the chants.

The phrase "Z1" is invariably preceded by a particular elaboration of the termination figure of the type-melody. We have already inspected this figure (refer to Example 11 and the discussion of the W phrases) and noted its connection with "Z1" of SICUT CERVUS, IN CONVERTENDO and DE PROFUNDIS.[19] The same association is found in Example 15, in NISI QUOD. It seems safe to assume that this less elaborate version of the termination figure would be found also in LAUDATE (had it survived undamaged), for this chant concludes with what is obviously an incomplete form of "Z1." (See below, Example 16; compare also the corresponding parts of the Gregorian and Old-Roman versions in Example 20.)

The Y phrase of NISI has been extended by the insertion (on the final syllable, after the penultimate note of the termination figure) of a long melisma developed by successive repetition[20] in the fashion of the *melodiae* of the Milanese Alleluias. It was perhaps this striking elaboration that led the singers to leave NISI unrevised.

The phrase "Y1," except for prosthetics and epenthetics is identical in all of the ten appearances. The syllables are placed with almost perfect regularity; the only exceptions are in HEU ME where, instead of a fourth prosthetic g, an extra syllable is accommodated by the epenthetic note c', and in DOMINE LIBERA and SICUT UNGUENTUM, where one of the normal prosthetics is avoided in favour of an epenthetic f. The syllables have been placed without regard for their accent.

---

[19] In these three chants, it will be remembered, because of the shortness of the second half of the psalm verse, there is no need of a Y phrase: "w" is followed directly by "Z1."

[20] The repetitions are marked with brackets in the example.

Example 16

The Phrases "Z," "Z1," "(Z1)" and "Z2"
in the Mass Cantus.

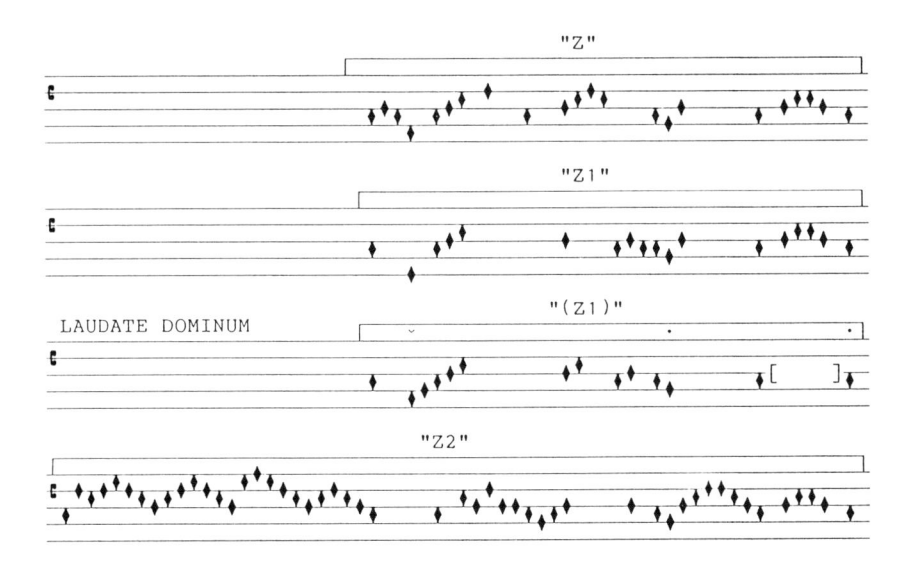

The phrases "Z" and "Z1" are the proper conclusions for all Mass Cantus with only one verse, and for second verses when a third verse follows. I suggested above that the phrase "Y" is the result of a later revision of the chants; it seems likely, since "Z1" is never found with "Y," that "Z" received its slightly more elaborate form at the same time. "Z2" is used always for last verses (i.e., the second, of ferial chants, and the third, of the Sunday Cantus).

It will have been noticed in Example 15 that the Y phrase of LAUDATE DOMINUM has suffered some damage; it is doubtless as a result of this damage that the final syllables of the verse have been assigned to the Z phrase, normally a closing melisma. These syllables have been marked for LAUDATE in Example 16.

Example 17

The Phrases "Y," "Y1" and "Z"
in the BENEDICTUS Canticles.

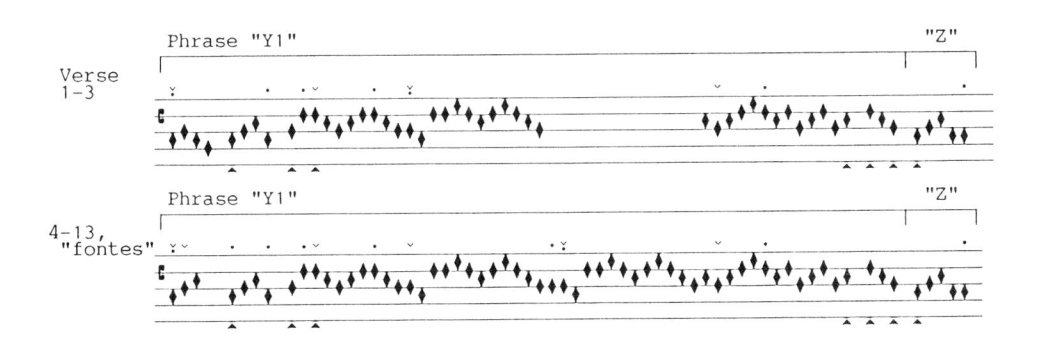

There are only two texts, one (et gloriosus in saecula) sung three times, the other (et superexaltate eum in saecula), eleven. The longer of the two melodies has been extended by the exact repetition of a passage sung only once in the shorter. Otherwise the two are nearly the same. With only two examples it is difficult to demonstrate method in the placement of the syllables, but except for the "accentual" form of the closing figure in verses 3 to 14, which (judging from verses 1 to 3, which also present a concluding proparoxytone) is entirely unnecessary, the last four syllables are assigned similarly in both.

Example 18

The Phrases "Y," "Y1" and "Z"
in the CANTEMUS.

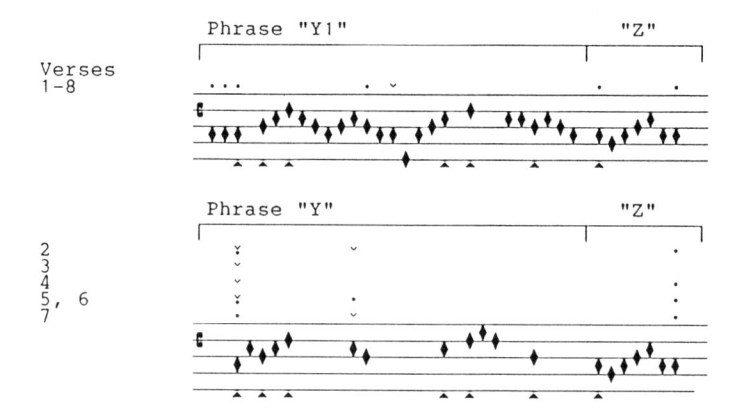

There are two melodies: one is sung twice to the same text, the other six times, to different texts. In the case of this latter, the two or three syllables are placed regularly, without regard for the accent. In Verse 3 and 7, as I mentioned above, the text has been awkwardly adapted; the Y phrase begins in mid-word.

VIII

THE DEVELOPMENT OF THE REPERTORY

The principal purpose of Examples 3 to 18, and of the commentary I have provided, has been to demonstrate the fundamental relationship of all of the constituent parts of the Cantus, a relationship that is owing (as I hope to have shown) to the operation in all of these phrases of two components. The first is an underlying structural formula, the second, a decoration appended to the *finalis* of this formula. But although the examples have obviously been arranged to demonstrate the similarity of the melodies, I have not wished to hide, in any way, the diversity in detail of these phrases, nor their momentary departures from type (whether accidental or deliberate). On the contrary, except only for the slight differences found in any one chant in different manuscripts (and these differences are remarkably few in the early sources used for the edition), the musical examples have presented an analysis of the melodies that includes all their idiosyncrasies.

Now that melodies have been presented in detail (dissected and splayed, as it were, in Examples 3 to 18), and now that the reader has been given the means to assess the general picture of the repertory presented by the summary of this musical analysis in Tables 2, 3 and 4, it is time to offer a few remarks about the development of the Cantus, the individual melodies and the repertory as a whole. I will begin with the second of the structural components, the appended cadential decorations, the phrases B, D, X and Z.

In Example 19 are brought together all complete forms of the phrases I consider to be cadential prolongations, the melodic flourishes that conclude (with the few exceptions that have been noted) the text-bearing phrases of the Cantus melody. The B and X phrases are variously decorated versions of a simple musical gesture, a motive that remains a recognizable constituent in the compound D and Z phrases.

Example 19

The Various Forms of the Cadential Flourish, the B, D, X and Z Phrases.

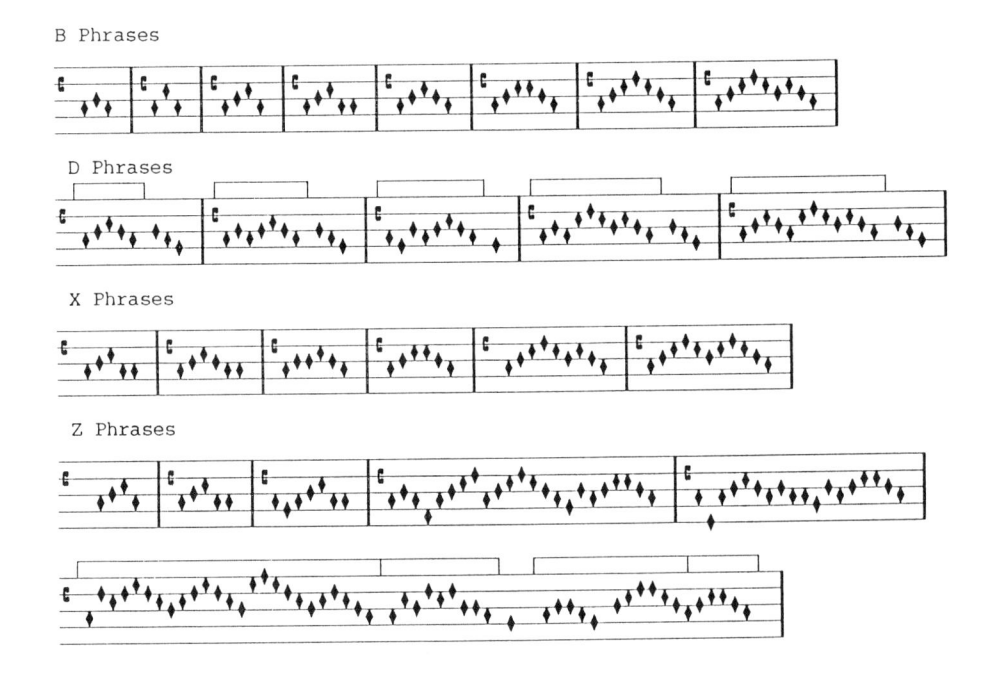

The briefest form of this cadential flourish (and perhaps the oldest, since it is frequently encountered in the Gregorian Tracts) was employed, as we have seen in Example 1, even in simple psalmody. This brief, "elemental," form will be found as the first item of Example 19 (it is the phrase "B2" of QUI REGIS and two other Cantus first-verses). It will be seen also to have survived as the first element of the compound phrases "D" and "D1" of the Mass Cantus, (slightly decorated) as the first part of "D" of the BENEDICTUS, and (perhaps) as the first part of phrase "Z" of the Mass Cantus.

Although this is the simplest form of the cadential prolongation (involving only the *finalis* and its upper neighbour), it is probably correct to see the version expanded to reach b as the normal form in the Cantus; those touching c', d' and even e' (phrases "b," "B1," "D," "D2," "X1," "Z" and "Z2" of the Mass chants), as later elaborations.

The "normal" form of the gesture, its simple melodic arch sometimes slightly elaborated, forms phrases "B" and "X" of the Mass Cantus and the canticles, and phrase "Z" of the CANTEMUS and BENEDICTUS. The normal form is also a recognizable constituent of the remaining compound cadential flourishes: it appears at the beginning of "D2" in the Mass chants, at the beginning of "D" in the BENEDICTUS and CANTEMUS canticles, and at the close of all the complete Z phrases of the Mass Chants.

The basis of all of the B and X phrases (even the versions with an expanded range, "B1" and "X1") is the same simple musical gesture – a gesture not confined to ecclesiastical chant, as those acquainted with the melodies of Bellini and Chopin will know – that serves to prolong the *finalis* in a single, decorative melodic arc beginning and concluding on g. All of the D phrases have been extended to conclude on f, sometimes, as in the third of the D phrases of Example 19 (the "D" of the BENEDICTUS and "d" of SICUT CERVUS), merely by appending this note to the basic motive (compare the phrases "d" and "Z1" of the latter chant), but usually by the addition of a three-note figure. I have suggested the proper relationship of the D phrases to the others by means of brackets, but I must confess to a certain diffidence in offering this kind of analysis when the phrases are so short.

The Z phrases of the Mass Cantus have been greatly elaborated. The basic motive, which survives in its simple form at the end of "Z," "Z1" and "Z2" (indeed, at the end of all undamaged Cantus verses), is preceded by an interpolation that seems to consist of a number of related arcs. That is to say, it appears to have been produced by the successive repetition and elaboration of this simple motive. (The process of elaboration by successive repetition is also observable in the late development of other florid Ambrosian chants.[1]) I have marked in Example 19 what seem to me to be to be the reiterations of the basic motive. As all who study the chant will know, the exact demarcations of such repetitions are often a matter of opinion, especially when there has been some elaboration. But if their exact boundaries and even the number of the reiterations might well be disputed, the structure and motivic basis of the elaborate melismas that close each verse of the Mass Cantus will hardly be in doubt.

From what has been said before it will already be clear that I have made a theoretical division of the Cantus phrases (one that corresponds, however, to the history I have proposed), characterizing some (phrases A, C, W and Y) as text-bearing, and others (B, D, X and Z) as decorative. While this division is borne out in general by the distribution of the text in the melodies as they are known to us presently (something the reader will already have observed), there are many exceptions that testify to a casual attitude on the part of the singers, and to a change in their conception of the standard melody.

Before the codification of the chants, which seems to have occurred for the Ambrosian rite only in the twelfth century, the Cantus were not autonomous melodies to be committed to memory individually like the songs of Schubert. In an oral tradition such a thing is hardly to be imagined. It was rather, for the singers, a question of adapting a single well-known melody, extemporaneously, to the texts assigned in the liturgy – a melody whose exact outlines were not fixed. It is unlikely, especially in later centuries when (whatever their earlier style) the chants had become very ornate, that a psalm-text would have been

---

[1] For another demonstration of the procedure of elaboration by repetition, see Bailey, *Ambrosian Alleluias*, pp. 82-88.

sung in exactly the same way on different occasions. There is no reason to think that the singers would have troubled to attempt it.

That in the course of centuries the Cantus became gradually more ornate does not seem a very contentious assumption. Even within the relatively short period represented by the manuscripts of the present Edition, something of this development may be visible. If corresponding parts of the melodies in the British Library manuscript (on paleographic grounds, the oldest source of the Ambrosian Antiphoner) and in the three other manuscripts are compared, the melodic interval of the third, with surprising frequency, will be found to have been bridged in the (presumably) later versions of the Chants. I have elsewhere been able to demonstrate progressive elaboration in the Milanese Alleluias,[2] but there are also many general examples. The (very natural) tendency of solo singers to make florid chants more florid, and an indication that the process is relatively rapid in an oral tradition, are to be seen in the comparison of melodies codified in the Gregorian manuscripts of the ninth and tenth centuries with the corresponding Old-Roman and Ambrosian melodies committed to writing only in the eleventh and twelfth. I might also mention, as another example of the continuous elaboration of ecclesiastical chant, the late practice of troping, which continued even after the general use of notation had established the final, official, form of the melodies.

When the Cantus melodies were plainer – closer to a simple psalm-tone, if perhaps never quite as stark – and as long as they continued to be recognized as versions of a recitation formula, the placement of the syllables was probably much more methodical than it appears at present. Of this early stage of the Cantus, nothing, of course, survives. But the Cantus became ornate, and this, it would appear, was enough to obscure the underlying recitation formula, and lead the singers to adopt unsystematic expedients. Having lost sight of its structure, they resorted, in most cases, to an ad hoc practice, adapting the embellished forms of the standard melody to the psalm texts in any way that served.

To this second stage of the Cantus, obviously, belong the Mass Cantus first-verses, (although, as we will see in a moment, some parts

---

[2] *Ambrosian Alleluias, passim.*

of these may be seen as evidence of tertiary development). Also to this second stage belong, less obviously, the canticles BENEDICTUS and CANTEMUS. Although (as we have observed) there is more evidence of order in the Canticles than in the Mass chants, it is an order very far removed from the simplicity of a simple recitation formula. Much of the apparent uniformity of the canticles, it must be remembered, is owing to the exact repetition of entire phrases of text and music. Practical considerations explain much of the rest, for it was doubtless because the verses of the canticles were sung one after another on the same occasion that their melodies diverged less than the Mass chants and an attempt was made to repeat the arrangement of the syllables in successive verses. But the latest adaptations of the standard formula to the verses of the canticles largely ignore the original structural divisions of the melodies. The decorative flourishes that prolong the *finalis* are treated regularly as cadences and (as we have seen in the third, fourth and seventh verses of the CANTEMUS) the divisions of the textual and musical phrases do not always coincide.

Other developments are also to be distinguished in the Cantus, although, of course, the order (or even the independence) of these later stages cannot now be determined. I am referring to interpolations (both within and between phrases), the substitution of extraneous musical material in place of standard phrases, the disposition of the syllables in accordance with accentual principles, the "normalization" (for want of a better word) of some parts of the melodies, and the creation of new, irregular settings.

I will begin with the latter. The standard melody for the Cantus is undoubtedly ancient, but there is reason to believe that some of the adaptations of the melody are more recent than others. The history of the Cantus-Tract is largely one of retrenchment. Although it seems clear that they were originally sung more generally, they came to be restricted to Lent and to penitential occasions, supplanted elsewhere by the Alleluias. Although it seems equally clear that whole psalms had been involved, the practice was truncated until, in Milan, the chants were reduced (the canticles aside) to one, two or three verses. But to some extent at least, this process was reversed in later years. New Tracts, not found in the earliest Gregorian books of the ninth century, appear regularly in the books of the tenth and eleventh. These chants were required in Lent for the more recent Sunday and weekday Masses, for votive Masses, either of a penitential character or falling between Septuagesima and Easter, and even for certain feasts whose celebration, according to later practice, was allowed in this formerly prohibited period. These additions to the repertory produced one interesting anomaly that should be mentioned. In eleventh-century sources, the Feast of the Holy Innocents, even though it does not fall within the period of penance, was assigned a Tract (unless it fell on a Sunday). And this was obviously because it was then conceived as a "sorrowful" chant. In this one instance, it is a Tract that has replaced an Alleluia.[3]

Although there are no such early manuscripts to document the growth of the Ambrosian repertory, it is reasonable to make the assumption that something similar occurred in Milan, and that a number of the Cantus found in the service books of the eleventh and twelfth century were introduced only during the preceding century or two.

There is some internal evidence that bears on this matter. The Holy Thursday Cantus QUI EDEBAT (whose adaptation, as we have seen, is untypical) might be one of the additions. Liturgical and musical considerations have already given us reason to question LAUDATE DOMINUM (with its second verse, QUONIAM CONFIRMATA), the only Cantus assigned to a specific Lenten Saturday. Also suspect is the Good Friday chant, SUPRA DORSUM, perhaps like *Eripe me*, its Gregorian counterpart, "nuperrime compilatum." SUPRA (like LAUDATE), has a text obviously chosen for the occasion, and its melody is rather too similar to that of SUPER FLUMINA – an obvious choice for a model, considering the resemblance of the incipits (compare, especially, the phrases "w" in Example 11). As the model had only one verse, the continuation of the Good Friday Cantus, i.e. DOMINUS IUSTUS, was fashioned after DOMINUS CUSTODIAT (the relationship of the two "A2" melodies in Example 4 is unmistakable) and DOMINE EXAUDI (compare the phrases "w" in Example 11). Once again, the chants are related by incipit. It is probably a further indication of the late intro-

---

[3] For a convenient summary of the Tract repertory see Apel, *Gregorian Chant*, pp. 313-14.

duction of these two Cantus that the adaptations of the second-verses of LAUDATE and SUPRA are not consistent with those of the other chants. The use of "A2" and "Z2" accords with the other last-verses, but the W, X and Y phrases are those of initial verses (please refer to Table 2).

Although it is not a question of chants for new occasions, but rather of the elaboration of chants already in place, one must also question the second- and third-verses of the Mass pieces. No one examining the Cantus could fail to notice that the musical settings of the subsequent verses are much more regular than the initial ones: more regular melodically (they are, as we have seen, scarcely differentiated at all), and more methodical with respect to the disposition of the syllables. These two styles, casual and regular, obviously represent different stages in the development of the chants. Since it can scarcely be supposed that the initial verses are later, it follows that the second- and third-verses were additions, possibly (although this seems rather improbable) replacing earlier versions that, had they survived, would exhibit the same kind of diversity as the first verses. It is likely, moreover, that the settings that are regular in formation were introduced not long before the codification of the chants, since their divergence (inevitable over a long period in an oral tradition) is so slight.

Although it seems unlikely that these regular settings of second- and third-verses in the Mass chants replaced earlier less regular ones, it seems to me quite probable that the phrases "Y" of the initial verses do. The adaptations of this phrase are almost perfectly regular, both in melody and in the disposition of the text. And the phrase "Y" stands, in these respects, in marked contrast with the other text-bearing phrases of the first-verses The assumption is, that the phrase "Y" replaced a variety of phrases "y" that, had they not been lost, would exhibit about the same degree of diversity as the other parts of the first-verses. This process of normalization (that is, the substitution of a single, standard, version for a number of melodies whose relationship had become attenuated over time) was obviously not carried out for the earlier parts of the first-verses, nor at all for NISI QUOD, whose phrase "y" would appear (as I have already suggested) to be the sole survivor of the earlier stage.

If "Y" is the result of a revision, so, it would appear, is "Z," which is always associated with it. "Z1," slightly less elaborate than "Z," is used to conclude the unrevised phrase "y" in NISI QUOD. It will be seen in Table 2 that it is also found in three other first-verses that – presumably since they have no Y phrase (in these three cases the second half of the psalm verse was very brief and there was no need of this part of the melody) – were allowed to remain as they were. Finally, it would seem to follow that "D1," which (as may be seen in Table 2) is associated with "Z1," belongs to an earlier stage of the Cantus than the more elaborate "D."

The unchanging melismas that are featured in the regularly-formed phrases "A1," "A2," "C1," "C2," "W1" and "Y1" (see Examples 4, 8, 12 and 15) may have been present in the added (or substituted) second- and third-verses from the beginning. But it is also possible, especially since the similarly normalized phrase "Y" does not have such features, that these were later interpolations. Of these, the very long first melisma of "C1" is much more extensive, and exploits a higher range than its counterpart in "C2" (curious features, since the general tendency is that such elaborations are carried furthest in the final verses). "C1" and "C2" share one melisma. It may be that, at an earlier stage, they shared both. The longer and more elaborate first melisma of "C1" is probably the later of the two.

To continue with the matter of later interpolations, the phrase "y" of NISI QUOD includes a long melisma – developed by successive repetitions (these are marked in Example 15) – that is obviously a later feature. This melisma, on the last syllable of the word "Dominus," is similar enough to the melisma, also on "Dominus," that has been inserted between the B and C phrases of IN CONVERTENDO (this insertion is represented in Table 2 by an asterisk) that one would appear to have been the source of the other.

The addition of phrases "a" and "B2" to the beginning of HEU ME (see Table 2) has evidently been made to provide scope for a descriptive melisma on the first word. The added musical material is not new, but the "word painting" that results most certainly is. I have already suggested that the verse HEU ME, the second-last of the psalm, was chosen instead of the usual final verse precisely because its first word presented this opportunity for dramatic treatment.[4] The comparisons given in Example 3 show that the model for the first part of HEU ME was ANIMA NOSTRA, where the extra A and B phrases were required for the very long first semiverse of the psalm. I have already mentioned that this circumstance explains why the continuation of the first phrase of HEU ME employs "A1" (as in ANIMA) rather than the "A2" that would be expected for third-verses. I mention it again because it is a further sign that the melody used for the opening of HEU ME has been borrowed.

Between the C and D phrases of ECCE QUAM is a melisma (it begins like the one added in the "W1" phrases, and in the continuation makes use of motives familar in the Cantus) on the word "jucundum." This too is to be explained as an example of late "word painting."

There remains to be discussed only the substitution of extraneous material for standard phrases. We may fairly leave aside the musical settings of the words that introduce and conclude the canticles.[5] It can hardly be doubted that these verses are later additions, and it is clear that no attempt has been made, in setting them to music, to employ the standard Cantus melody. Apart from these, extraneous material is found only in the CANTEMUS.

The beginning of the canticle proper has been set to a "foreign" melody (see Table 4), apparently to provide a smooth transition between the added introduction (which occupies a lower range and in all the early manuscripts concludes on f) and the standard Cantus melody (which is entirely in a higher range and has g for a final). It will be seen in the Edition that the beginning of the canticle does conform to type in *MUh*, but circumstances suggest that this is the result of a late revision carried out in the interest of tonal consistency.

---

[4] It comes to mind that this striking detail may have been suggested by the liturgical dramas, which were already widespread in the eleventh century. In a number of them, similar emotional interjections are sometimes set to affecting melismas. See, for example, "O dolor" in the Lament of Rachel (N. Greenberg, ed., *Play of Herod* (New York, 1965), pp. 94-96, or "quid ploras" (A. Hughes, ed., *The New Oxford History of Music*, II (Oxford, revised first edition, 1955), 187).

[5] "Hymnum Danielis," "Tunc hi tres," "Tunc cantabat Moyses," etc.

A more extensive substitution of extraneous material is found in verses 4 and 7. There, the expected A and C phrases have been replaced (see Table 4). The substituted melody has been assigned the letter "O," rather than simple asterisks, in order to show its reappearance). The ad hoc nature of this substitution – whatever the source of the melody – is betrayed by its awkward adaptation in verse 4. There, phrase "O" is supplemented, quite unnecessarily, by an additional foreign interpolation (indicated in the Table 4 by the asterisk). The corrupt state of the CANTEMUS, at any rate of some of its verses, is indicated in another way as well. It will be remembered that in verses 3, 4 and 7, the divisions of the text phrases and the musical phrases do not always coincide. Willi Apel has pointed out that such instances, where "musical units cut right across the textual divisions," are signs of "decadent days."[7]

---

[7] *Gregorian Chant*, p. 274.

IX

AMBROSIAN, GREGORIAN, OLD-ROMAN AND OLD-BENEVENTAN

In the earliest Gregorian and Ambrosian books, the number of occasions for Tracts and Cantus is roughly the same: of the latter, there are 18, of the former, 17. The Old-Roman Gradual[1] contains 20 Tracts, four of which can be identified as Gregorian additions. This rough similarity in the size of the repertories is perhaps to be expected, in view of the general agreement between the Milanese and Roman calendars and the restriction of these chants, in both liturgies, to occasions of penance. When the number of verses is considered, however, the Gregorian and Old-Roman repertories are seen to be rather larger than the Milanese: 59 and 88,[2] as compared to 47 Ambrosian verses. And if we take into

---

[1] Margareta Landwehr-Melnicki, ed., *Die Gesänge des altrömischen Graduale* [Vat. lat. 5319] (Kassel and Basel, 1970). The introduction to the edition is by Bruno Stäblein.

[2] This figure counts the number of verses designated in the manuscript, however the number of Old-Roman verses is rather closer to the Gregorian figure than this number would suggest. It is difficult to make an exact comparison, since in the matter of the verse-divisions, the Gregorian, Old-Roman and Ambrosian versions of the chants frequently disagree.

account that 22 of this latter number are found in the two Ambrosian canticles alone, the discrepancy will be seen to be that much greater. None of the Gregorian and Old-Roman Tracts (except only *Laudate dominum*, whose two verses comprise all of Psalm 116) has fewer than three verses; more than half of the Cantus have only one.

Although the early Gregorian and Ambrosian repertories are roughly similar in size, there is less agreement in other respects. Indeed, there are certain general differences in the liturgical assignments that should be noted. Although Cantus are supplied in the Ambrosian books for Lenten weekdays, there are no Tracts, at least no proper Tracts, for these feriae; on the other hand, for the feasts that fall within the period when the Alleluia was excluded, there are no proper Cantus, yet there are eight such feasts that are assigned Tracts in the Gregorian books.

It may seem surprising, considering the much closer relationship between the Gregorian, Old-Roman and Milanese liturgy in the choice of texts and liturgical assignments in the case of certain other Mass chants (the Ingressae-Introits, for example, and the Alleluia verses), that there is so little agreement between the Ambrosian and Roman practice in the case of the Cantus and Tracts. In only a few instances is the same text chosen, and even in these cases, only those of Holy Saturday have the same liturgical assignment.

However, this lack of agreement in the matter of choice of text and liturgical assignment is accompanied by striking agreement in the musical procedure. There is only one authentic type-melody for the Tracts (the eighth-mode melody), only one for the Cantus. Moreover, the Gregorian, Old-Roman, Old-Beneventan (as it would appear from the few examples that are known to have survived) and Ambrosian melodies, although thoroughly differentiated in detail, are obviously related – most likely through a common ancestor. These circumstances are another indication that the Tracts and Cantus belong to an early stratum of the ecclesiastical chant.

Since the beginning of this century, there have appeared several studies of the Tracts. One of the most influential of these studies, by Dom Paolo Ferretti,[3] included analyses of the Gregorian melodies, anal-

---

[3] *Estetica gregoriana* (Rome, 1934), French translation, *Esthétique grégorienne* (Tournai, 1938).

yses that are supported by examples drawn from only a few of the chants, but would appear (to the unwary at least) to represent the repertory as a whole. Ferretti's analyses present a false picture of a musical practice that is, in fact, far less regular than his over-simple account suggests. The shortcomings of the learned Benedictine's work (which contains, nevertheless, a great many valuable observations) have not gone unnoticed. Willi Apel remarks (in *Gregorian Chant*), concerning the "principles governing the succession and function of the standard Tract-phrases . . . , that most of [Ferretti's] statements are incorrect."[4] But although Apel does go on to chart, without attempting to take account of details, the recurrences of related phrases in the eighteen Tracts found in the earliest Gregorian books, a really satisfactory analysis of the Gregorian repertory has yet to appear.

A thorough analysis of the Gregorian Tracts will obviously be required before their relationship to the Ambrosian melodies can be properly assessed; and the Old-Roman repertory will require no less attention. Just as obviously, these studies cannot be undertaken here. For the moment, I can only offer a comparison of those few chants that adapt a related melody to the same psalm-verse, and a few interesting conclusions that arise from these comparisons. As for these conclusions, some of them must inevitably – since, like Ferretti's, they are based on a sampling of pieces, not the whole repertory – be seen as tentative. It must be said, however, that the Tracts that represent the Gregorian repertory in the following comparisons, although the choice has been made for purely practical reasons, seem in no way untypical.

But before these particular comparisons are made, a few general observations will perhaps be useful. To begin with, there is, between the Tracts and Cantus, overall agreement in structure. In both, the text-bearing portions of the melody can be shown to be variously elaborated versions of a basic reciting formula. In the Gregorian, Old-Roman and Old-Beneventan versions of the chants, as in the Ambrosian, there are what I have referred to earlier as "prolongations" of the last notes of the text-bearing phrases. These important ornamental figures, which do not

---

[4] Page 317.

seem to occur as regularly in the Tracts, are in all versions (obviously, little can be said about the Old-Beneventan repertory) much more stable than the phrases they serve to conclude. The Ambrosian, Gregorian and Old-Roman versions of these figures are not in every instance the same. All appear to have undergone a similar kind of embellishment, however it would be difficult to show that the elaborations of the three versions are directly related; it is just as likely that these developments took place independently and locally. But these musical figures have obviously the same function, and are a striking demonstration of the fundamental relationship of Tract and Cantus.

In the Gregorian chants, as in the Ambrosian, phrases will be found to conclude on f, as well as on g. However, the occurrence of the f-phrases is not, as is the case in the Cantus, firmly associated with the psalmodic caesura. Indeed there seems to be nothing, except perhaps a desire for tonal variety, that would explain the Gregorian practice. Concerning the choice between musical phrases ending on f and on g, Ferretti could only offer the following (not very helpful) observation: "les mélographes aiment à [les] faire alterner."[5]

The *mélographes* may indeed have liked to do so, but such alternation is by no means the rule: there is at least one Tract in which four g-phrases occur in succession.[6] Phrases concluding on f occur very frequently at the caesura, but also as the setting for the first phrase of a psalm-verse or its last (see below, Example 20 (d)), or even successively. Moreover, the association of musical phrases concluding on f with subsequent phrases beginning on the same note, an association that is unvarying in the Ambrosian chants, is not always found in the Tracts. (In Example 20 (d), below, in the Gregorian version of *Qui regis*, the cadential prolongation just before the caesura, the figure that corresponds to the Ambrosian D-phrase, concludes on f, but it is followed by a musical phrase beginning on g.) The impression given is that the Gregorian g-phrases and f-phrases, with respect to the structure of the psalm verses, are more or less interchangeable – an observation that

---

[5] *Esthétique*, p. 137.

[6] The arrangement of the g- and f-phrases in the old Tract-repertory has been charted by Apel (*Gregorian Chant*, p. 319).

accords very well with the hypothesis put forward at the beginning of this present analysis.

The adaptation of the type-melody to the first phrase of the initial verses of the Tracts, the oldest ones at least, is generally (although by no means always) so similar that one suspects that what I have called a "normalization" has been carried out, a revision like those I have already postulated for certain (other) parts of the Cantus. For the Ambrosian opening phrases the situation is, it will be remembered, quite different: they are generally quite idiosyncratic. As for the other text-bearing phrases of the Tracts, they are more like the corresponding phrases of the Cantus, that is, they exhibit considerable variety – although, as in the Ambrosian versions, "occasionally the sections of two Tracts are melodically similar to one another."[7] It has been remarked of the Tracts generally (we have seen that the same is true of the Cantus), that the second halves of the melodies "are less variable than the first."[8]

I mentioned earlier that the Gregorian cadential flourishes, the (normally) melismatic parts that correspond to the B, D, X and Z phrases in the Cantus, are perhaps less consistently used than the Ambrosian. In one particular respect, the difference between the two practices is distinctive. In the Mass Cantus, there is a standard concluding formula for single-verse chants (phrases "Y"-"Z"), another (phrases "Y1"-"Z") for second-verses (when a third verse is to follow), and another (phrases "Y1"-"Z2") for concluding verses. The final verses of the Tracts, all the early ones at least, do employ a standard concluding melisma, but there is no consistent formula for the conclusion of the verses that precede. These features articulating the structure of the Cantus (as well as others involving the beginnings of the verses and the regular use of the phrases "A1" and "A2") would seem to be relatively late. But although such features are more consistently found, and more thoroughly integrated, in the Ambrosian Mass chants than in the Gregorian, the case of the canticles is quite different. The Gregorian version of *Cantemus* concludes with the same special formula found in all the other Tracts; in the Ambrosian canticles (CANTEMUS and BENEDICTUS) the final verses are not distinguished in any way.

---

[7] Helmut Hucke, in *The New Grove*, XIX, s.v. "Tracts."
[8] Ibid.

TABLE 9
GREGORIAN TRACT–VERSES
WITH AMBROSIAN COUNTERPARTS

TRACT VERSE	GREGORIAN ASSIGNMENT
Qui regis	for the Saturday of the Advent Ember Days and Annunciation
De profundis	for Septuagesima Sunday
Laudate dominum (verse ii) *Quoniam confirmata*	for the Wednesday and Saturday of the Lenten Ember Days, the Saturday of the September Ember Days, Holy Saturday and the Vigil of Pentecost
Supra dorsum meum *Dominus justus concidet*	set as parts of the Tract *Saepe expugnaverunt* for the fifth Sunday of Quadragesima

The verse *Supra dorsum* (Psalm CXXVIII, 3) is treated (in both the Gregorian and Old-Roman books) as though it were the second part of the verse *Etenim non potuerunt mihi*. Similarly, *Dominus justus* (usually considered to be verse 4 of the psalm) is set as the second half of *Prolongaverunt iniquitates suas*. There is, therefore, little to be learned from a direct comparison of these verses with their Ambrosian counterparts, beyond a general similarity of procedure (which will be obvious enough from the other examples) and a general relationship – equally obvious – between the Ambrosian and Gregorian melodies.

| *Domine exaudi* | for the Wednesday of Holy Week |

Domine exaudi, although given as a Tract in many of the later Gregorian books (and also in the books of the Old-Roman and Old-Beneventan tradition), employs a second-mode melody and is properly a Respond. It is so designated in the Sextuplex manuscripts. (Hesbert, *Sextuplex*, pp. 92-93.)

Table 9 (continued)

Cantemus domino   for Holy Saturday and the Vigil
(verse ii) *Hic deus meus*   of Pentecost
(verse iii) *Dominus conterens*

The Tract *Cantemus* has three verses, all of which are found also in the Cantus, but circumstances are again such that a direct comparison of the Gregorian and Ambrosian versions would reveal very little. The singers who adapted the standard melody to the Tract and the Cantus have (as far as the musical structure is concerned) interpreted the phrases of the poem quite differently. What is treated as one five-member verse in the Gregorian version forms the first three verses in the Ambrosian. What makes the matter even more difficult, the first words of the Cantus (as we have already noted) have been set to a foreign musical phrase. The Ambrosian second verse, HIC DEUS MEUS (as we have also seen), is virtually a free composition; the Gregorian employs the standard type-melody. As for the third verse, DOMINUS CONTERENS, a comparison of the two versions would not, perhaps, be entirely pointless, but neither is it straightforward. The Gregorian version does not divide the first semiverse; the Ambrosian, as we have seen, does. The Tract employs the standard Gregorian concluding-melisma; but although there is a corresponding formula in the Ambrosian Mass Cantus (the phrase "Z2"), DOMINUS CONTERENS is not, in the Milanese version, the last verse, and in any case, in the Ambrosian canticles the final verse is not distinguished in this (or any other) fashion.

Sicut cervus   for Holy Saturday and the Vigil
                                                 of Pentecost

The Gregorian Tract-verses in Table 9, all of which are found in the books of the ninth century, have Ambrosian counterparts. For most there are also Old-Roman versions. The exceptions are *Dominus conterens* and *Sicut cervus*, although for this latter chant the Old-Beneventan form survives. In Example 20, Ambrosian, Gregorian, Old-Roman and Old-Benventan versions of five Tract and Cantus verses are compared. In the transcriptions I have not differentiated melodic nuances such as quilismas and liquescents (for the present purposes the bare notes are sufficient), nor have I taken into account any variants that might exist in the different manuscripts of the Gregorian, Old-Roman and Beneventan tradition.[9] Not wishing to force the comparisons, I have usually aligned the melodies simply, syllable by syllable, even though more melodic correspondences (usually readily apparent in any case) could have been suggested by a more complicated arrangement. I have departed from this syllabic alignment only to show important similarities that might otherwise have gone unnoticed.

---

[9] The sources of the melodies (other than the Cantus) in Example 20 are: the *Graduale Romanum* (Tournai, 1945), the Melnicki edition of the Old-Roman Mass chants already cited, and Benevento MS VI.40 (*PM*, XIV [Tournai, 1931]).

Example 20

Ambrosian, Gregorian, Old-Roman
and Old-Beneventan Chants Compared.

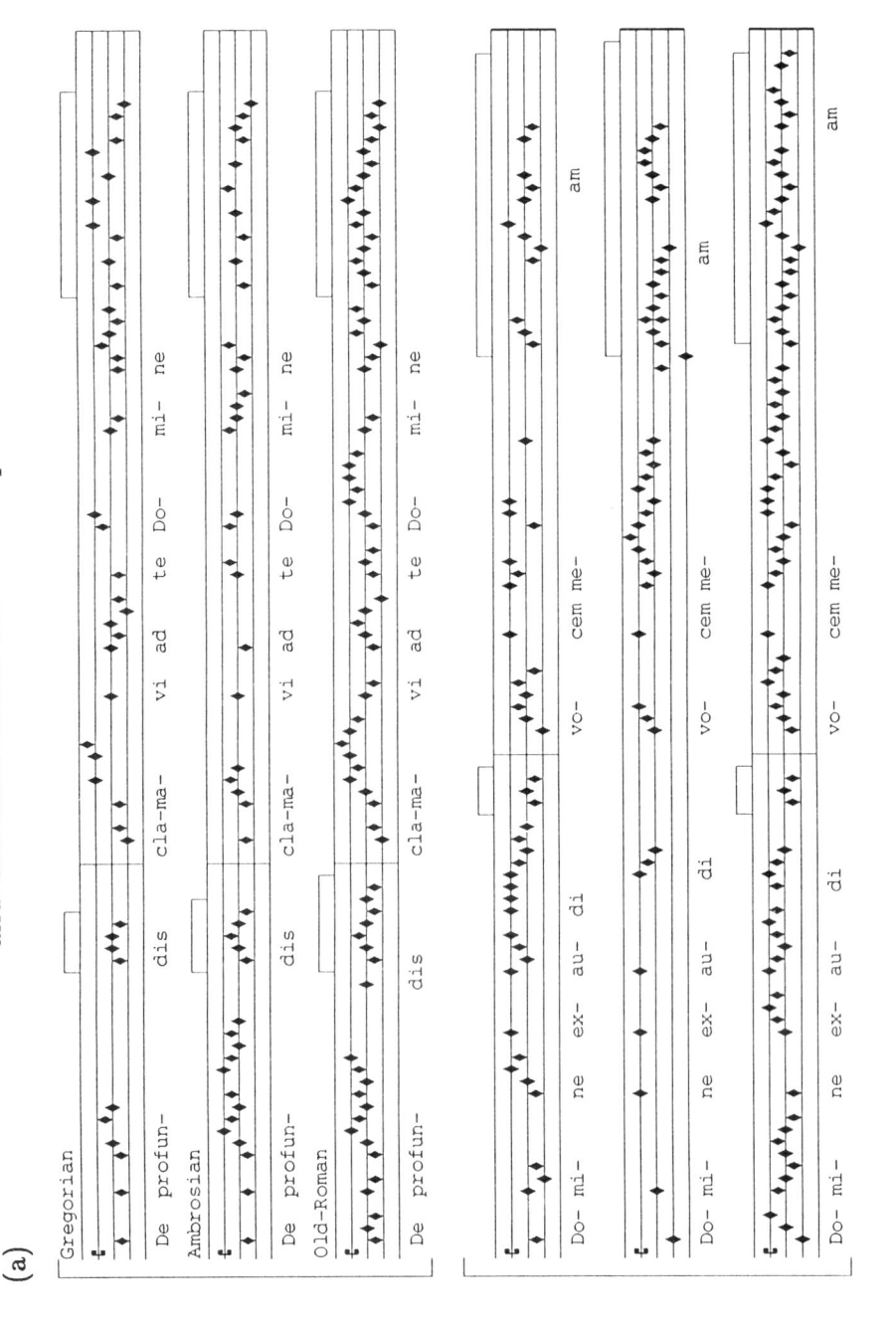

Example 20 (continued)

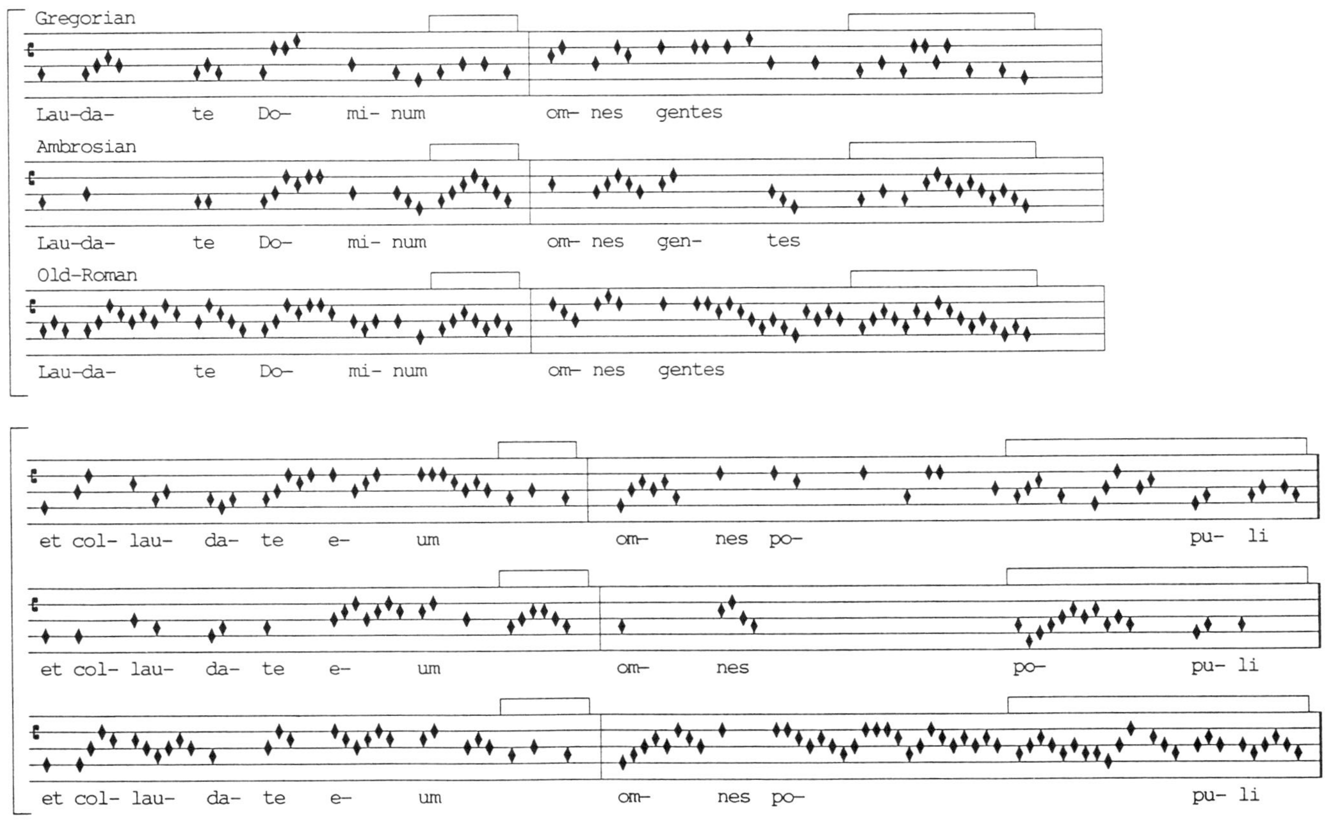

Example 20 (continued)

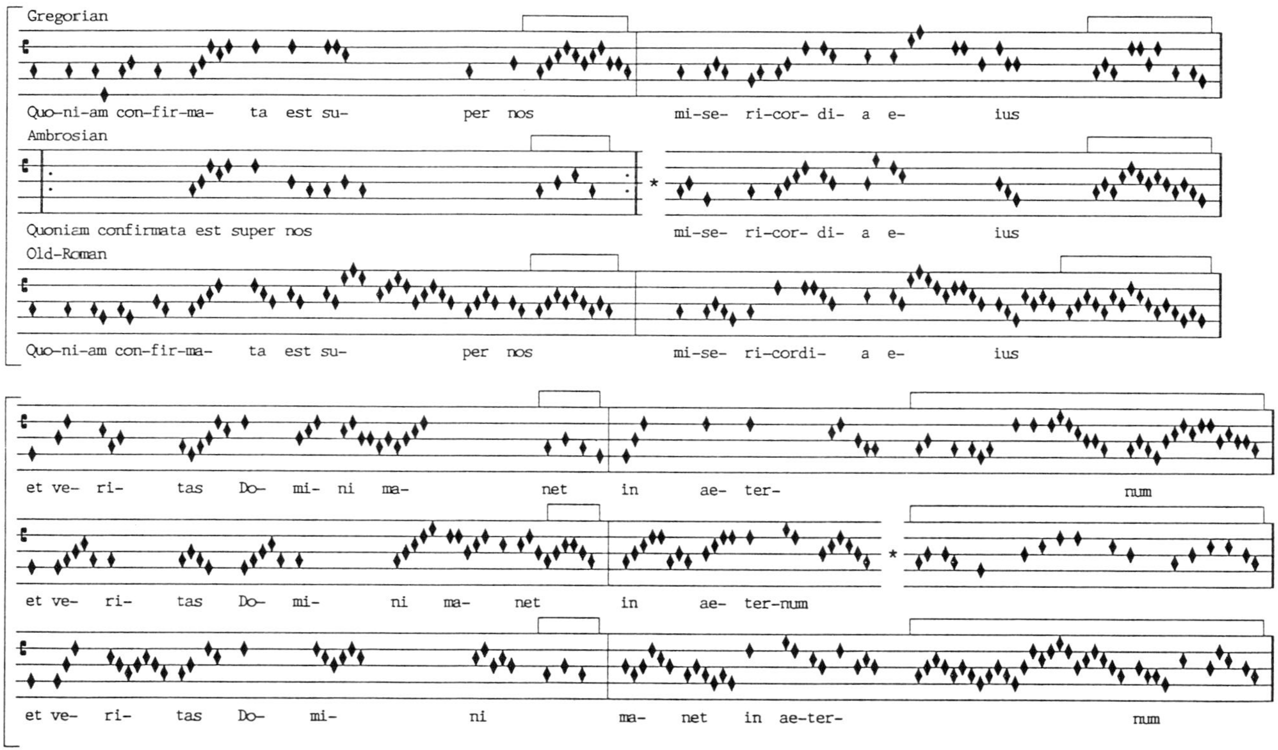

Example 20 (continued)

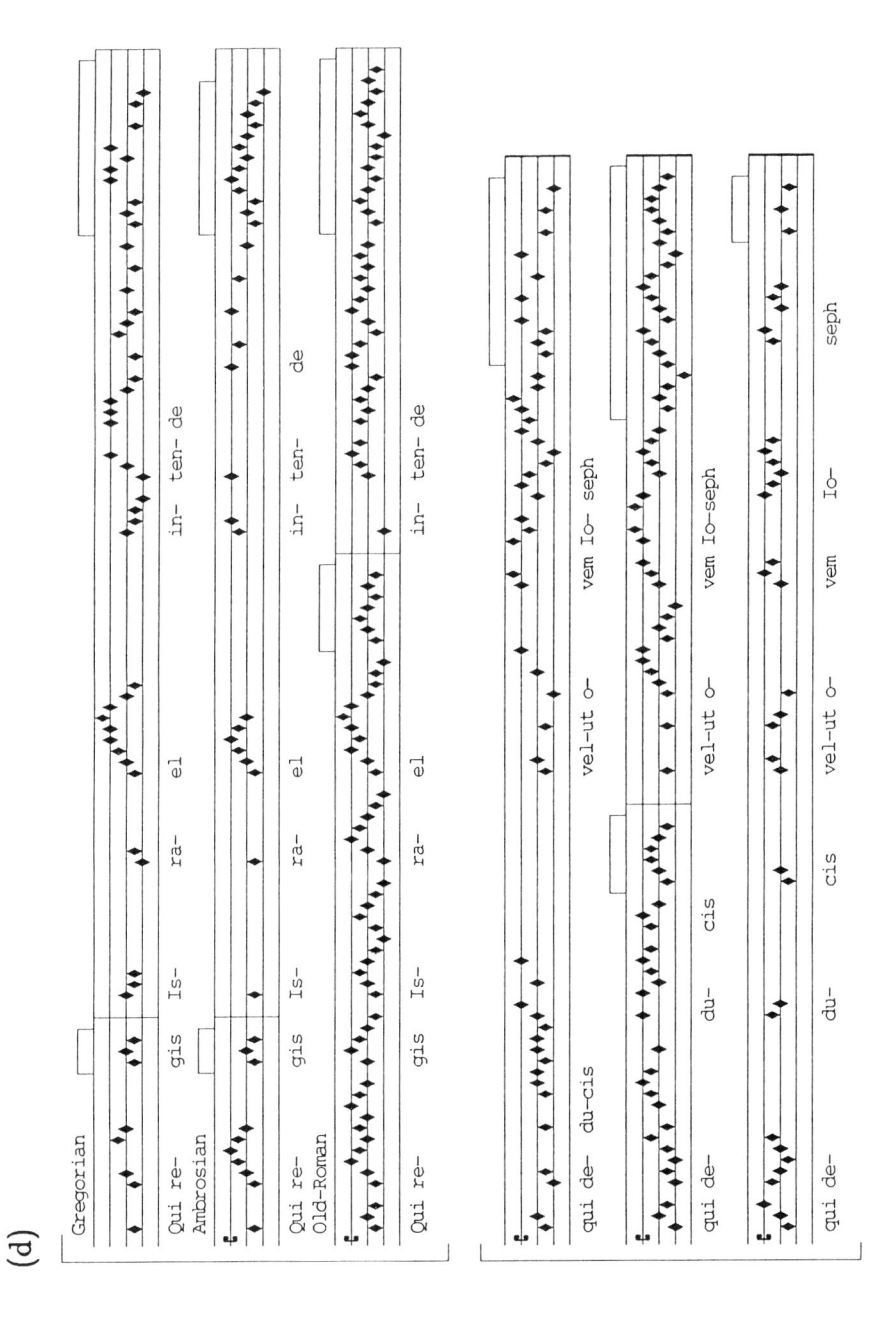

Example 20 (continued)

Example 20 (c) requires some explanation. In the Cantus verse QUONIAM CONFIRMATA I have omitted two melismas (later elaborations, as I have already suggested). The position of these melismas is indicated with asterisks, and what is missing can be recovered easily from the Edition. In this same Cantus I have also omitted, for practical reasons, the text set to Phrases "a" and "B" (this too can be recovered from the Edition). Although the Cantus employs the same basic melody as the Gregorian and Old-Roman versions for the first part of *Quoniam confirmata*, the Milanese adapted this melody to the long text differently – not by means of prosthetics, but by repeating (exactly) the notes that comprise these phrases. This repetition is indicated with the usual double-bar sign.

I will consider first the matter of overall structure. In LAUDATE DOMINUM, QUONIAM CONFIRMATA and QUI REGIS the four text-bearing parts of what we have seen to be the normal Cantus melody (the A, C, W and Y phrases of the analytical tables given above) and the four cadential prolongations (the B, D, X and Z phrases) will be seen to have Gregorian and Old-Roman counterparts. (In the Gregorian and Ambrosian QUI REGIS, the first semiverse is divided, and the B phrase inserted, after "regis"; the division, and the B phrase, occur after "Israel" in the Old-Roman version, but the correspondence of structure is nonetheless clear.)

The familiar four-part structure is not found in all the chants of Example 20. In the Ambrosian DE PROFUNDIS, the second semiverse (for obvious grammatical reasons) has been treated as a unit; there is no X phrase. However, in the Gregorian and Old-Roman versions of this chant (grammar notwithstanding), a figure that corresponds to the Ambrosian X phrase does divide the second half of the psalm-verse. The second semiverse of SICUT CERVUS is undivided in the Gregorian, Ambrosian and the Old-Beneventan versions, and there is nothing in this chant that corresponds to the X phrase. In the Old-Beneventan Tract the first semiverse is also undivided. As it happens there is no bipartite Cantus verse, but if an Ambrosian setting had been required for a psalm verse whose sense did not allow a division of either half, in such a case the the structure that would be expected (namely, AB WZ) corresponds to that of the Old-Beneventan version of *Sicut cervus*.

Although there is not, in every case, a perfect correspondence in structure between the Ambrosian, Gregorian, Old-Roman and Old-Beneventan chants compared in Example 20, there is an obvious and fundamental similarity in structural principle that – even if there were not other more particular indications – would attest to a common parentage.

But of course there are many such indications. First of all, there is a general melodic relationship. It would be premature to conclude that what I have suggested as the underlying tonal structure of the Cantus (a structure that corresponds to the psalm-tone of Example 1) is also the exact tonal basis of the Gregorian, Old-Roman and Old-Beneventan Tracts – although that would appear to be the case for the chants we have examined, and is historically plausible in view of Rome's central position in the development of western ecclesiastical chant. But even if the details of their *initium* and *terminatio* should prove to be local options, a cursory overview of these local repertories is sufficient to show that, for all, the ideal shape of the psalmodic formula is a melodic arch whose apex (c′) is the principal reciting-tone, and whose tonal architraves are the notes (g) with which the formula begins and ends.

The relationship of the Ambrosian, Gregorian, Old-Roman, and (as far as one can tell from the little that survives) the Old-Beneventan cadential prolongations is even more obvious. These too are based on a melodic arch, at its simplest formed by the *finalis* of the reciting formula and the upper neighbour of this note. But the unembellished figure (g a g), although it appears frequently enough, is very often (in the case of the Cantus, usually) expanded to reach b, c′, or higher. The Milanese D phrases (and in most cases, it would appear, what corresponds to these phrases in the Tracts) have been extended, as well as expanded.

We have seen some evidence already in support of the hypothesis, presented at the beginning of this analysis, that this extension of the cadential prolongations to conclude on an f immediately before the caesura of four-part Cantus was originally (however important this feature may have seemed later) an inessential detail; that this f was added to prepare for the idiosyncratic opening (on this same note) of the W phrases; that the cadential elaborations ending on f are not essentially different from the others concluding on g. This hypothesis is considerably strengthened by the situation in the Old-Roman version of *Qui regis* (Example 20 (d)). This is a quadripartite Tract-melody, in which the cadential prolongation before the caesura (the D phrase, as it were) will be seen to conclude on the note g (the following phrase begins also on g). Of course the Old-Beneventan version of *Sicut cervus* (Example 20 (e)) presents the same situation, but in fact this example only confirms what we already know. In this instance the first semiverse is not divided, and we have seen that in such cases the Ambrosian versions customarily conclude the first half of the psalm verse on the note g (see Table 1, the Cantus-verses, LEVAVI OCULOS, DOMINE EXAUDI, BENEDICAM DOMINUM and DOMINUS IUSTUS).

PREFACE TO THE EDITION

The Milanese did not divide the music for their Mass and Office (except in the latest period, when Gregorian influence prevailed) between an Antiphoner and a Gradual. The Ambrosian Mass and Office chants are found together, although usually bound into two books, one, the *pars hiemalis*, for the winter season (the period from November 10, the vigil of feast of St Martin, to Holy Saturday) the other, the *pars aestiva*, containing the chants for the rest of the year. The principal occasions for the Cantus fall, of course, in the winter period; in the *partes aestivae* one finds only the Cantus (or merely cues to the chants) for feasts[1] important enough to have a vigil Mass, all of these chants borrowed (although never more than the first verse) from other occasions.[2]

---

[1] And for the Requiem Mass, when it is included.

[2] For the vigils of St Martin, St Ambrose St James, St Lawrence and John the Baptist, LEVAVI was sung; for Sts Protasius and Gervasius, ECCE QUAM BONUM; for Sts Nazarius and Celsus, Sts Peter and Paul and for All Saints, NISI QUOD. The choice of feasts to be celebrated with vigils is to some extent a regional option. The above assignments are found generally, but one would expect, for example (whether the manuscripts make any specific provisions or not), that a vigil was customary for the feast of the saint to whom the local church was dedicated. For the feast of the Assumption and the feast of the Nativity of the Virgin, the vigils were introduced only later, and Psalmelli are found in place of Cantus.

The manuscripts referred to in this edition as *L*, *Mh*,[3] *D* and *Vh* are the oldest copies of the *hiemalis*, the first three from the twelfth century, the last from the thirteenth. Where a melody is missing in one of these manuscripts, a fourth version has been supplied from *MUh*, a manuscript written in 1387.

THE SOURCES

Siglum	Manuscript	Date	FPCA[4] Catalogue Number
L	London, British Library, add. Ms 34209 (published in facsimile[5] in 1896)	XII	50
Mh	Milan, privately owned (formerly known as the Ms Varese-Eredi Bianchi)	XII	53
D	Milan, Biblioteca Capitolare del Duomo, Ms F.2.2 (known as the "Metropolitano")	XII	55
Vh	Vimercate, S. Stefano, Ms ssp B	XIII	218
MUh	Muggiasca, S. Lorenzo, without number (known also as the Vendrogno Ms)	1387[6]	62

---

[3] The "h" (for *hiemalis*) is used where both parts of the chant book survive.

[4] M. Huglo, L. Agustoni, E. Cardine, E. Moneta Caglio, *Fonti e paleografia del canto ambrosiano* (Milan, 1956). The catalogue of manuscripts compiled by Huglo et alii includes more complete descriptions than are given here and also much other useful information about the sources. *Fonti* had a complicated publication history, and it is important to note carefully the corrections and addenda. It is not always the best opinion concerning the dating and provenance that is found in the body of the book.

[5] *PM*, V. A transcription of the antiphoner was published as volume VI in 1900.

[6] At the conclusion of *MUh* is a note: "Expletum est anno Domini MCC-

The provenance of L is unknown. As for the other manuscripts, it may be assumed, at least, that they had been in use in the churches where they were found (*Mh*, in Varese).

There are a few obvious errors and omissions in the melodies. What is missing, when the omission is clearly inadvertent, has been supplied, but always from a parallel passage in another Cantus from the same source. It is important to note that there has been no conflation of versions from different manuscripts. Once or twice, errors (obvious enough in any case) have been corrected from subsequent appearances of the same melody in the same manuscript. However it should be noted that the melodies sometimes differ slightly in detail when copied more than once, even in the same hand.

This edition, whose aim has been to present the melodies as simply as possible, is not intended for paleographers; for their purposes nothing less than a facsimile would serve (for some details, only the manuscript itself). The transcriptions indicate no notational nuances except (by means of a hollow note) the *punctum liquescens*; but in any case, the Guidonian notation used in the Ambrosian chant books (with local variants, the same as that used in Rome and extensively throughout the northern half of the peninsula) no longer distinguished the quilisma and other such ornaments found in earlier chant manuscripts.[7]

In the interest of clarity of presentation, I have avoided the slurs that are a feature of some modern chant transcriptions. The position of the syllables is made clear in the Edition by the spacing; and as for the neume groupings, I have decided, after careful consideration, not to indicate them. The arrangement of the notes of melismas into groups of two, three, four and more is sometimes ambiguous in Guidonian notation, even when the extremely fine lines of ligation remain perfectly legible in the manuscript (which is very often not the case). The impor-

---

CLXXXVII die 17 decembris per presbyterum Fatium de Castoldis ben[efitiatum] eccl[es]iae s[an]c[t]i Michaelis ad cluxam M[edio]l[an]i porte ticinensis. F[a]c[tu]s in honore s[an]c[t]i Laurentii communitatis Mugiaschae. Eram annorum XXIX quando feci hunc librum." See Huglo, *Fonti*, p. 50.

[7] The quilismas included in Suñol's publication of the Ambrosian service books are editorial additions.

tance of such notational details may be gauged from the observation that the scribes commonly change the groupings in subsequent appearances of a melody in the same source, and even in subsequent appearances of a motive in the same chant. There will be no one, surely, to suppose still that such indications (especially in manuscripts of such late date) encode the secret of chant rhythm.

In order to facilitate references to the analyses given in Tables 2, 3 and 4, a single bar-line has been used in the Edition to mark the principal musical divisions of the verses. In the normal four-part chants, these bar-lines occur before the C, W, and Y phrases (in some of the Cantus, of course, the C or the Y phrase is not required). The musical articulation does not always correspond with the caesura and other divisions of the text as they are given in modern editions of the psalms and canticles. In a few instances (the occurrences have all been mentioned in the commentary, above), the musical division occurs in mid-word, and in such cases the bar line has been simply omitted in the transcription. A double bar has been used to mark the ends of verses.

Since the aims of this edition are limited (there has been no attempt to derive the "correct" form of the melodies, although a good deal might be said about such an undertaking), it has been possible to present the chants almost without critical apparatus.

The *traits verts* added in *L* to indicate the occurences of b-flat have not been included – this decision made easier by the ready availability of *Paléographie musicale* VI, where the *traits* (or most of them at least) are marked, and by the circumstance that fading has made it impossible to be sure, in every case, whether they were intended.[8] It is generally agreed, on paleographic as well as musical grounds,[9] that these extra staff lines are revisions made by a second hand.[10] There can be lit-

---

[8] The problem is even more severe, obviously, in the monochromatic facsimiles published in *PM* VI.

[9] The editors of *PM* VI (p. 26) remark, concerning the *bémolisations*: "Elles révèlerait . . . une ignorance complète de la tonalité ancienne, et s'écarteraient des indications transmises par d'autres documents ambrosiens."

[10] That it is a "much later" hand, as the monks of Solesmes insist (*PM* VI, 26), seems not so clear.

tle doubt, as the authentic b-flats in *MUh* and later manuscripts (and other evidence as well) indicate, that at least some *bémolisation* was customary in the Cantus, whether explicitly marked or not. It is entirely possible, therefore, that the b-flats of the British Library manuscript were in the nature of a clarification of the practice, not a novelty.

Although the manuscripts have not survived entirely unscathed, it is generally possible to make out the intentions of the scribes. One or two passages in *L* are particularly faint (their reading was helped by an ultra-violet lamp[11]); very difficult, too, are the last pages of *D*, containing the Holy Saturday Chants. *Mh*, as will be noticed in the edition from the number of substitutions of readings from *MUh*, has a number of lacunae, involving, particularly, the last pages with the chants for Holy Saturday.

The transcription of the notation is generally quite straightforward, although it has been difficult in a few instances where one of the elements of a neume (the first note of the clivis and climacus, for example) is normally formed by a compound gesture of the pen, to decide whether one note was intended or two. In such cases, unless the components are unambiguously separate, the uncertain signs have been interpreted as single notes. It is interesting that at these very points of difficulty in the notation, the sources will as often as not disagree, some giving two notes, some one. This disagreement is itself a clear indication that such double notes are to be regarded as inessential details, but I am inclined to go further and suggest that some of the "nuances" derive entirely from notational ambiguities.

The texts of the psalm and canticle verses have been given in standard Latin, although, of course, the manuscripts present the usual diversity of medieval spellings. There is one exception. Although "hi" is the normal form, it has been necessary to retain the unusual spelling "hii" in the phrase ("Tunc hii tres") that introduces the Good Friday version of the BENEDICTUS canticle; in all the sources of the Edition, "hii" is set as two syllables. I have added only minimal punctuation.

---

[11] The present transcriptions of the Cantus in *L* do not always agree with those published in *PM* VI. It is consoling to observe that no one, not even a monk of Solesmes, is free from error.

There are a very few intentional text variants: "meam" for "tuam" in the verse DOMINUS CUSTODIAT (doubtless to accord better with the "meum" of the opening verse of the Cantus), an "et" inserted in the verse BENEDICITE ANANIA AZARIA (this is in the nature of a correction, since the "et" is properly in the Ambrosian HYMNUM TRIUM PUERORUM). All these variants have been included in the edition.[12] There are also a number of quite obvious mistakes ("descendet" for "descendit" (in all four sources for SICUT UNGUENTUM), "maris" for "mari," "est" for "es," "domino" for "domini," "laudabile" for "laudabilis," "gloriosum" for "gloriosus," "edebant" for "edebat," etc.). These obvious slips have been corrected without comment. Differences between the manuscripts in the placing of the syllables in the melodies have, of course, been noted.

The tabs on which are written the page numbers visible in the photographs of *L* published by the Monks of Solesmes[13] are not part of the manuscript, and cover an earlier foliation. But since most of my readers will have readier access to the facsimile than to the British Library, it seemed best to refer to pages rather than folios.

---

[12] The texts of the Cantus given in Suñol's *Antiphonale* include a number of readings, some doubtless intended as corrections, that are not found in the Ambrosian chant books, at least not in any of the oldest ones.

[13] *PM* V.

THE EDITION

QUI REGIS ISRAEL

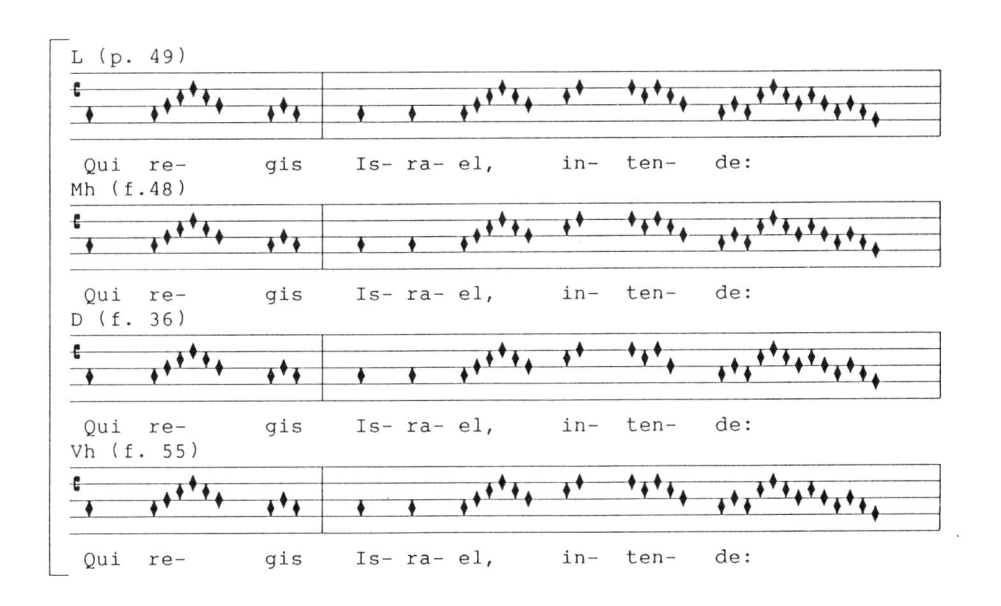

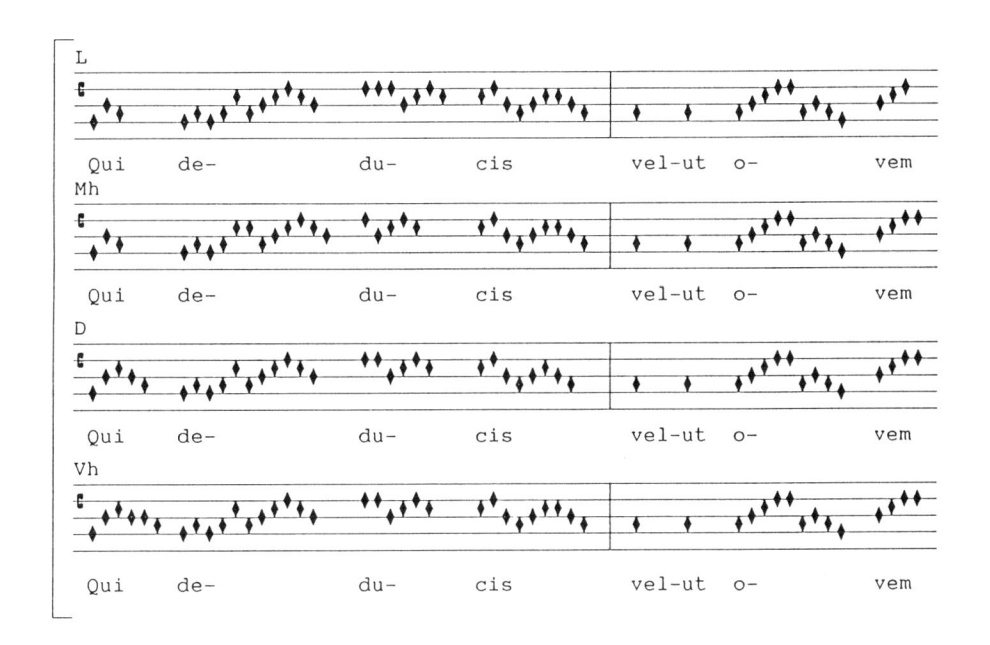

L (p. 49)

Qui re- gis Is- ra- el, in- ten- de:

Mh (f.48)

Qui re- gis Is- ra- el, in- ten- de:

D (f. 36)

Qui re- gis Is- ra- el, in- ten- de:

Vh (f. 55)

Qui re- gis Is- ra- el, in- ten- de:

L

Qui de- du- cis vel-ut o- vem

Mh

Qui de- du- cis vel-ut o- vem

D

Qui de- du- cis vel-ut o- vem

Vh

Qui de- du- cis vel-ut o- vem

QUI REGIS ISRAEL (continued)

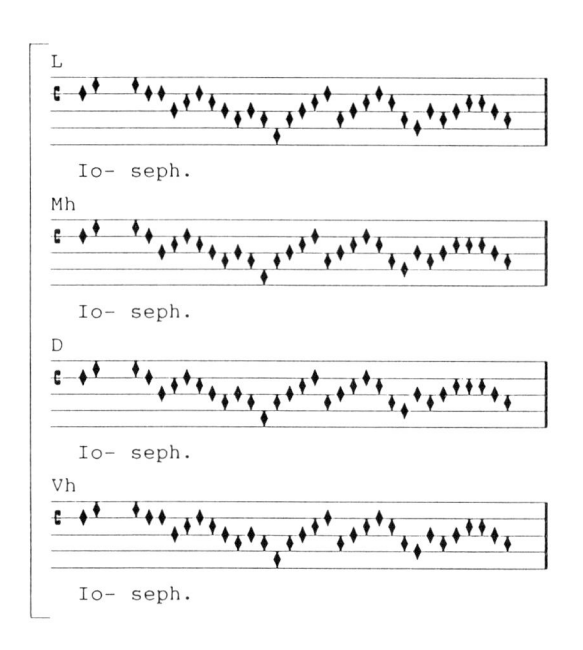

L

Io- seph.

Mh

Io- seph.

D

Io- seph.

Vh

Io- seph.

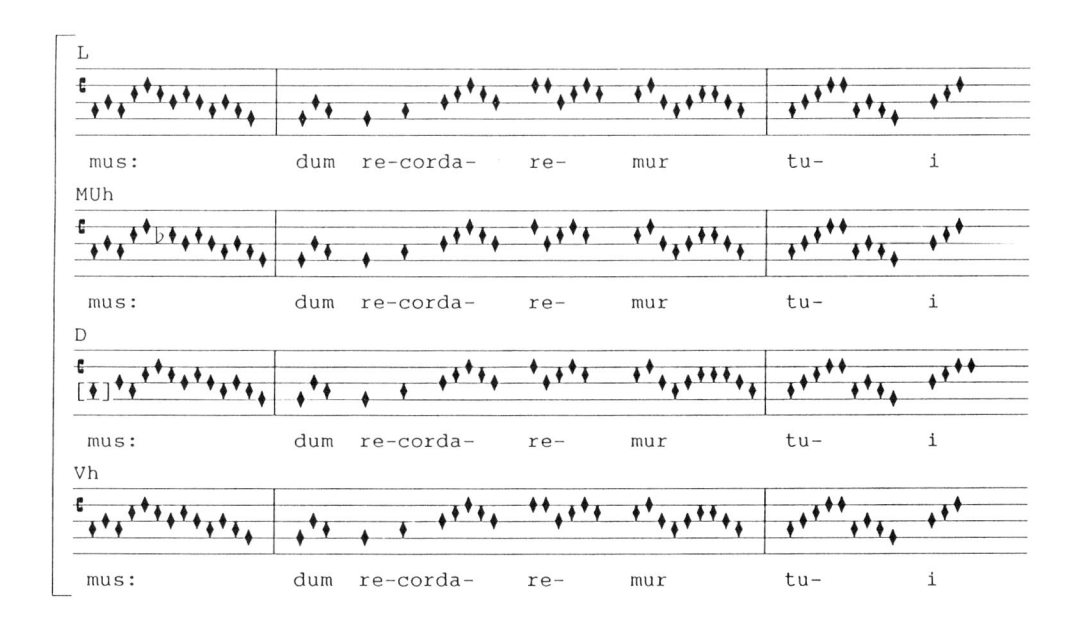

SUPER FLUMINA BABYLONIS

SUPER FLUMINA BABYLONIS (continued)

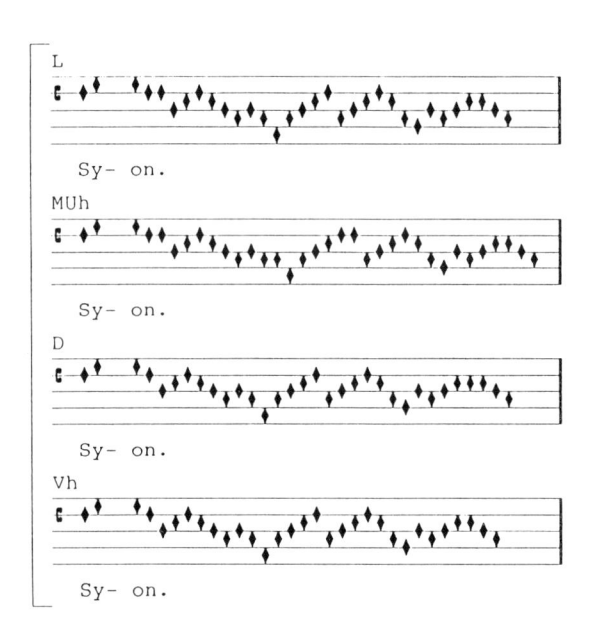

L

Sy- on.

MUh

Sy- on.

D

Sy- on.

Vh

Sy- on.

NISI QUOD DOMINUS

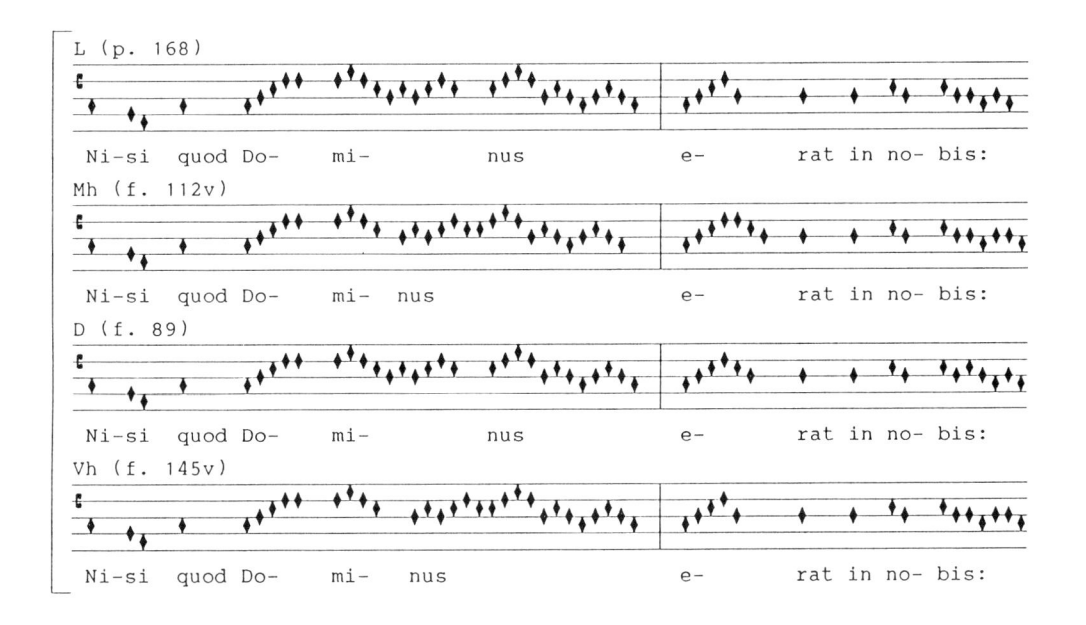

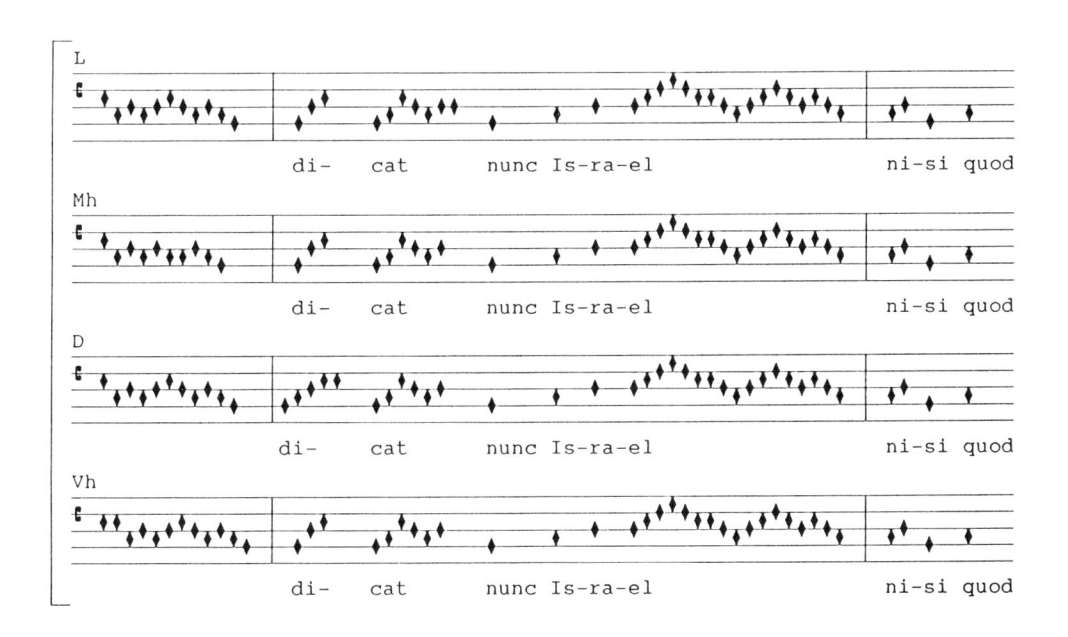

NISI QUOD (continued)

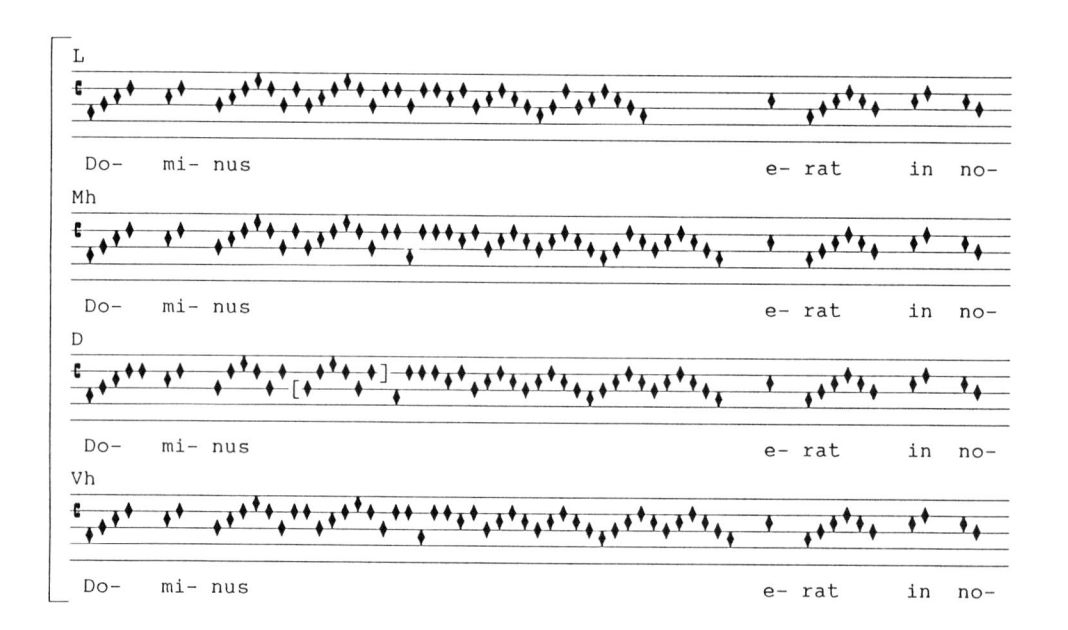

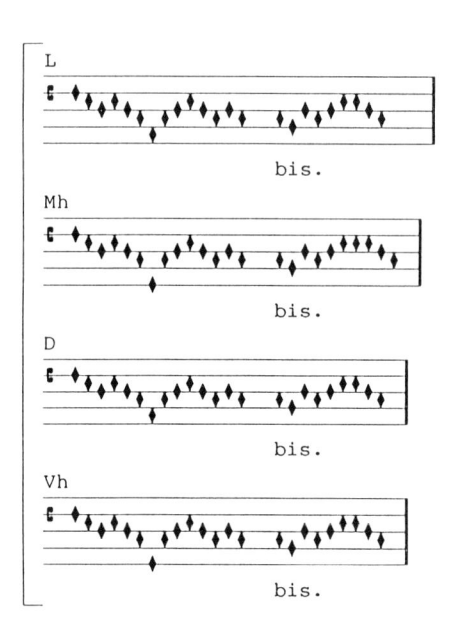

L: Do- mi- nus e- rat in no-
Mh: Do- mi- nus e- rat in no-
D: Do- mi- nus e- rat in no-
Vh: Do- mi- nus e- rat in no-

L: bis.
Mh: bis.
D: bis.
Vh: bis.

(ii) ANIMA NOSTRA EREPTA

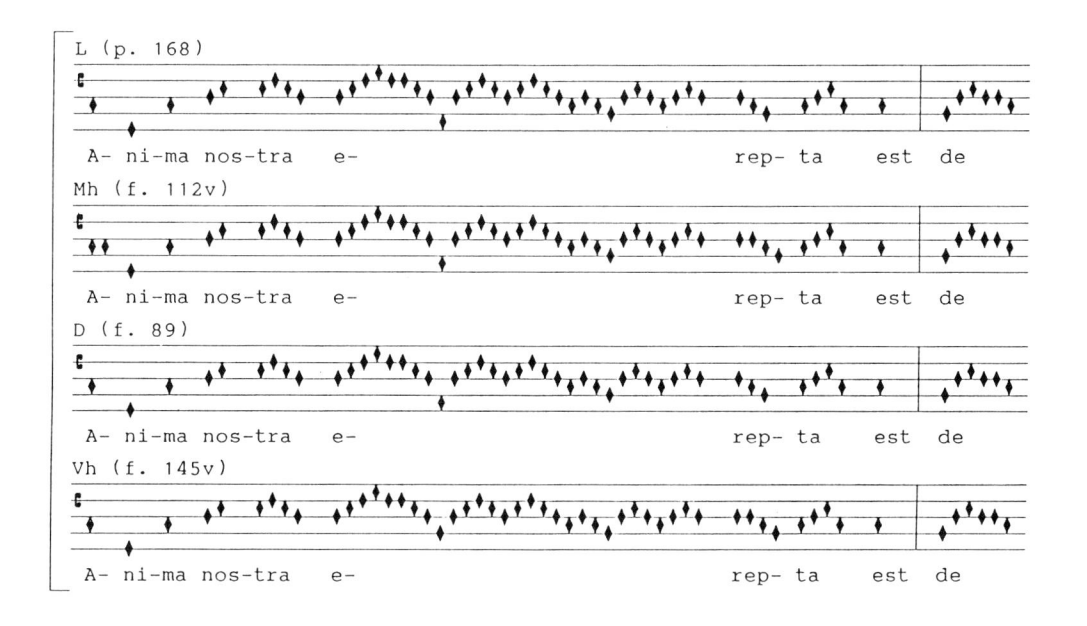

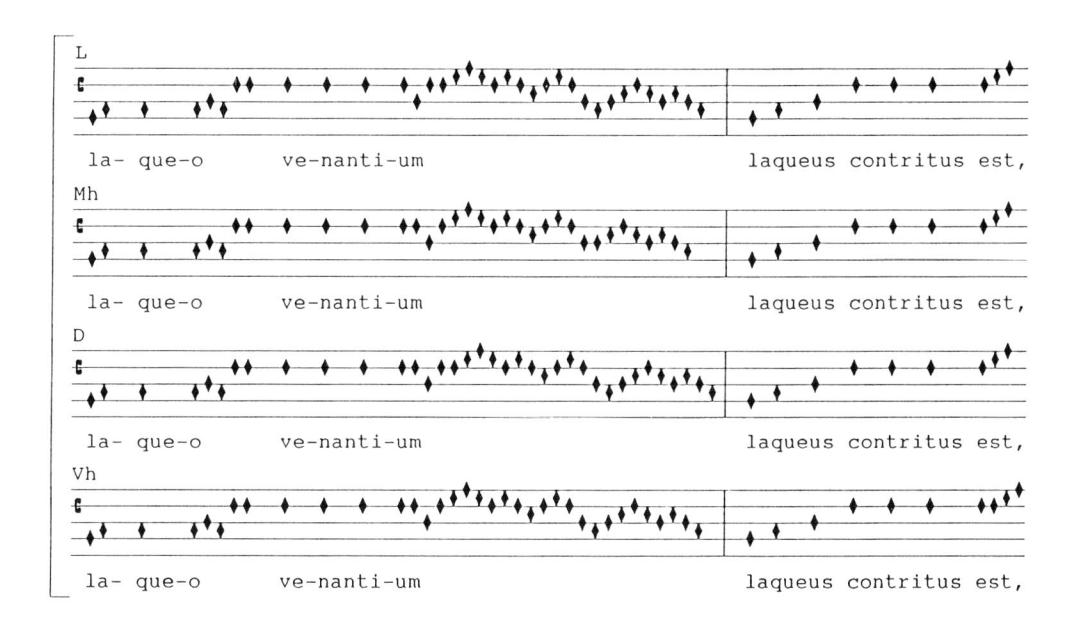

L (p. 168)

A- ni-ma nos-tra e- rep- ta est de

Mh (f. 112v)

A- ni-ma nos-tra e- rep- ta est de

D (f. 89)

A- ni-ma nos-tra e- rep- ta est de

Vh (f. 145v)

A- ni-ma nos-tra e- rep- ta est de

L

la- que-o ve-nanti-um laqueus contritus est,

Mh

la- que-o ve-nanti-um laqueus contritus est,

D

la- que-o ve-nanti-um laqueus contritus est,

Vh

la- que-o ve-nanti-um laqueus contritus est,

ANIMA NOSTRA (continued)

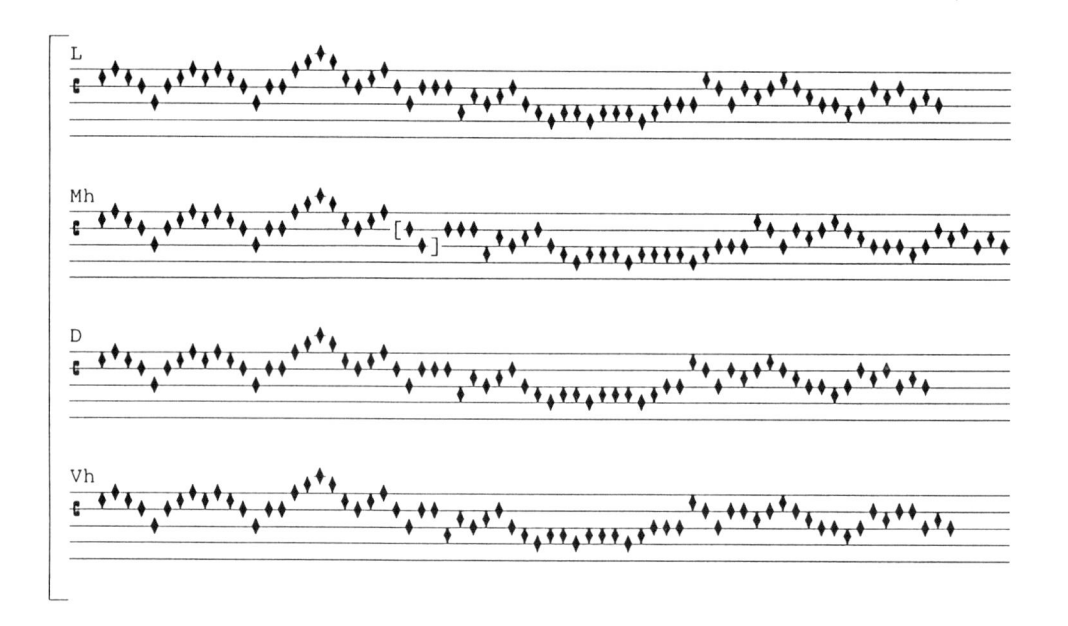

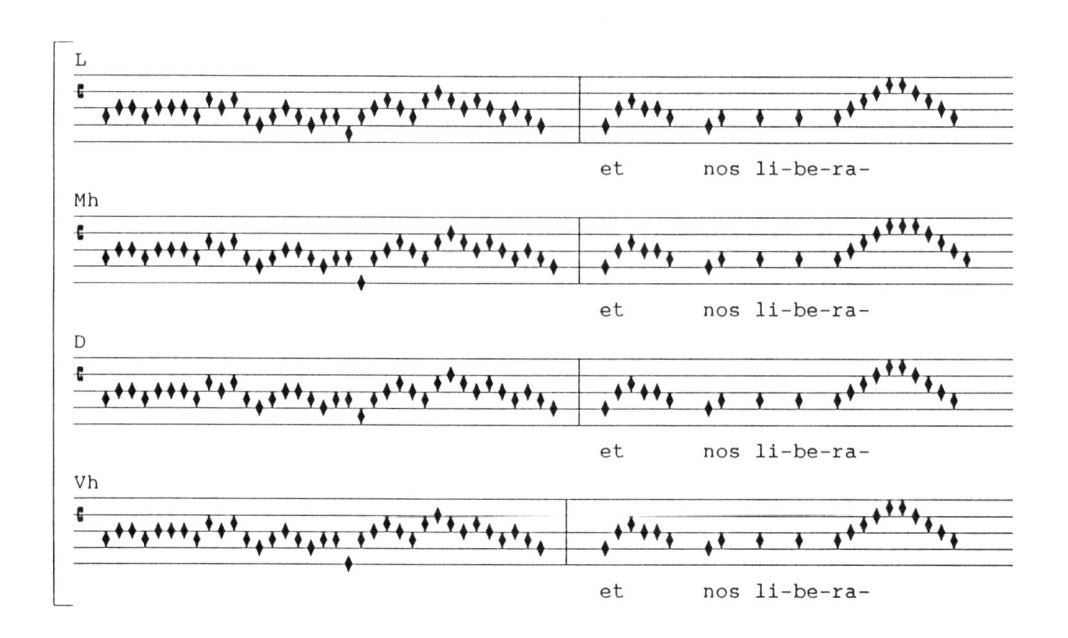

et nos li-be-ra-

ANIMA NOSTRA (continued)

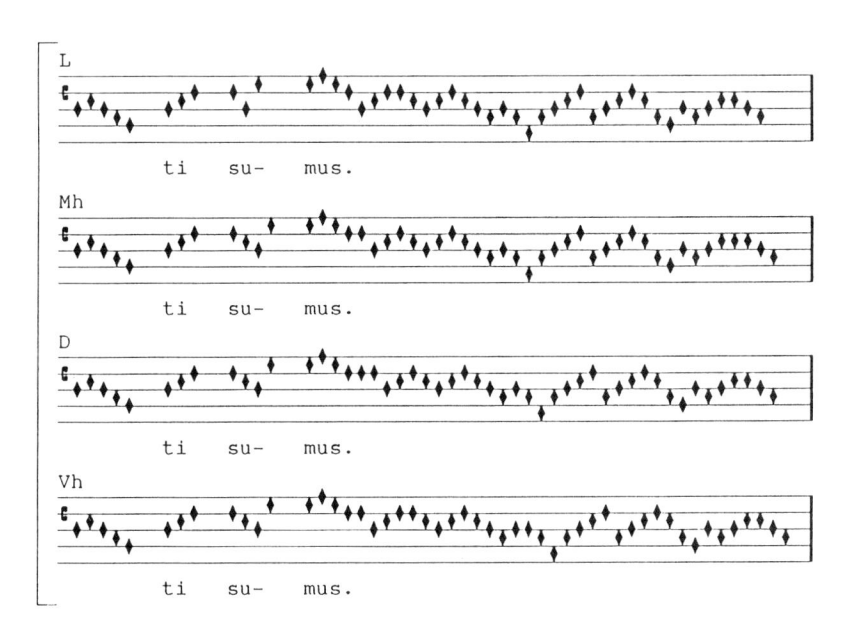

L: ti su- mus.

Mh: ti su- mus.

D: ti su- mus.

Vh: ti su- mus.

(iii) ADIUTORIUM NOSTRUM A DOMINO

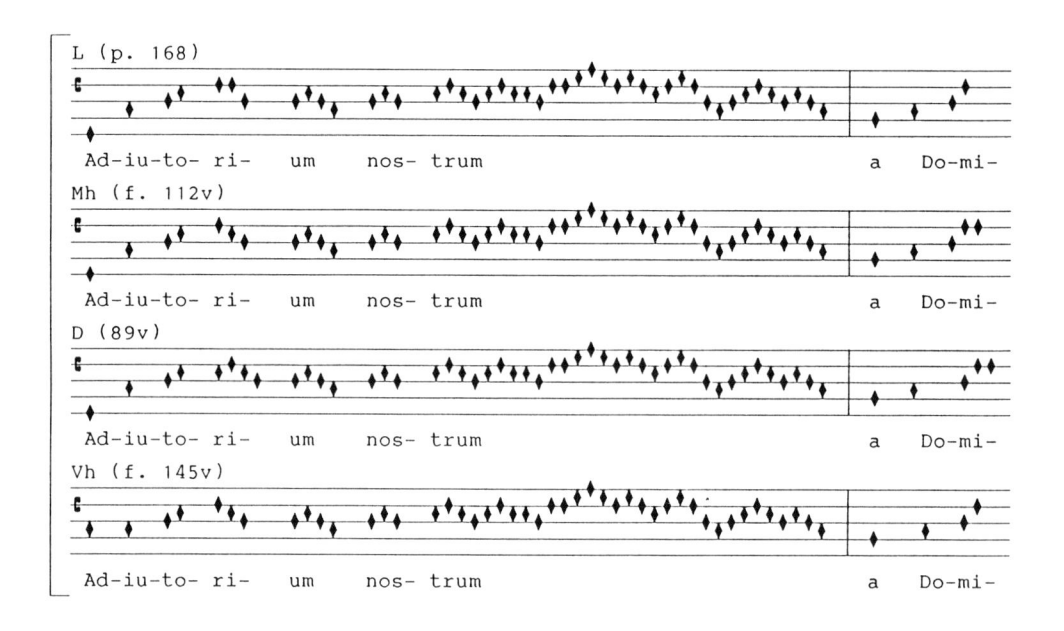

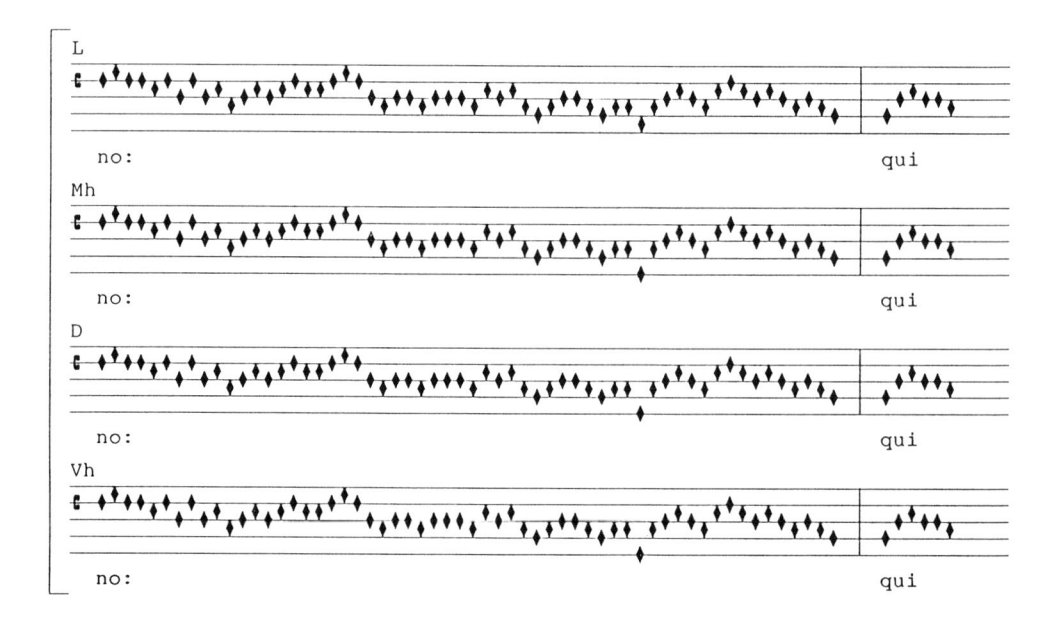

ADIUTORIUM NOSTRUM (continued)

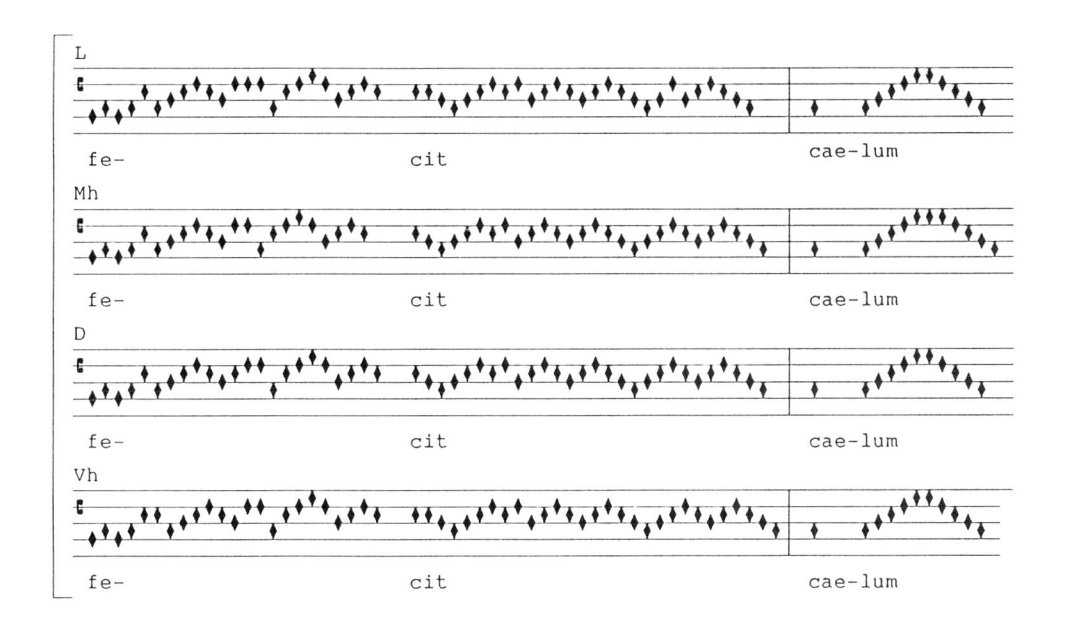

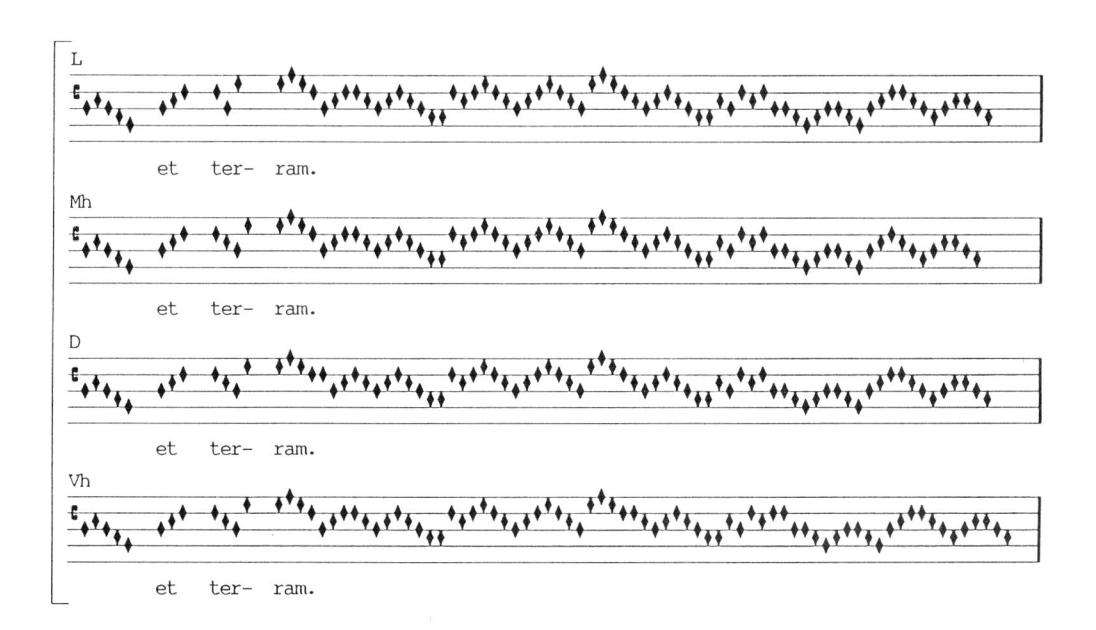

AD DOMINUM CUM TRIBULARER

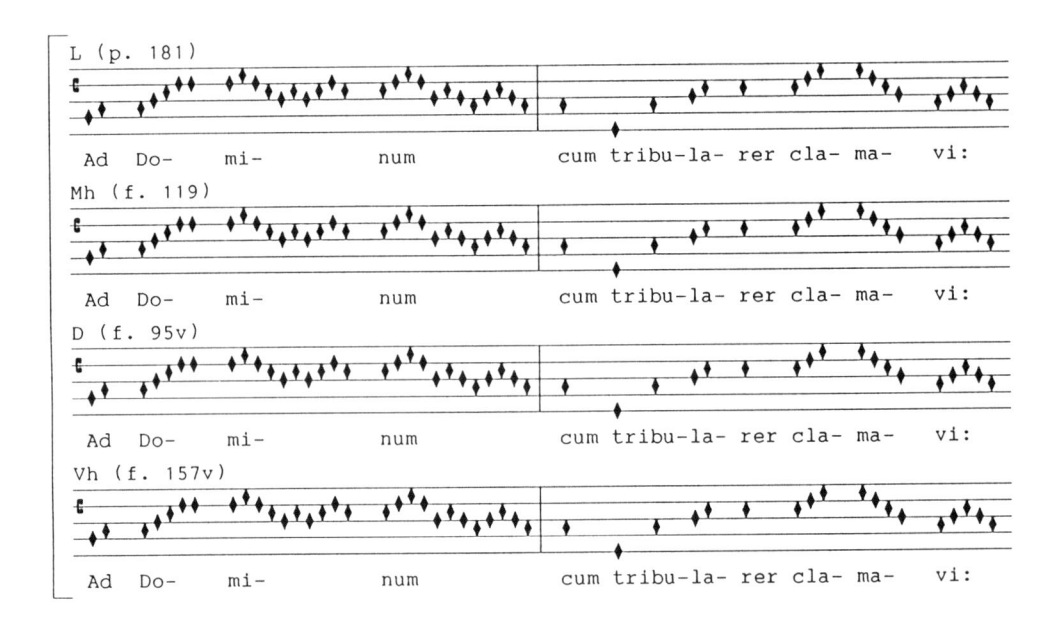

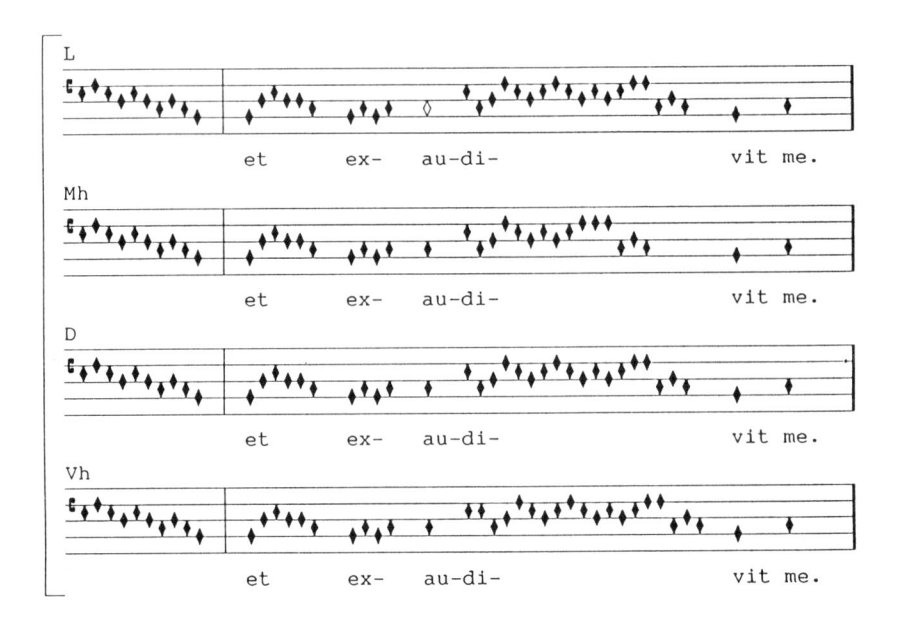

(ii) DOMINE LIBERA ANIMAM

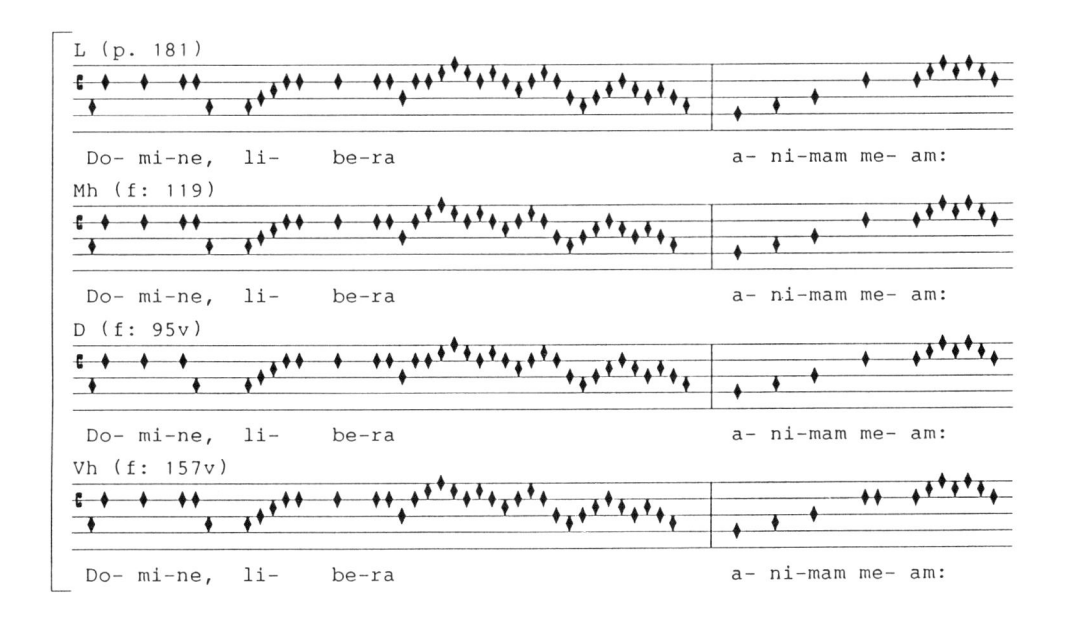

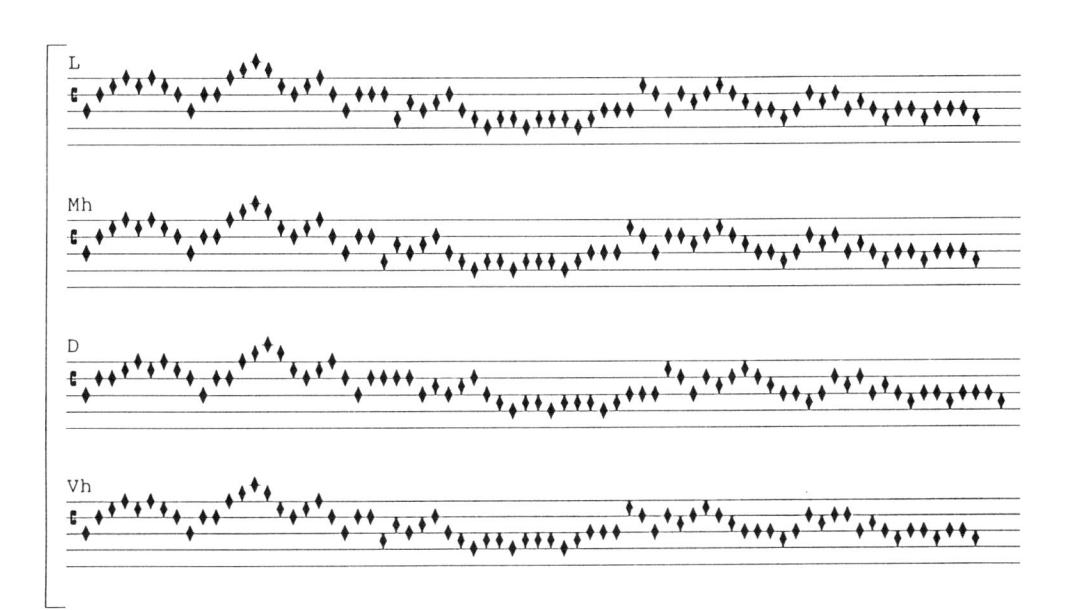

L (p. 181)

Do- mi-ne, li- be-ra a- ni-mam me- am:

Mh (f: 119)

Do- mi-ne, li- be-ra a- ni-mam me- am:

D (f: 95v)

Do- mi-ne, li- be-ra a- ni-mam me- am:

Vh (f: 157v)

Do- mi-ne, li- be-ra a- ni-mam me- am:

DOMINE LIBERA (continued)

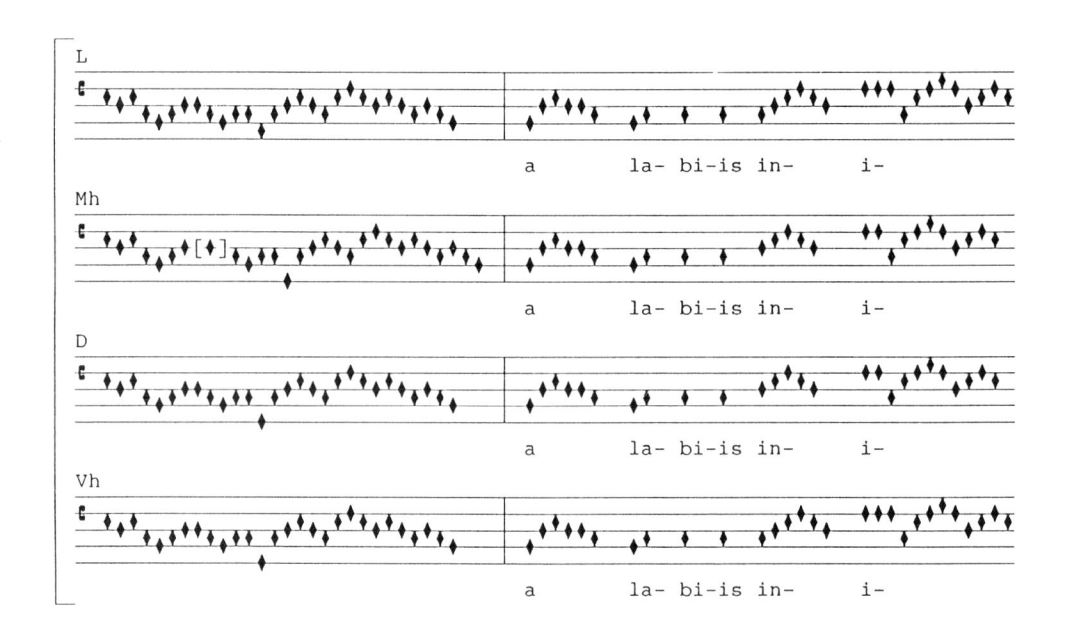

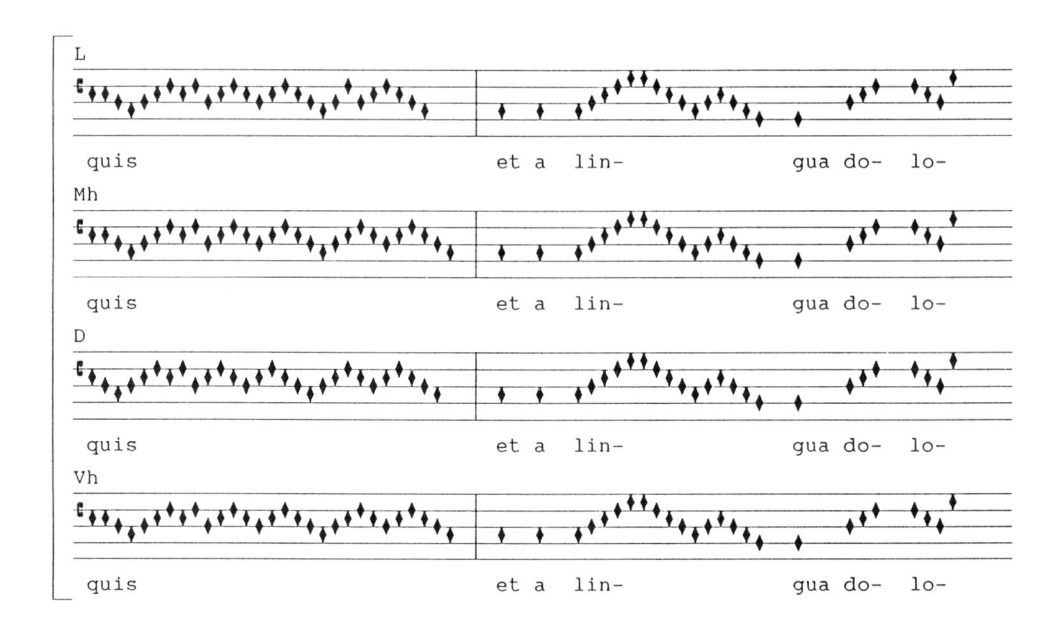

a la-bi-is in- i-quis et a lin- gua do- lo-

DOMINE LIBERA (continued)

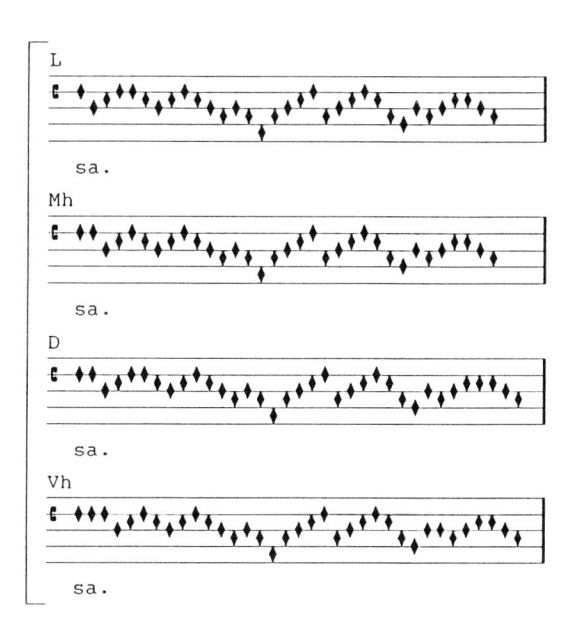

L

sa.

Mh

sa.

D

sa.

Vh

sa.

(iii) HEU ME QUOD INCOLATUS

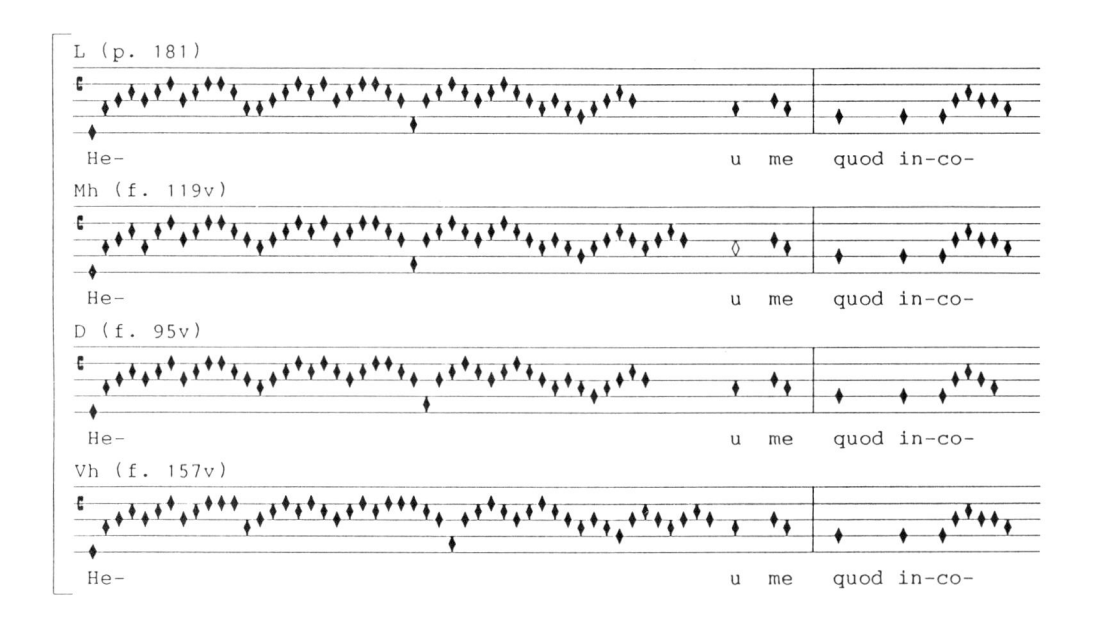

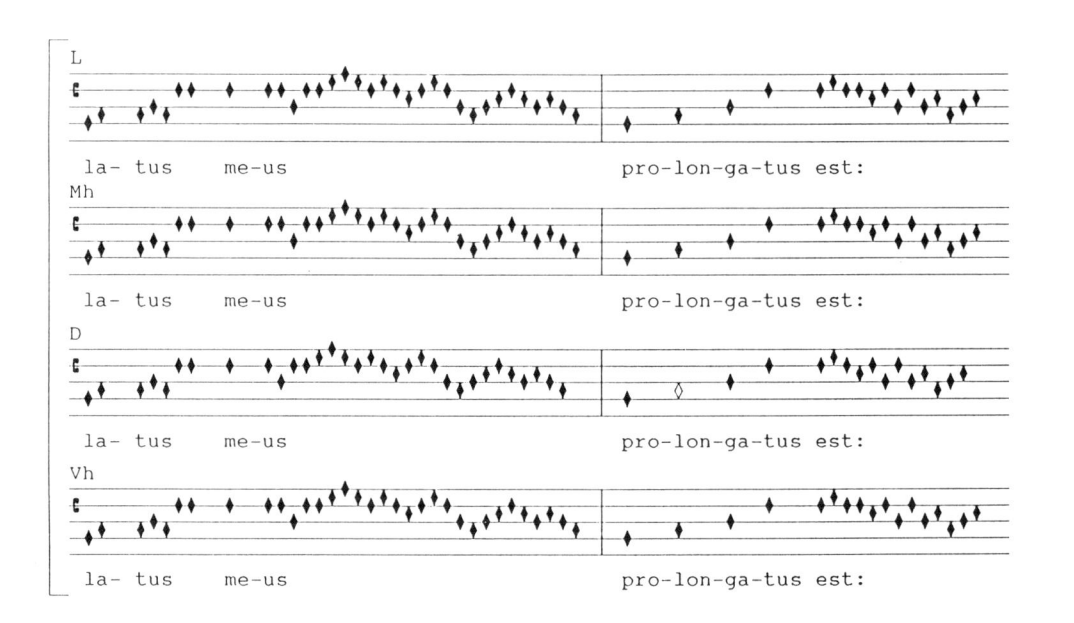

L (p. 181)
He- u me quod in-co-

Mh (f. 119v)
He- u me quod in-co-

D (f. 95v)
He- u me quod in-co-

Vh (f. 157v)
He- u me quod in-co-

L
la- tus me-us pro-lon-ga-tus est:

Mh
la- tus me-us pro-lon-ga-tus est:

D
la- tus me-us pro-lon-ga-tus est:

Vh
la- tus me-us pro-lon-ga-tus est:

HEU ME (continued)

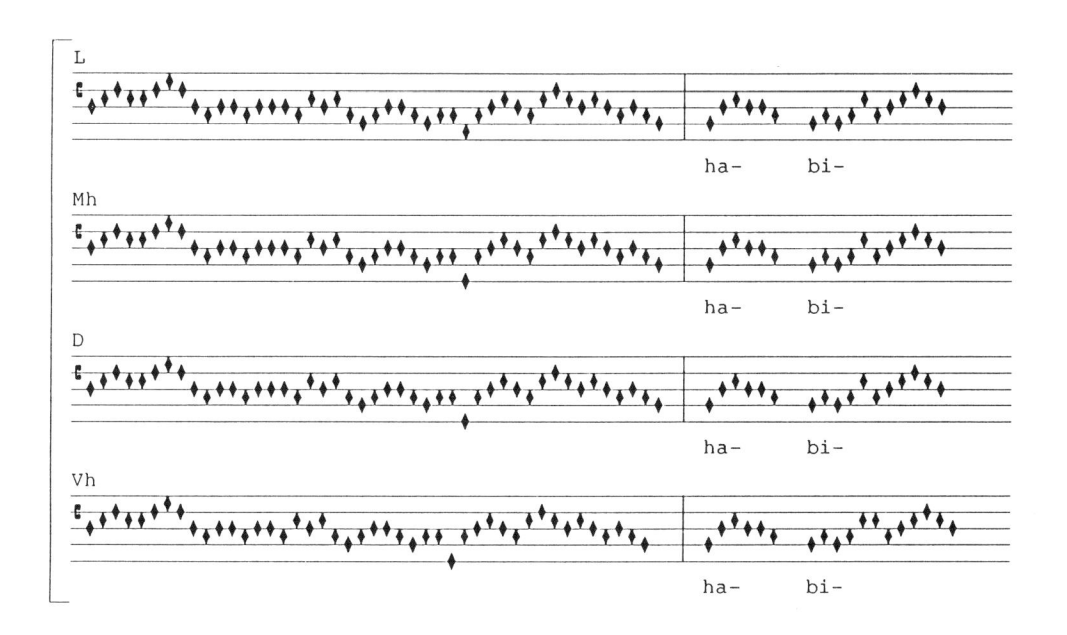

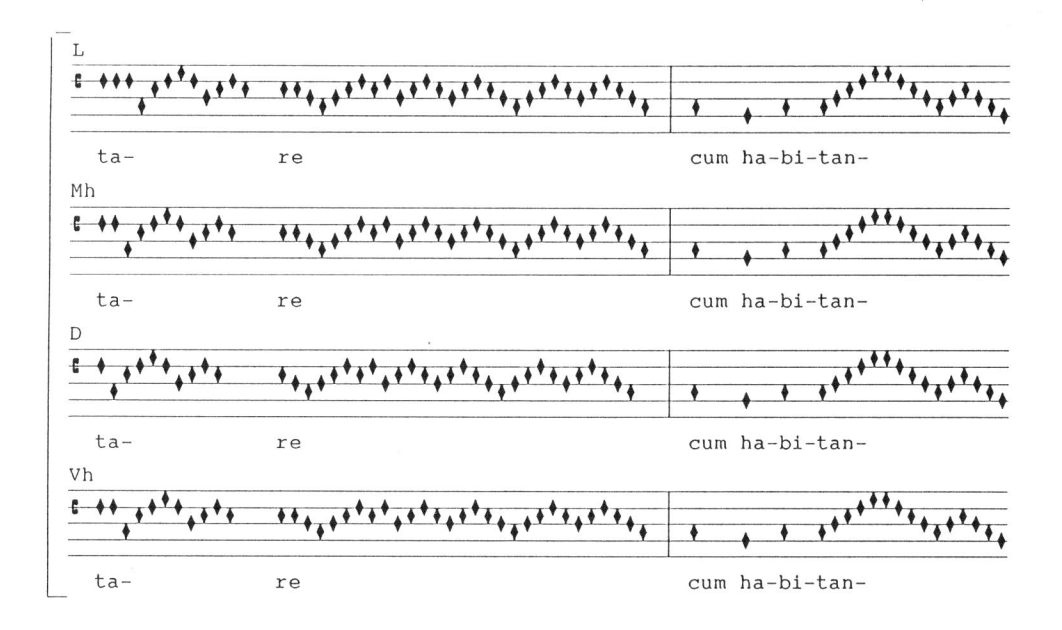

HEU ME (continued)

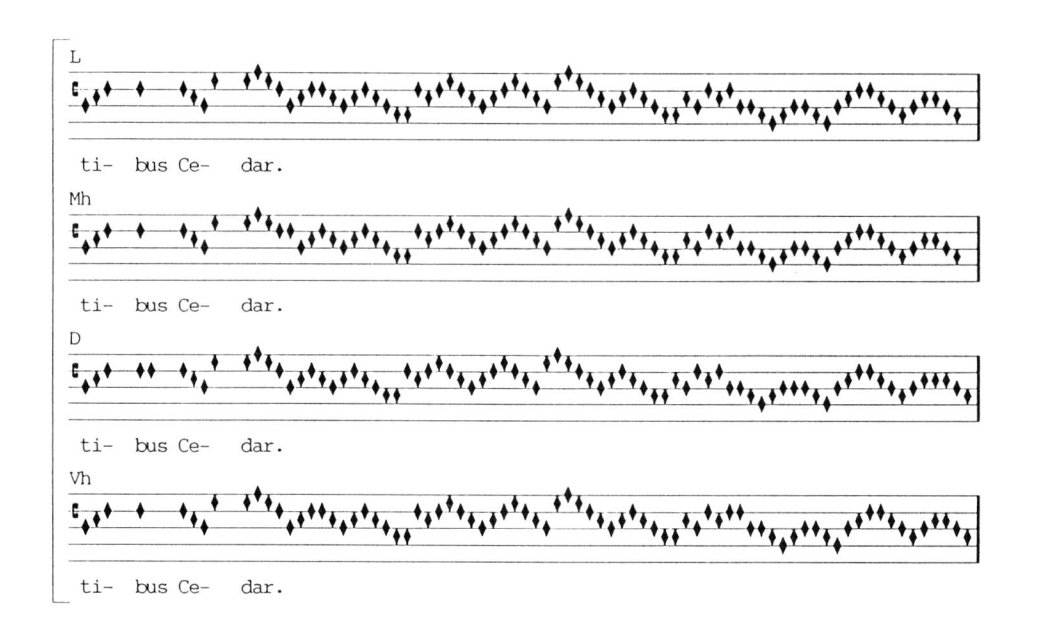

LEVAVI OCULOS MEOS

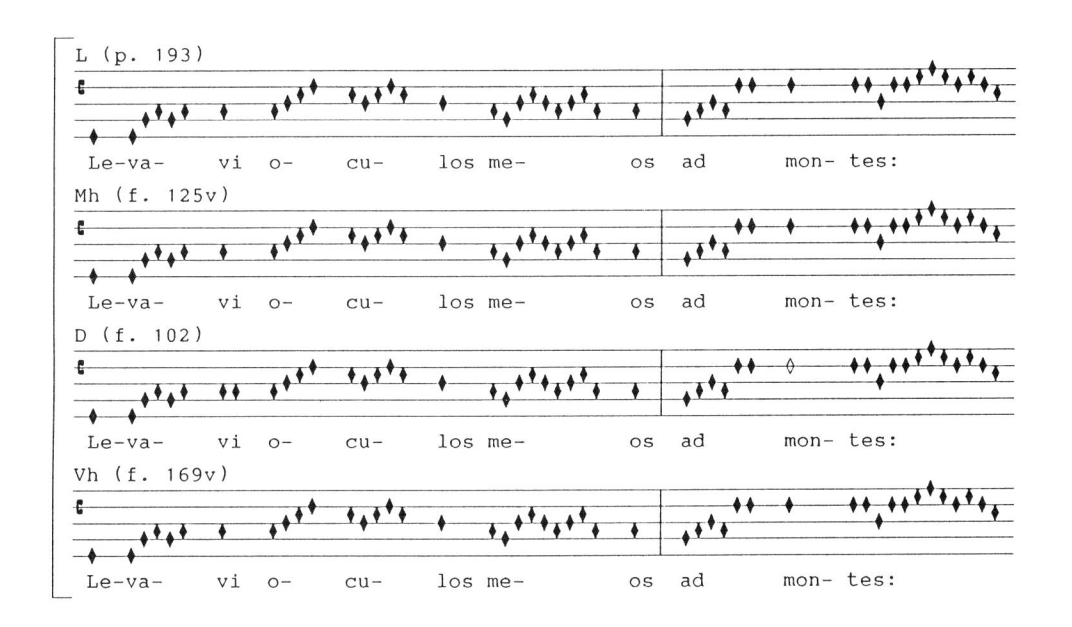

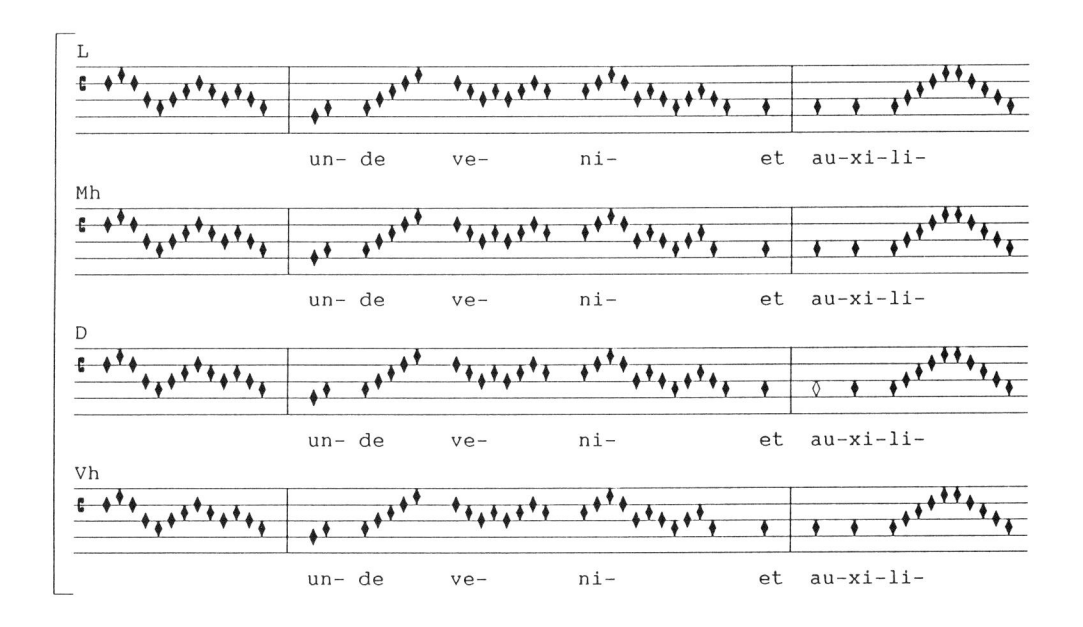

LEVAVI OCULOS MEOS (continued)

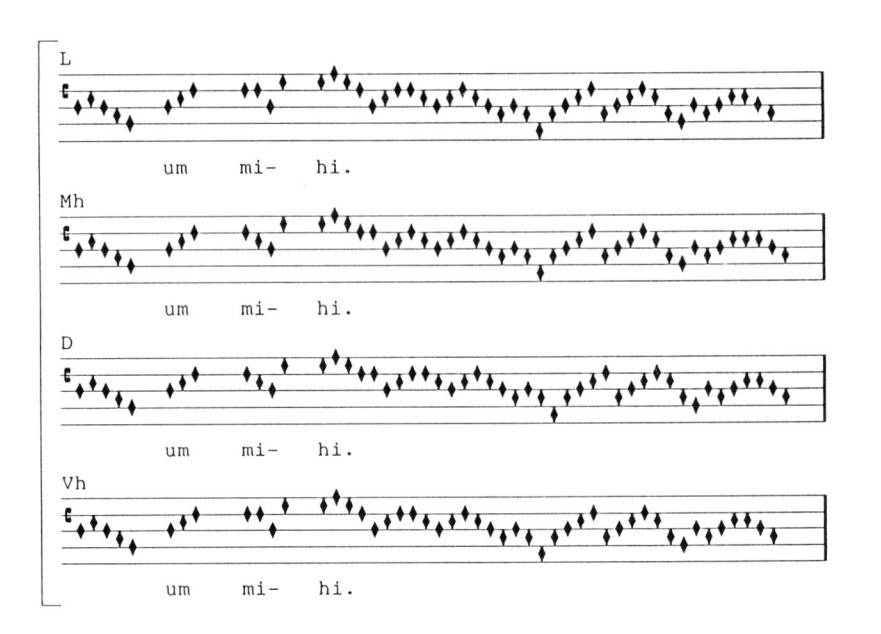

L

um mi- hi.

Mh

um mi- hi.

D

um mi- hi.

Vh

um mi- hi.

(ii) AUXILIUM MEUM A DOMINO

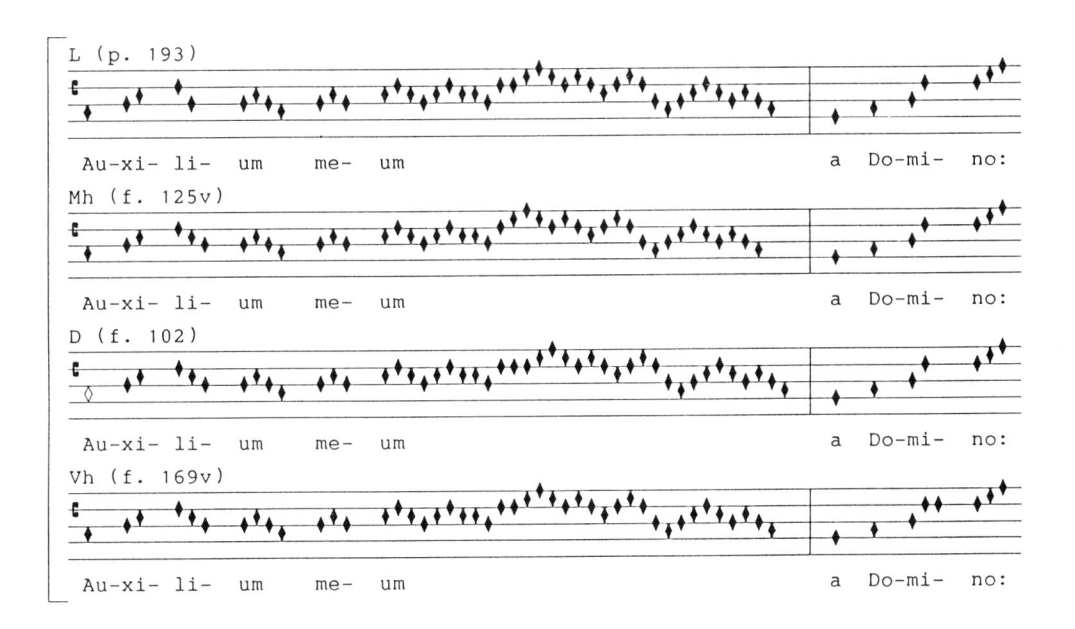

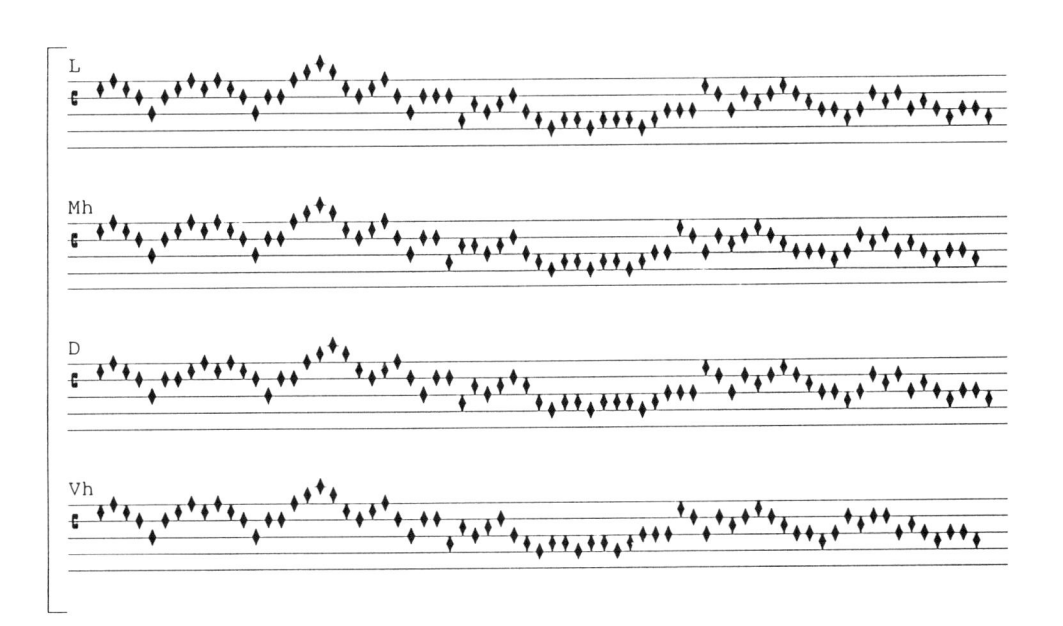

AUXILIUM MEUM (continued)

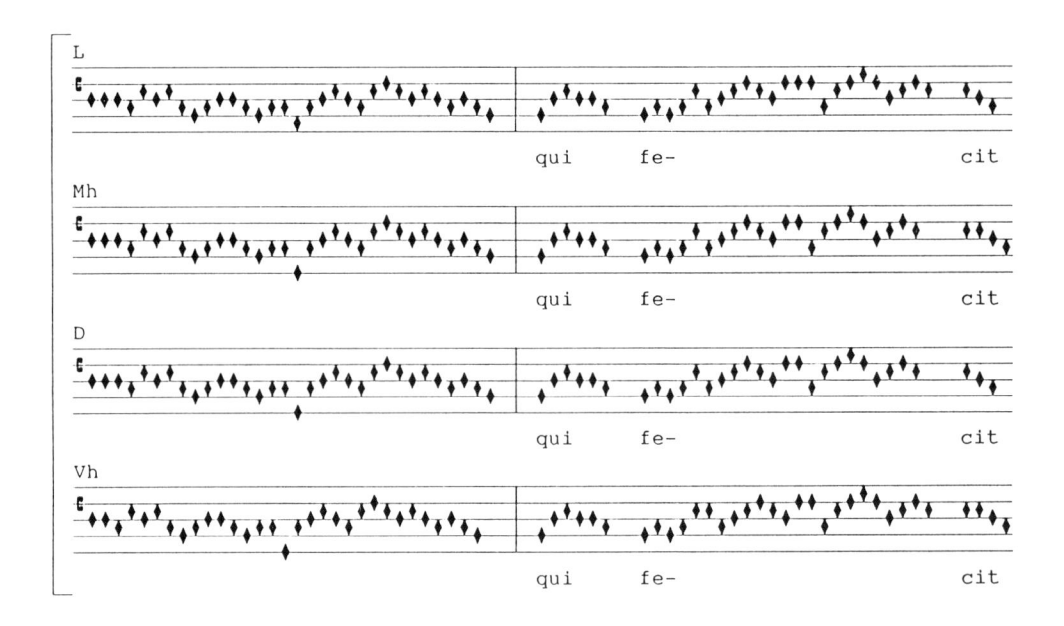

L: qui fe- cit
Mh: qui fe- cit
D: qui fe- cit
Vh: qui fe- cit

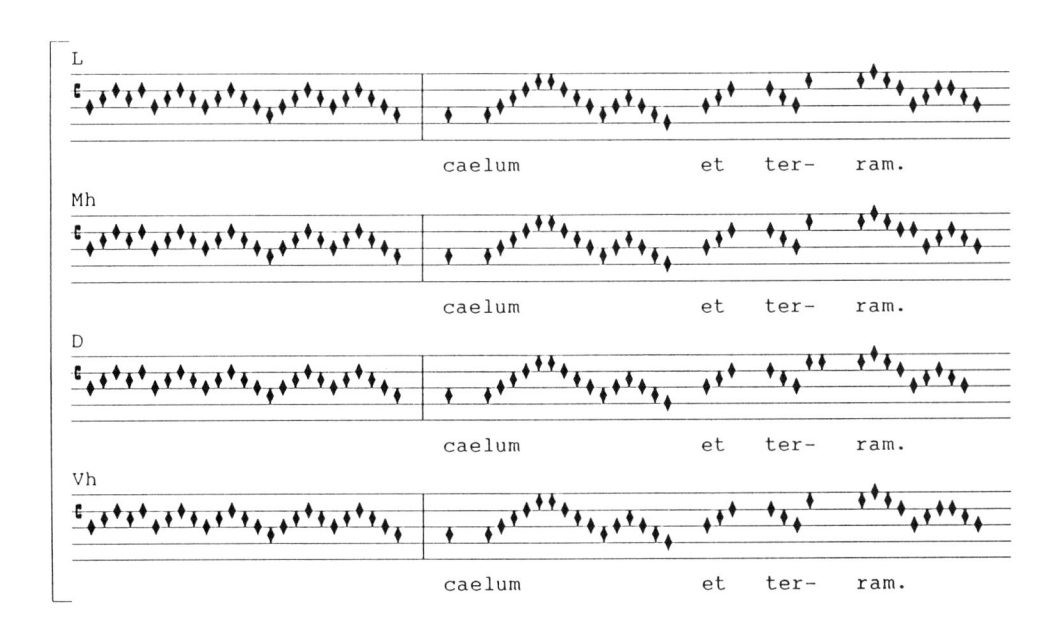

L: caelum et ter- ram.
Mh: caelum et ter- ram.
D: caelum et ter- ram.
Vh: caelum et ter- ram.

AUXILIUM MEUM (continued)

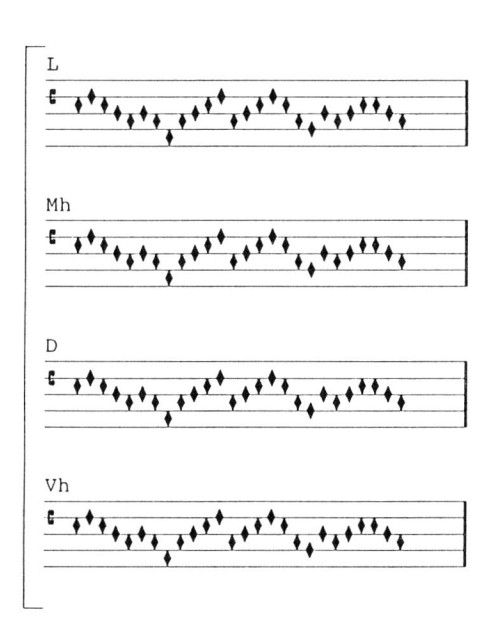

(iii) DOMINUS CUSTODIAT ANIMAM

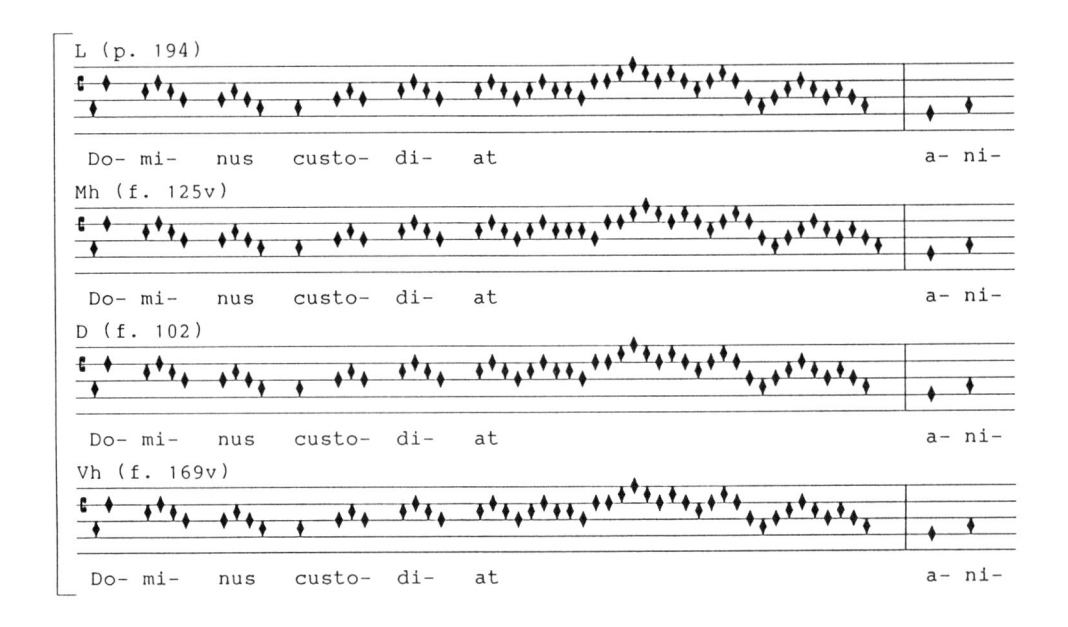

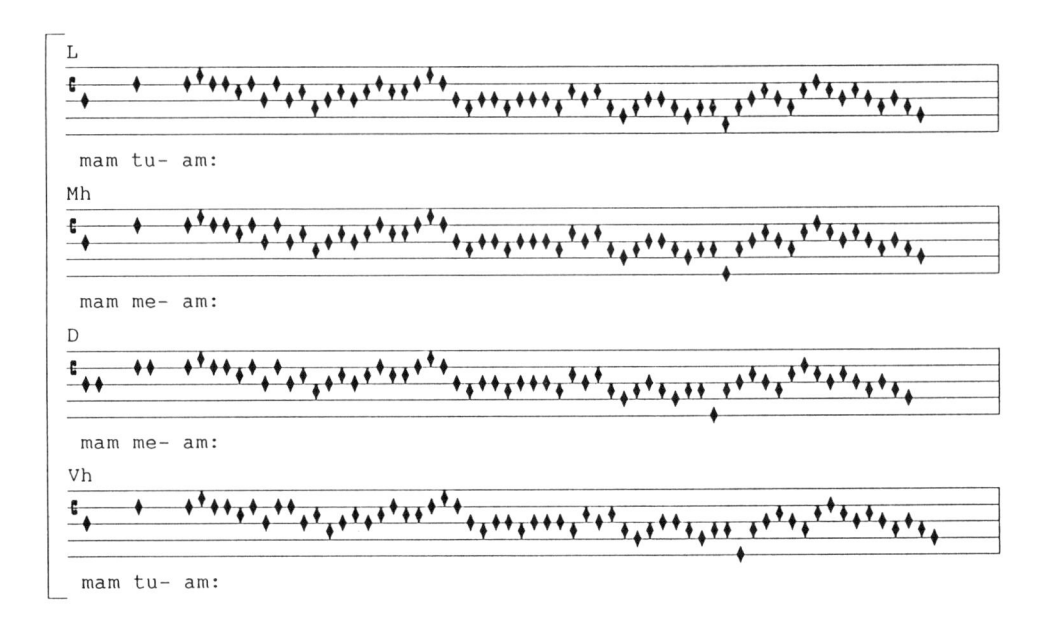

L (p. 194)
Do- mi- nus custo- di- at a- ni-

Mh (f. 125v)
Do- mi- nus custo- di- at a- ni-

D (f. 102)
Do- mi- nus custo- di- at a- ni-

Vh (f. 169v)
Do- mi- nus custo- di- at a- ni-

L
mam tu- am:

Mh
mam me- am:

D
mam me- am:

Vh
mam tu- am:

DOMINUS CUSTODIAT (continued)

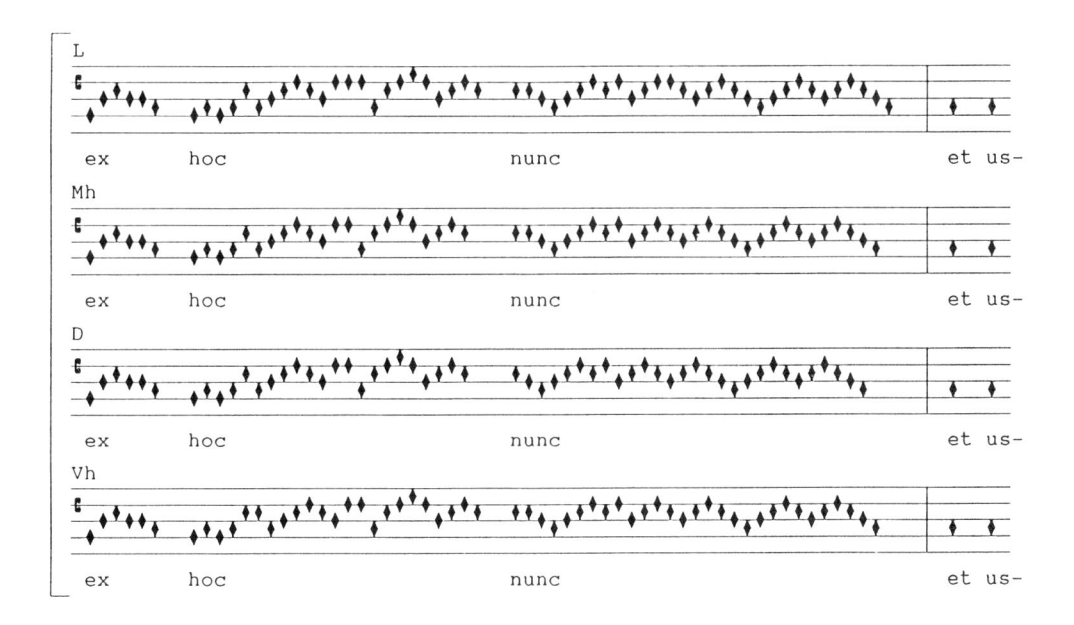

L: ex hoc nunc et us-
Mh: ex hoc nunc et us-
D: ex hoc nunc et us-
Vh: ex hoc nunc et us-

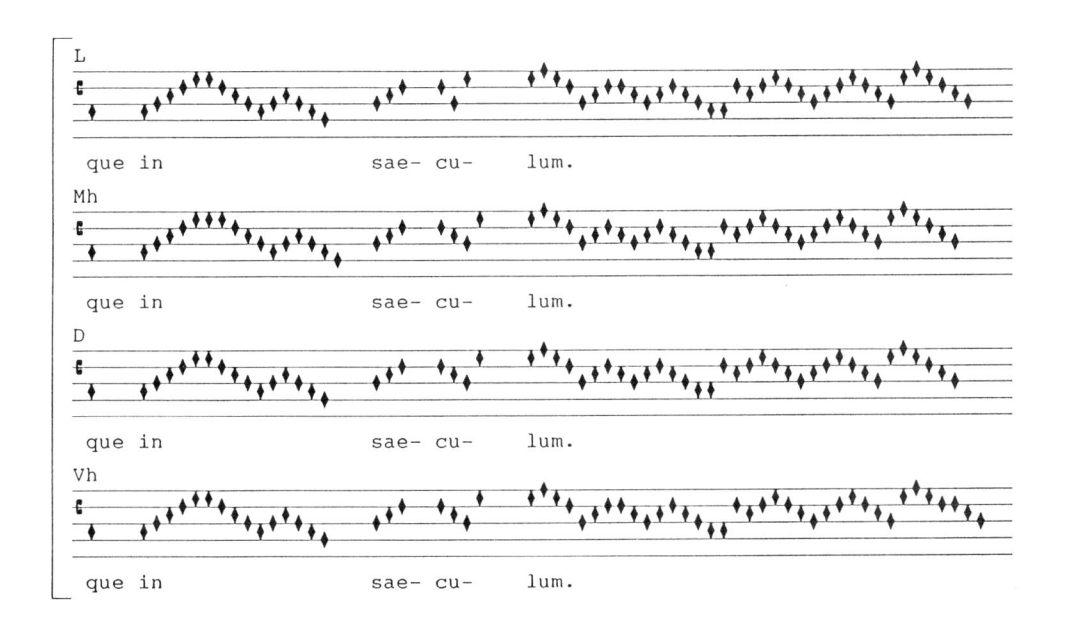

L: que in sae- cu- lum.
Mh: que in sae- cu- lum.
D: que in sae- cu- lum.
Vh: que in sae- cu- lum.

DOMINUS CUSTODIAT (continued)

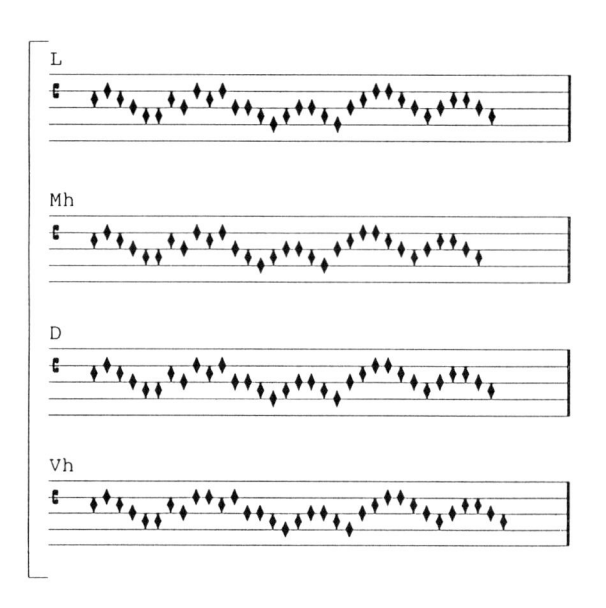

ECCE QUAM BONUM

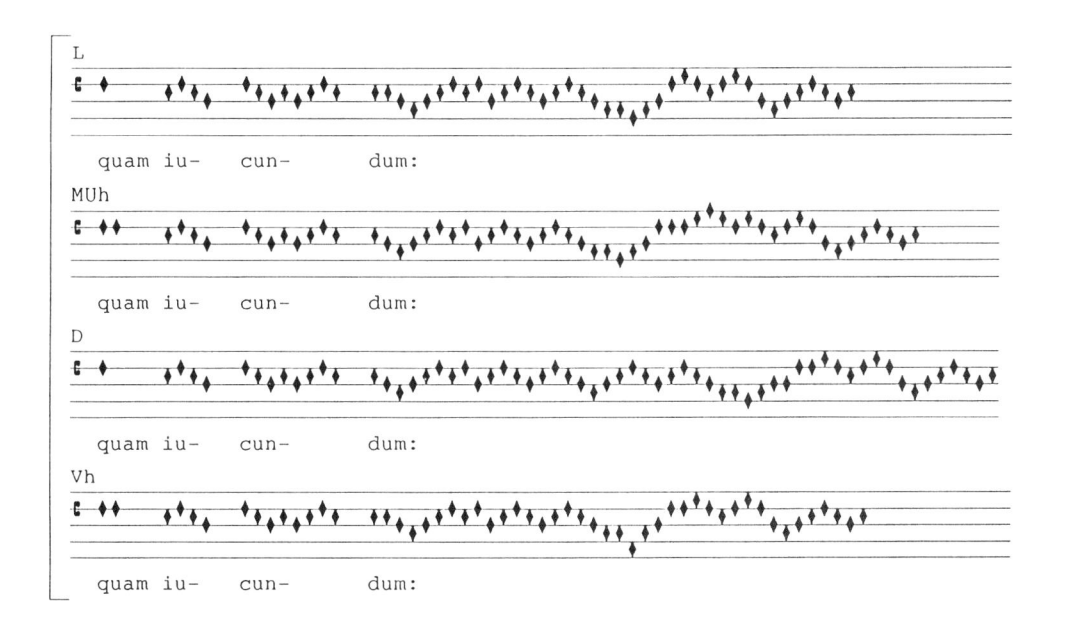

ECCE QUAM (continued)

L: ha- bi- ta- re

MUh: ha- bi- ta- re

D: ha- bi- ta- re

Vh: ha- bi- ta- re

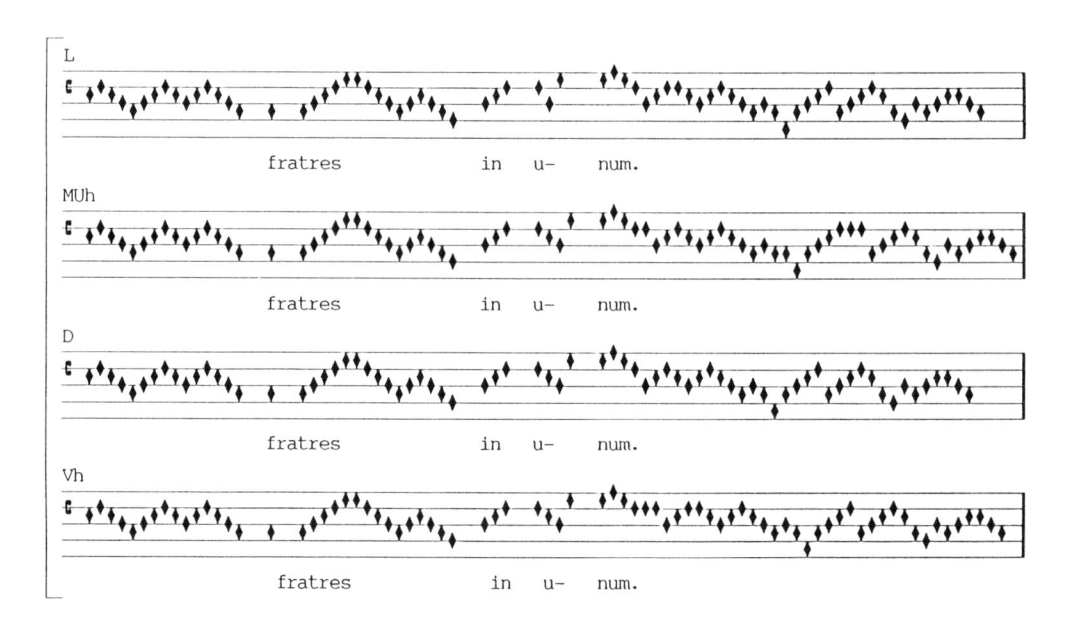

L: fratres in u- num.

MUh: fratres in u- num.

D: fratres in u- num.

Vh: fratres in u- num.

(ii) SICUT UNGUENTUM IN CAPITE

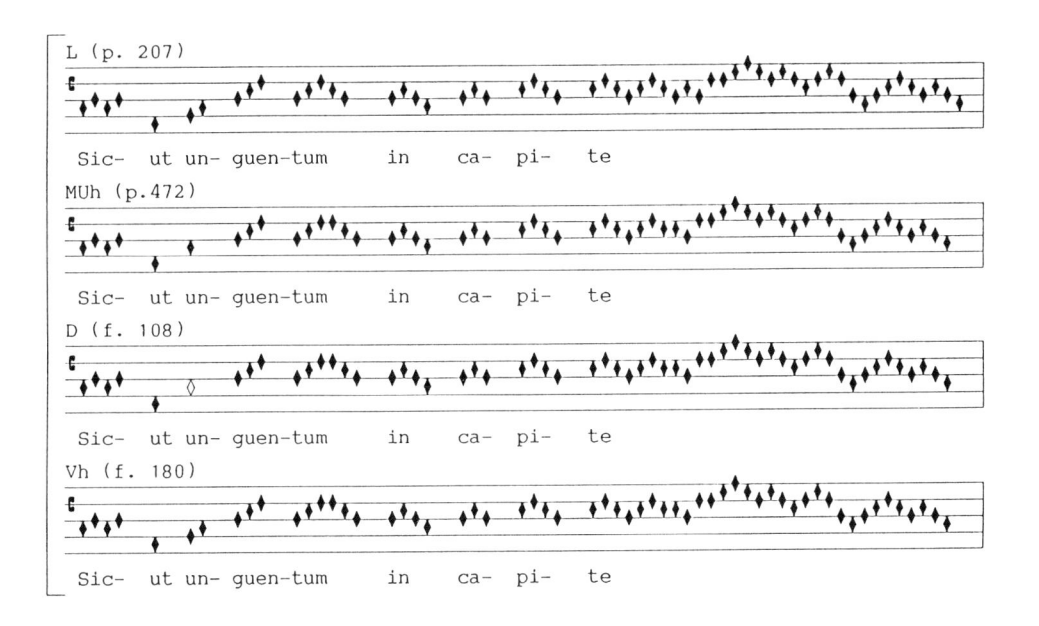

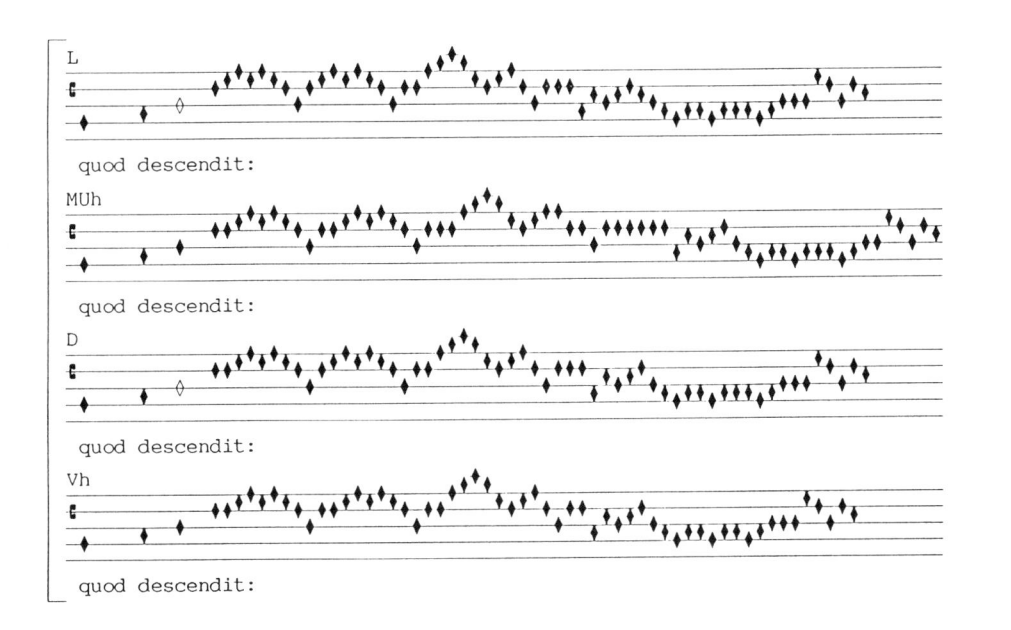

L (p. 207)

Sic- ut un- guen-tum in ca- pi- te

MUh (p.472)

Sic- ut un- guen-tum in ca- pi- te

D (f. 108)

Sic- ut un- guen-tum in ca- pi- te

Vh (f. 180)

Sic- ut un- guen-tum in ca- pi- te

L

quod descendit:

MUh

quod descendit:

D

quod descendit:

Vh

quod descendit:

SICUT UNGUENTUM (continued)

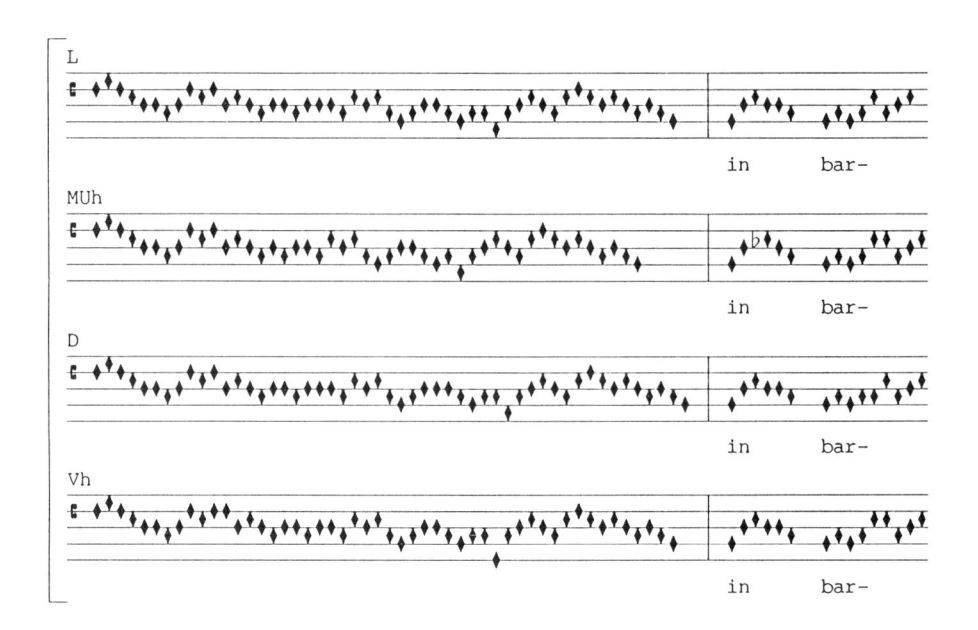

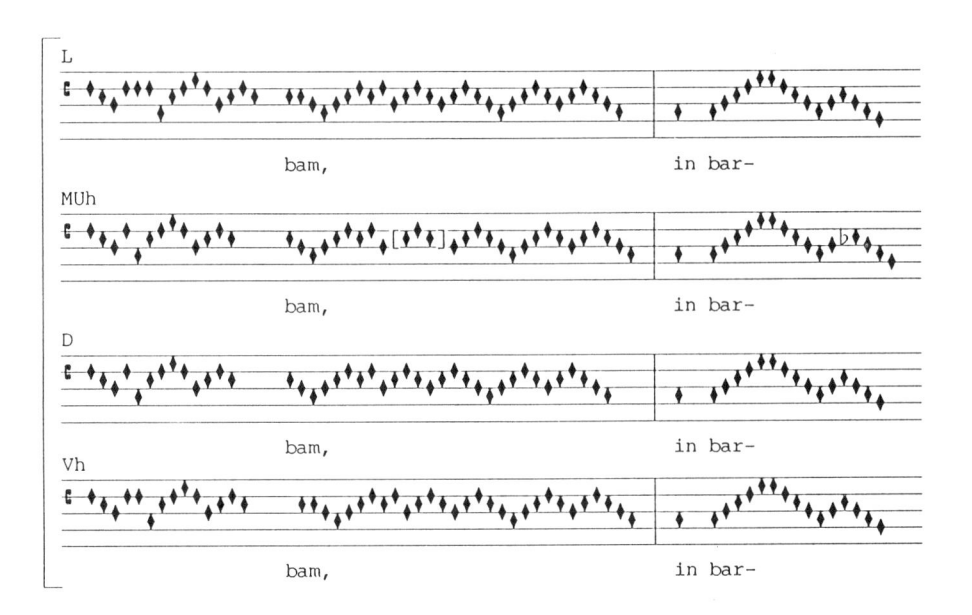

SICUT UNGUENTUM (continued)

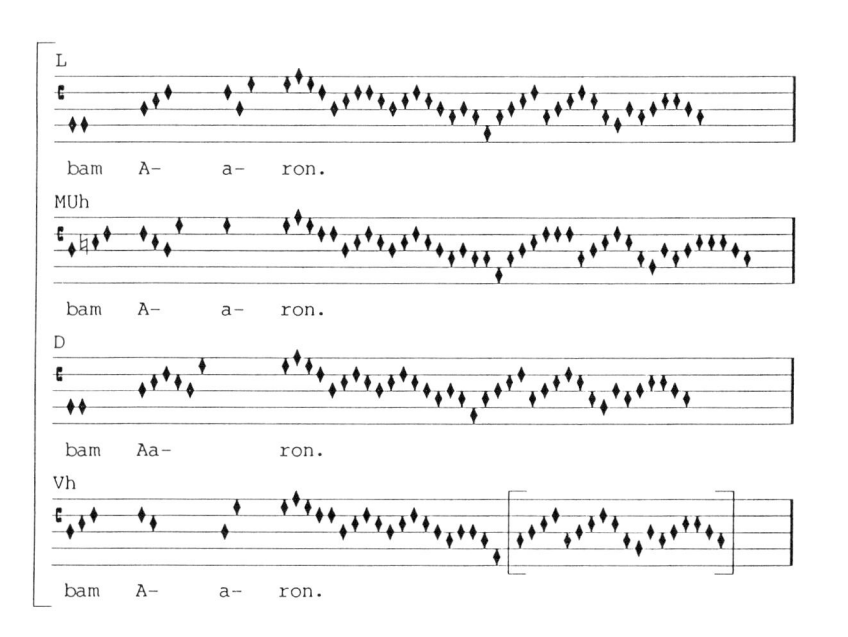

(iii) QUIA ILLIC MANDAVIT

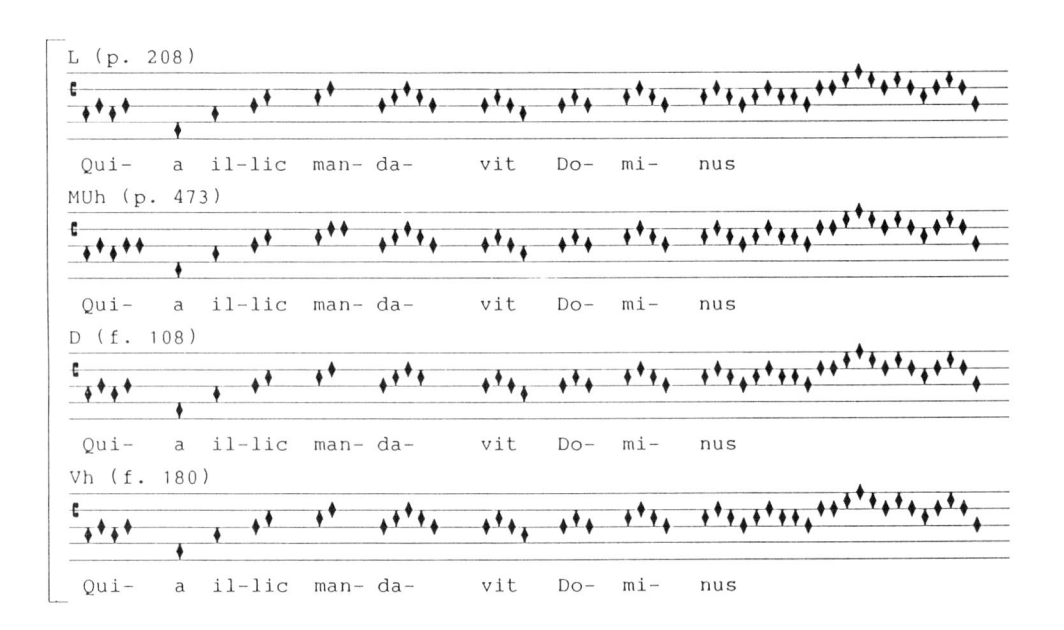

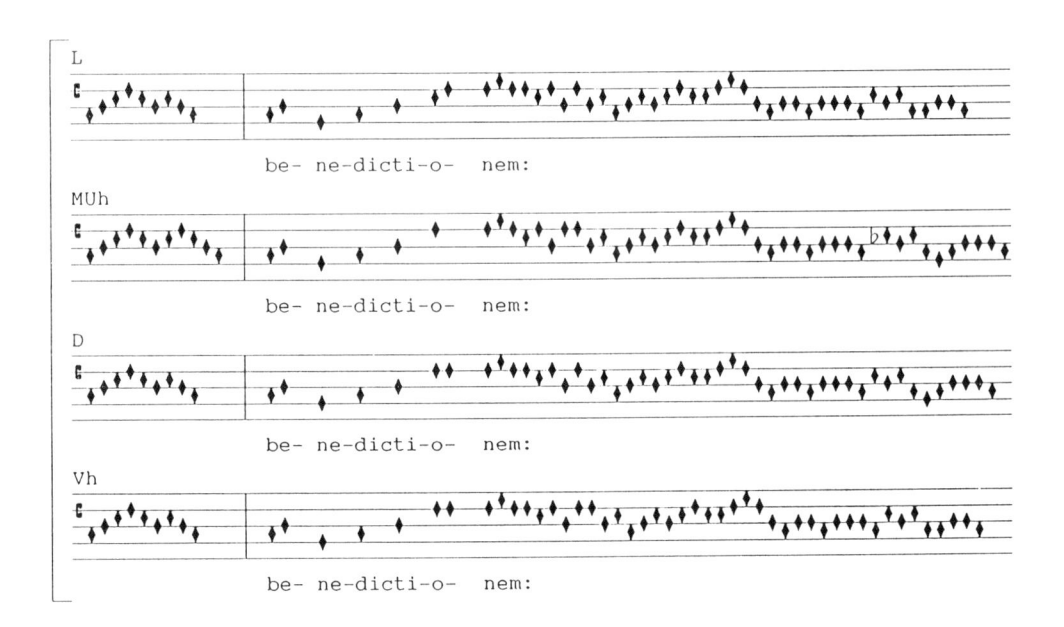

L (p. 208)

Qui- a il-lic man- da- vit Do- mi- nus

MUh (p. 473)

Qui- a il-lic man- da- vit Do- mi- nus

D (f. 108)

Qui- a il-lic man- da- vit Do- mi- nus

Vh (f. 180)

Qui- a il-lic man- da- vit Do- mi- nus

L

be- ne-dicti-o- nem:

MUh

be- ne-dicti-o- nem:

D

be- ne-dicti-o- nem:

Vh

be- ne-dicti-o- nem:

QUIA ILLIC MANDAVIT (continued)

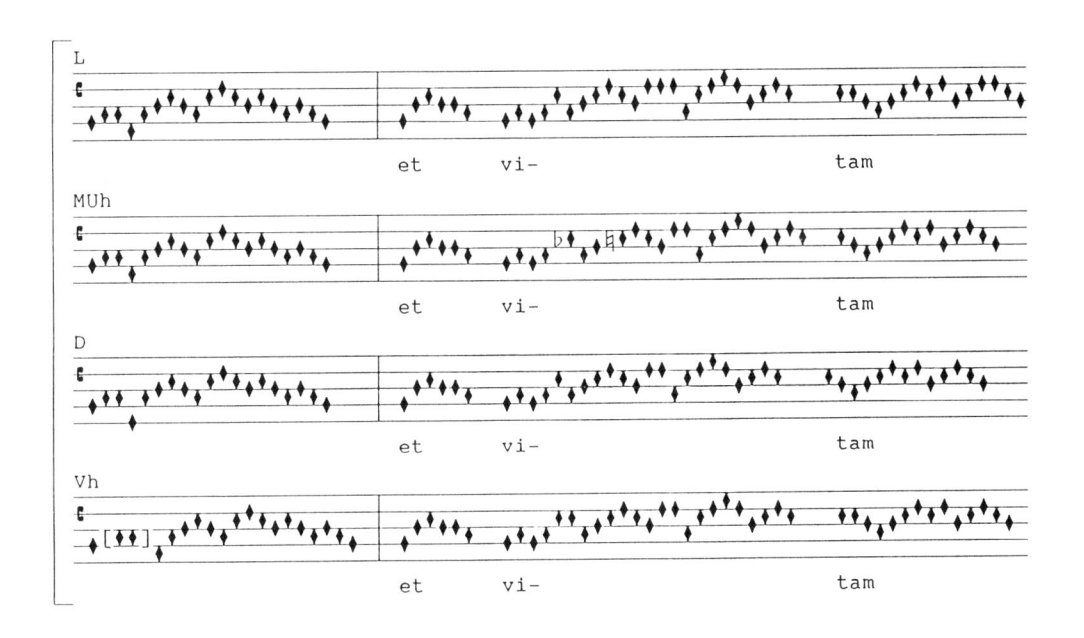

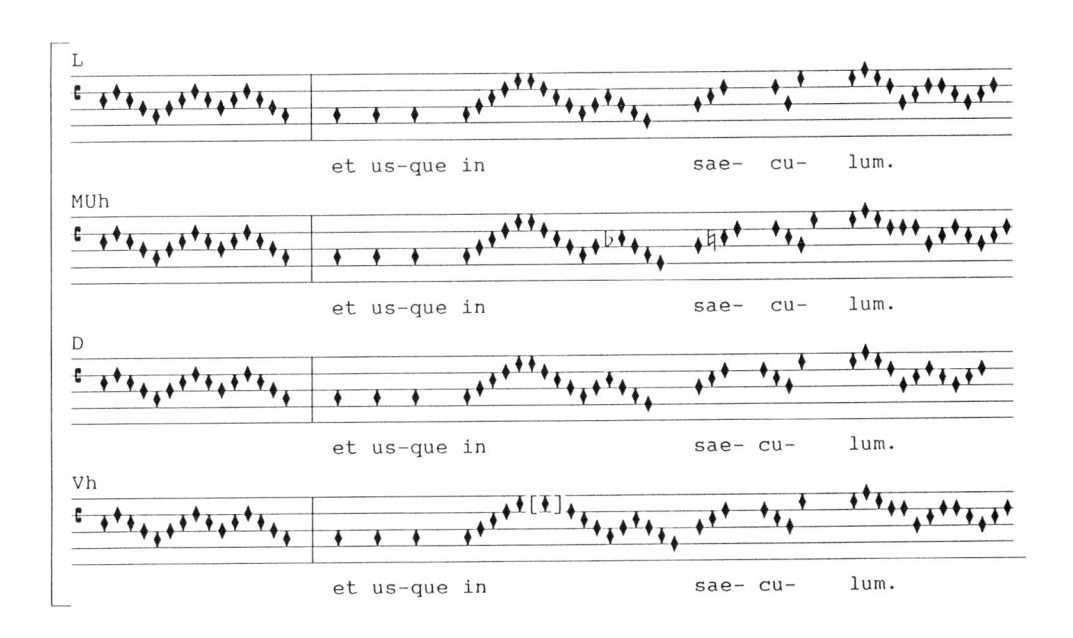

QUIA ILLIC MANDAVIT (continued)

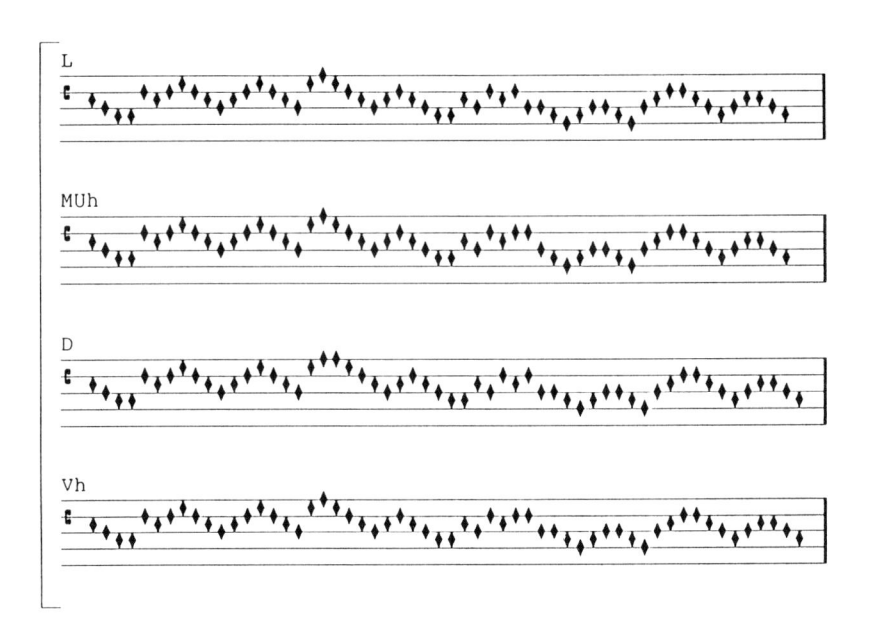

CONSERVA ME DOMINE

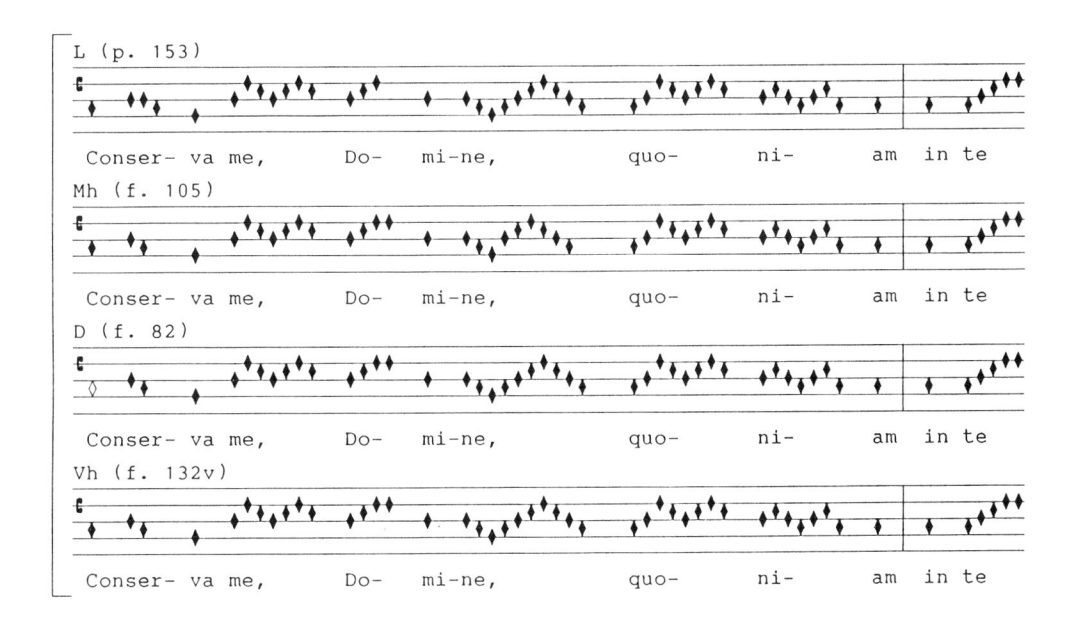

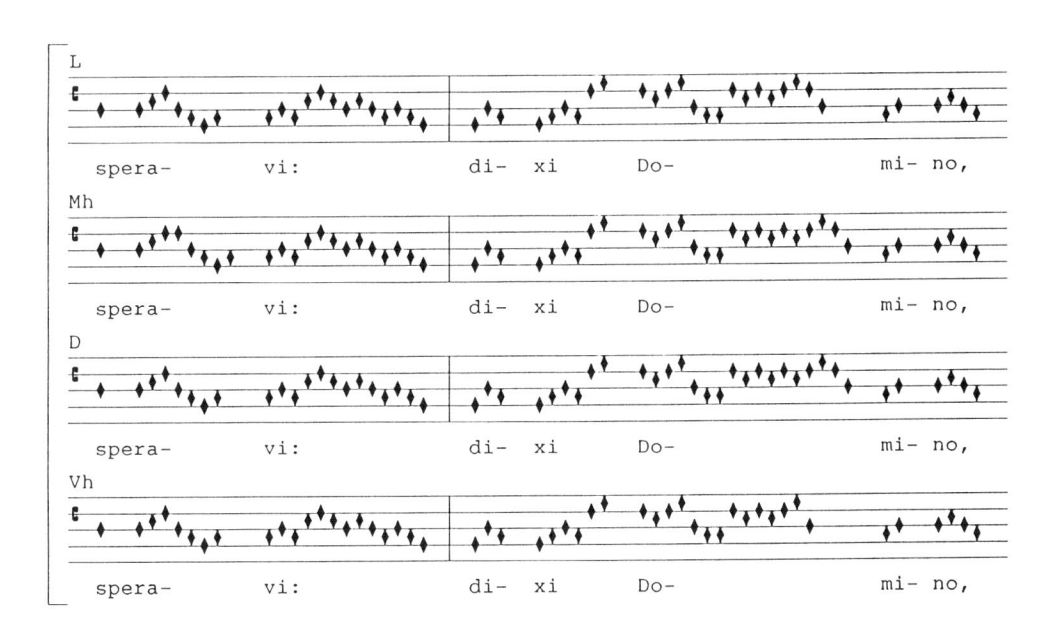

CONSERVA ME (continued)

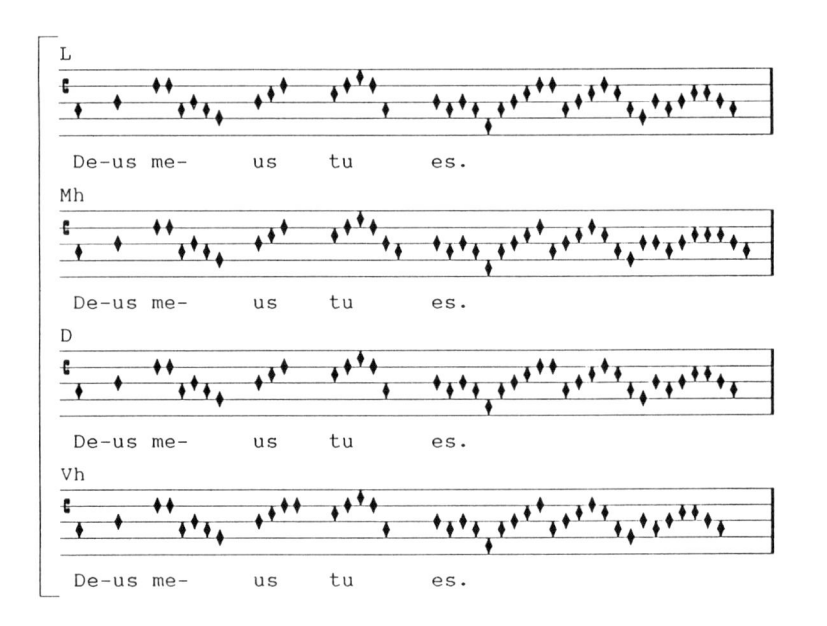

L

De-us me- us tu es.

Mh

De-us me- us tu es.

D

De-us me- us tu es.

Vh

De-us me- us tu es.

IN CONVERTENDO DOMINUS

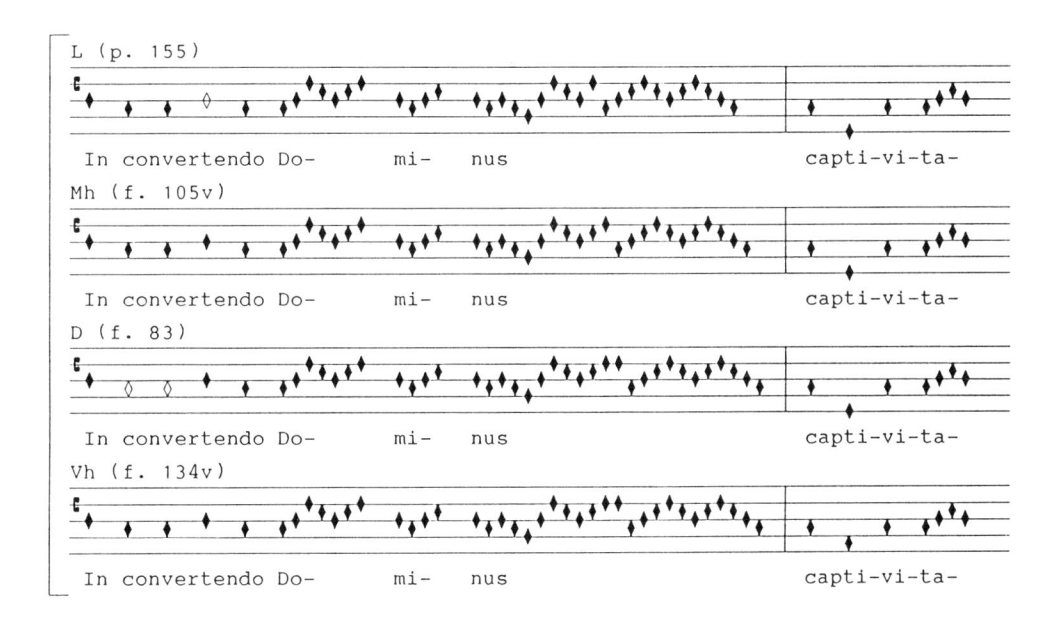

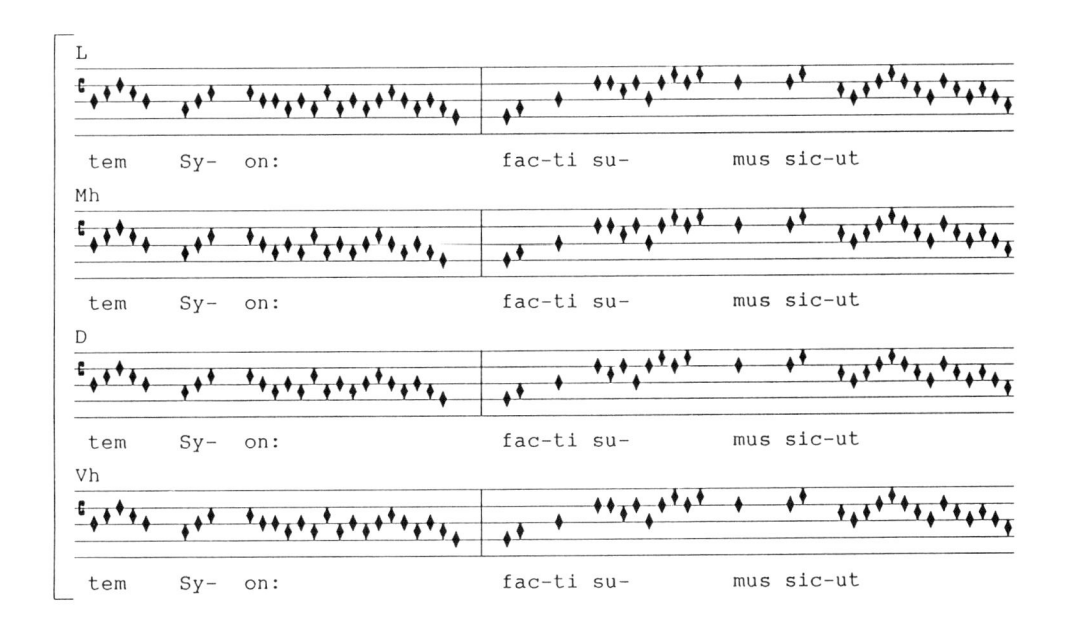

IN CONVERTENDO (continued)

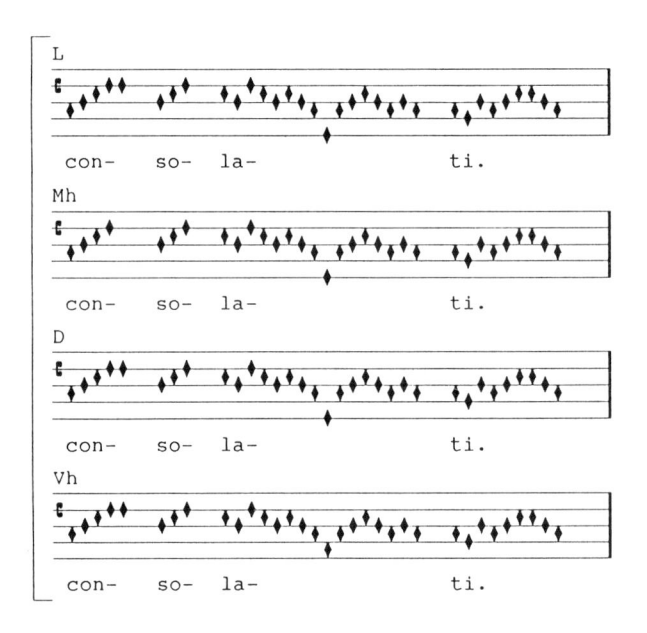

L

con- so- la- ti.

Mh

con- so- la- ti.

D

con- so- la- ti.

Vh

con- so- la- ti.

DE PROFUNDIS CLAMAVI

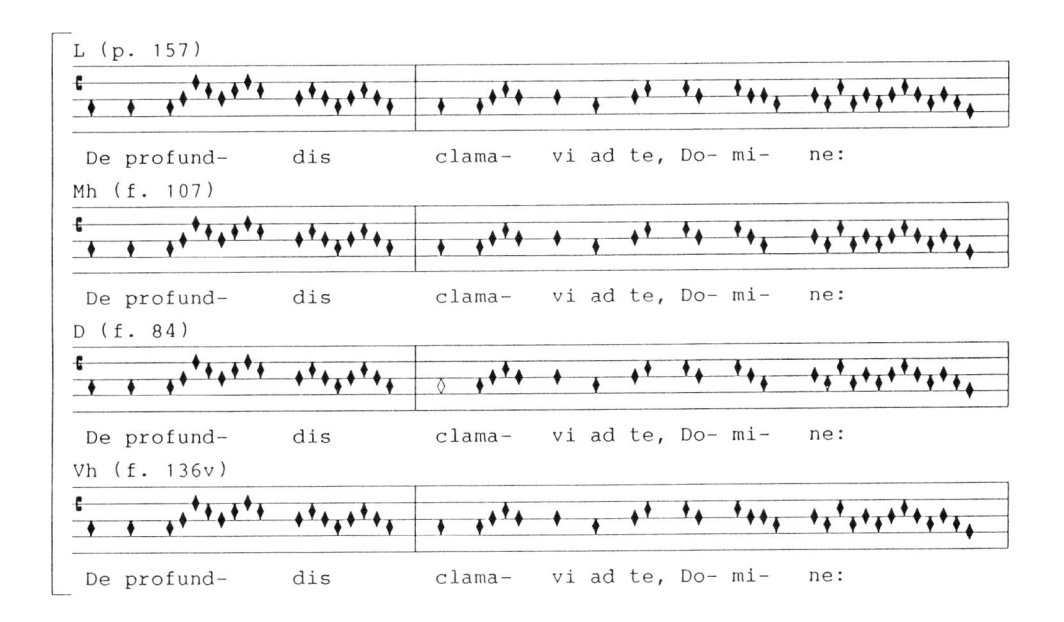

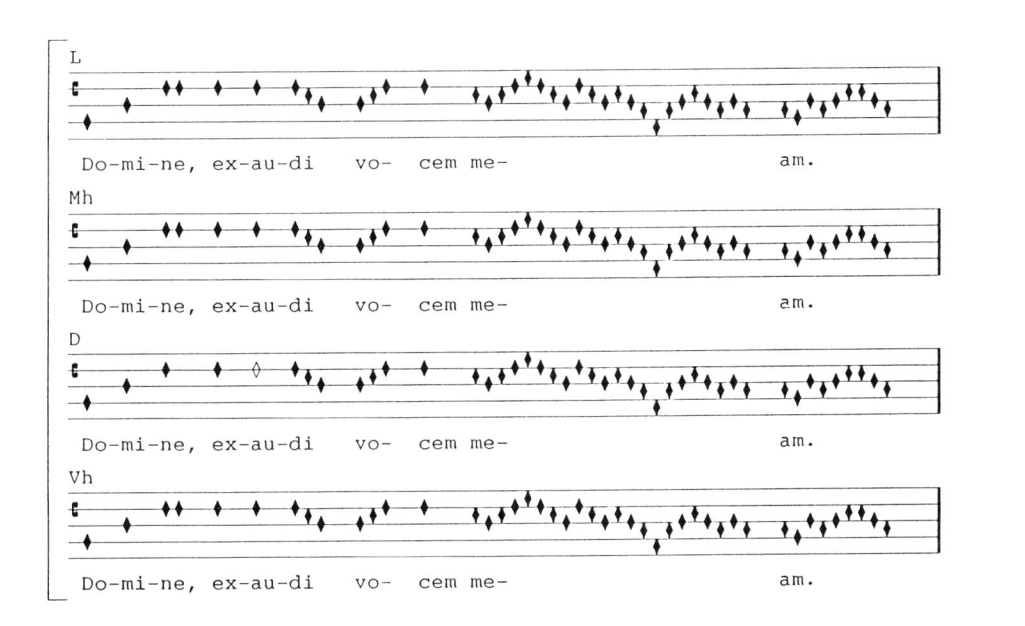

L (p. 157)
De profund- dis clama- vi ad te, Do- mi- ne:

Mh (f. 107)
De profund- dis clama- vi ad te, Do- mi- ne:

D (f. 84)
De profund- dis clama- vi ad te, Do- mi- ne:

Vh (f. 136v)
De profund- dis clama- vi ad te, Do- mi- ne:

L
Do-mi-ne, ex-au-di vo- cem me- am.

Mh
Do-mi-ne, ex-au-di vo- cem me- am.

D
Do-mi-ne, ex-au-di vo- cem me- am.

Vh
Do-mi-ne, ex-au-di vo- cem me- am.

DOMINE EXAUDI ORATIONEM

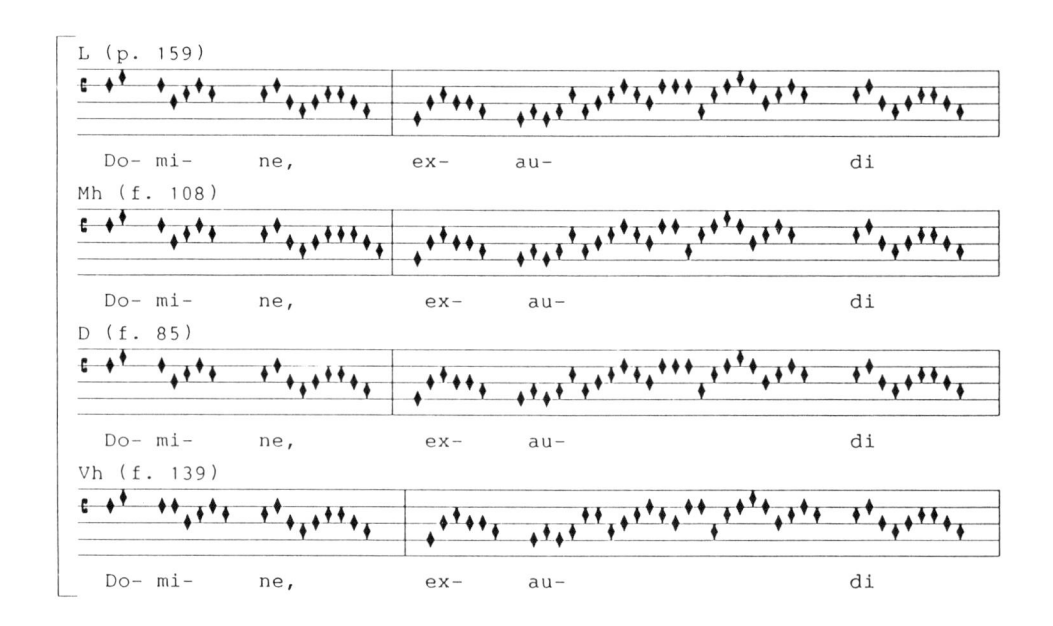

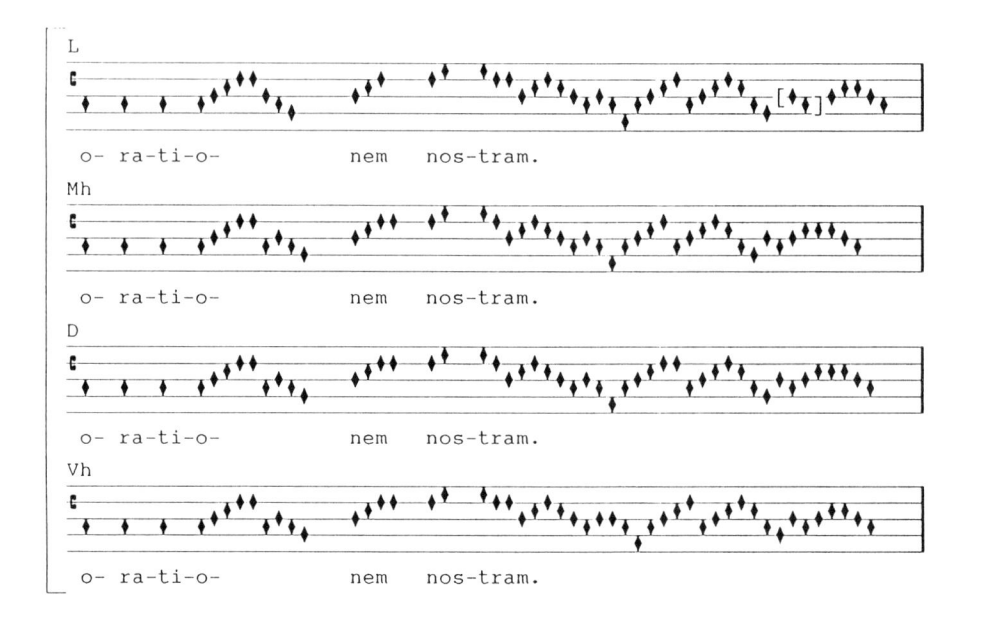

L (p. 159)
Do- mi- ne, ex- au- di

Mh (f. 108)
Do- mi- ne, ex- au- di

D (f. 85)
Do- mi- ne, ex- au- di

Vh (f. 139)
Do- mi- ne, ex- au- di

L
o- ra-ti-o- nem nos-tram.

Mh
o- ra-ti-o- nem nos-tram.

D
o- ra-ti-o- nem nos-tram.

Vh
o- ra-ti-o- nem nos-tram.

BENEDICAM DOMINUM

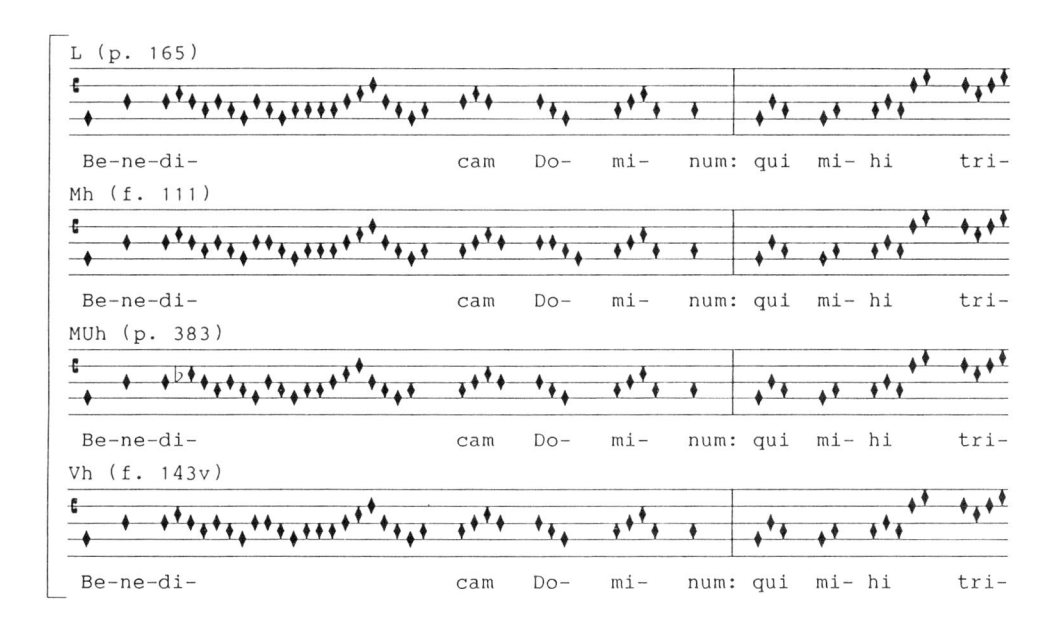

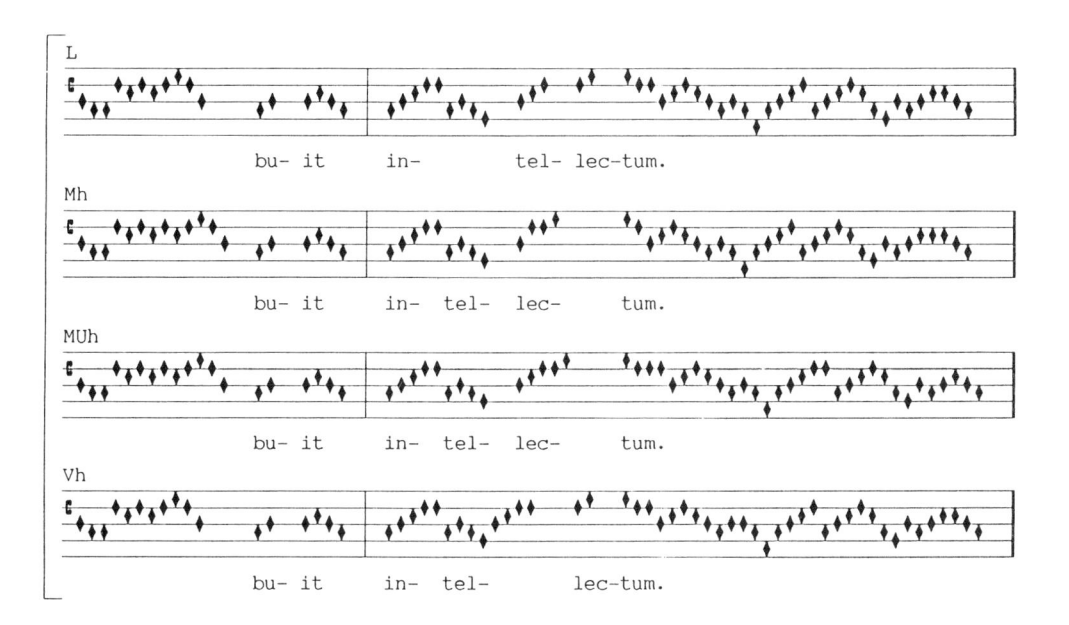

LAUDATE DOMINUM OMNES GENTES

L (p. 218)

Lauda-te Do- mi-num om-nes gen-tes: et col-

Mh (f. 137)

Lauda-te Do- mi-num om-nes gen-tes: et col-

D (f. 113v)

Lauda-te Do- mi-num om-nes gen-tes: et col-

Vh (f. 188v)

Lauda-te Do- mi-num om-nes gen-tes: et col-

L

lau- da- te e- um om-nes po- pu- li.

Mh

lau- da- te e- um om-nes po- pu- li.

D

lau- da- te e- um om-nes po- pu- li.

Vh

lau- da- te e- um om-nes po- pu- li.

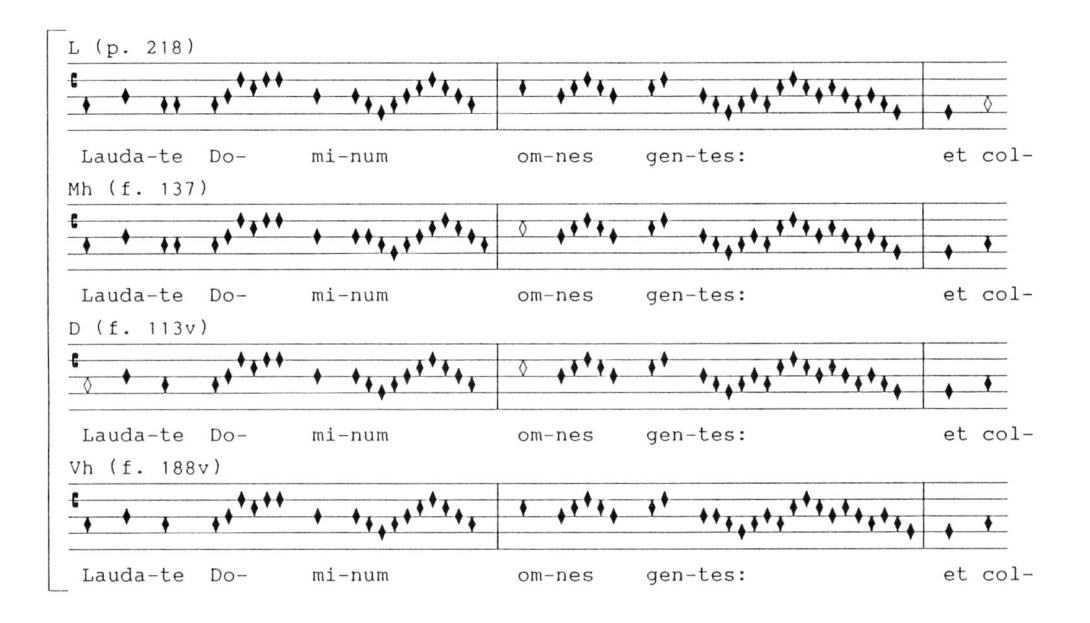

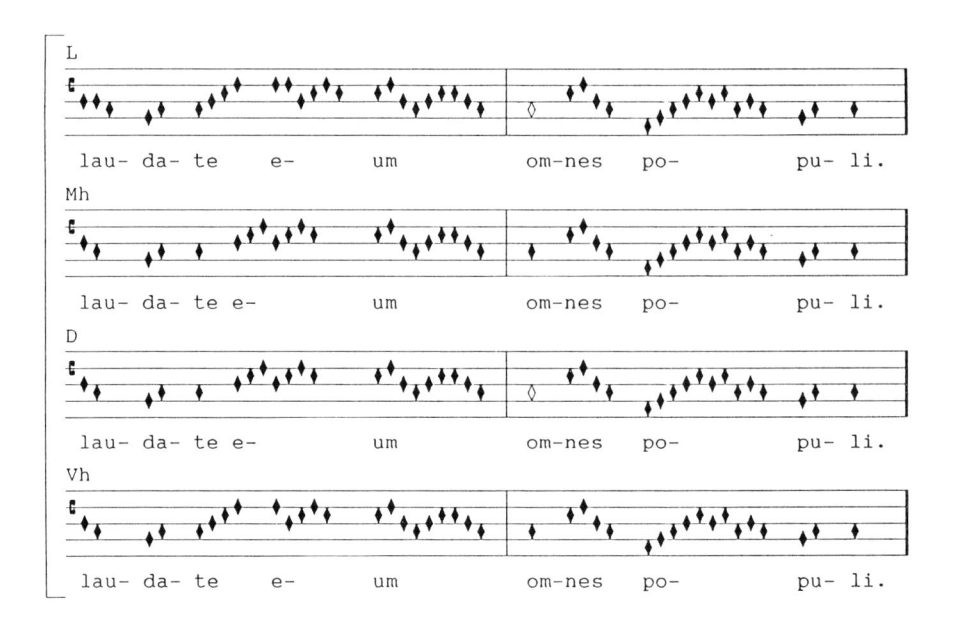

(ii) QUONIAM CONFIRMATA EST

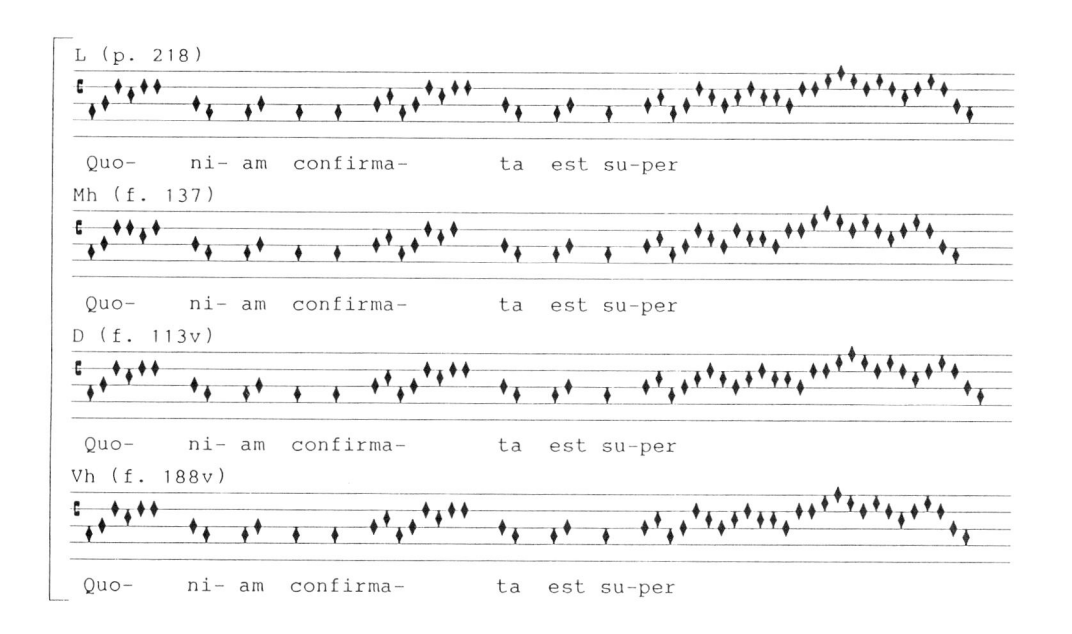

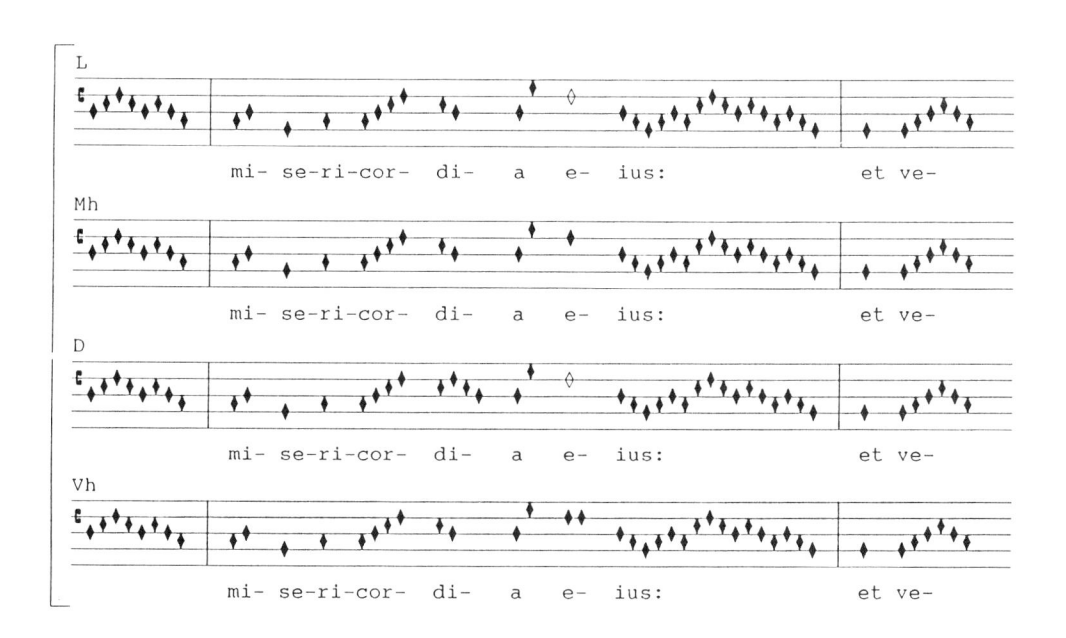

QUONIAM CONFIRMATA (continued)

ri-tas Do- mi-ni ma- net in ae- ter-num

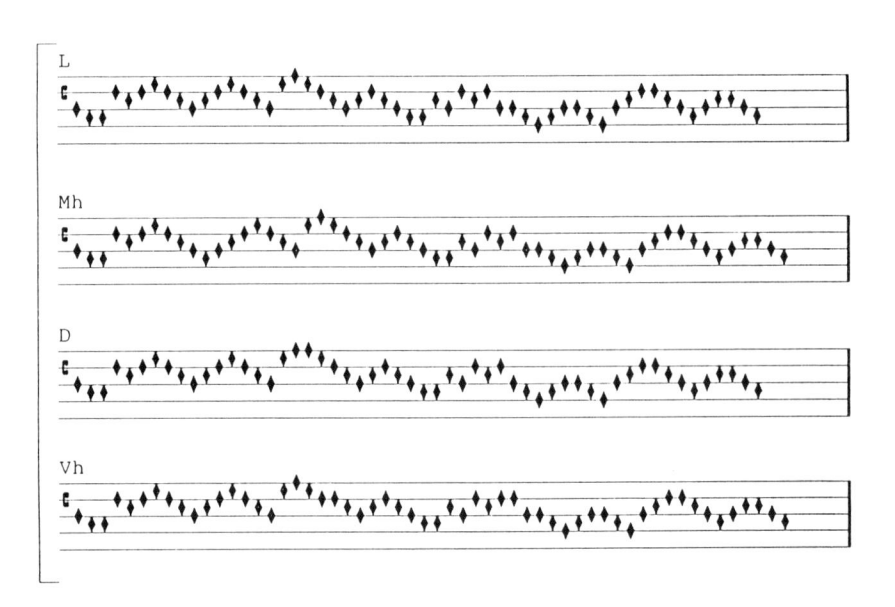

QUI EDEBAT PANES

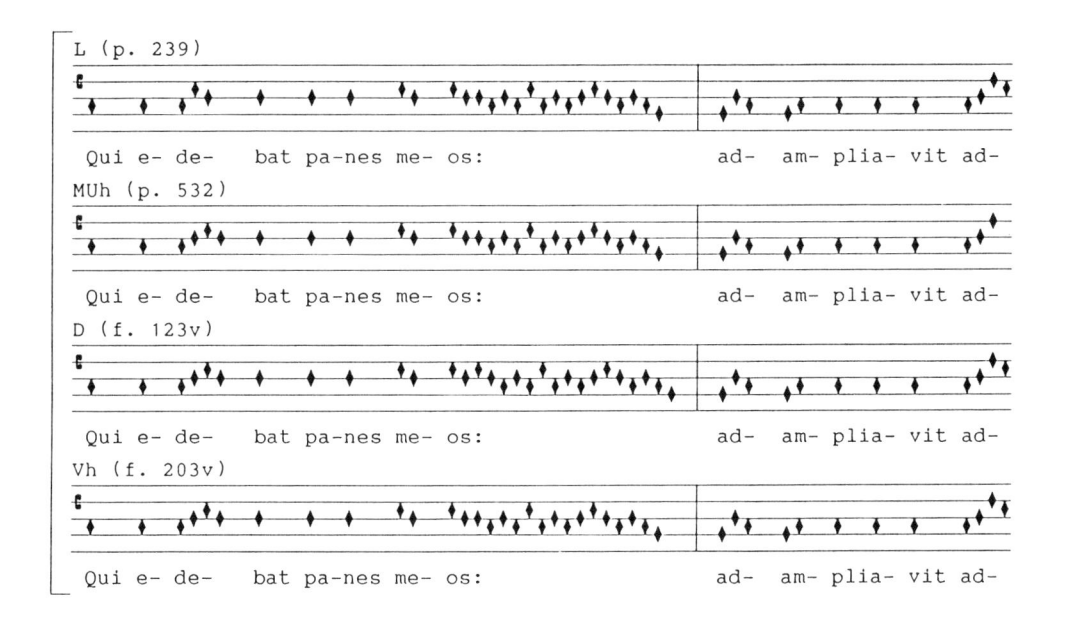

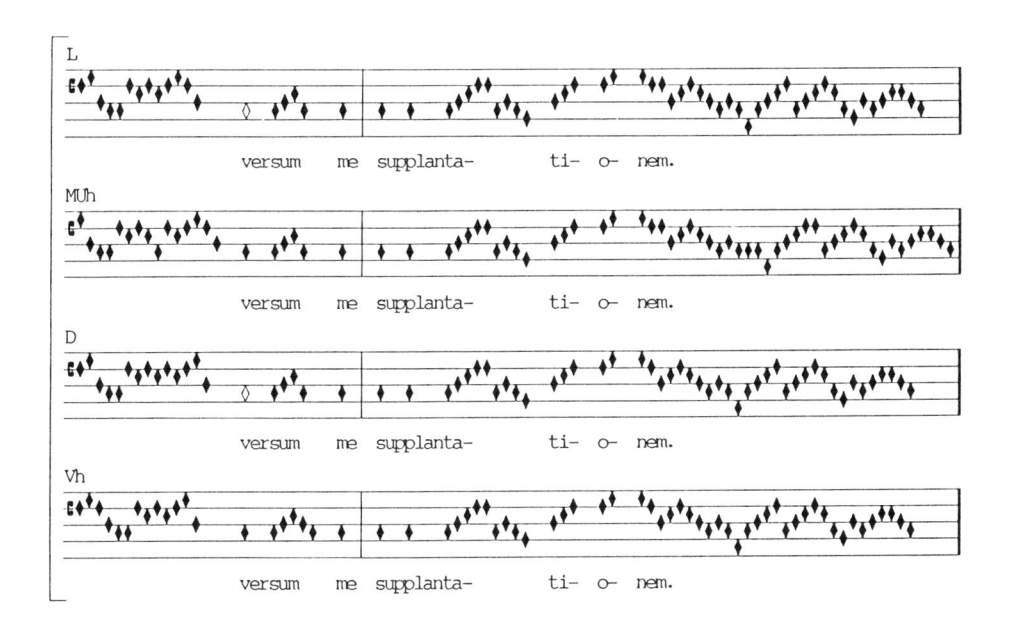

L (p. 239)
Qui e- de- bat pa-nes me- os: ad- am- plia- vit ad-

MUh (p. 532)
Qui e- de- bat pa-nes me- os: ad- am- plia- vit ad-

D (f. 123v)
Qui e- de- bat pa-nes me- os: ad- am- plia- vit ad-

Vh (f. 203v)
Qui e- de- bat pa-nes me- os: ad- am- plia- vit ad-

L
versum me supplanta- ti- o- nem.

MUh
versum me supplanta- ti- o- nem.

D
versum me supplanta- ti- o- nem.

Vh
versum me supplanta- ti- o- nem.

SUPRA DORSUM FABRICAVERUNT

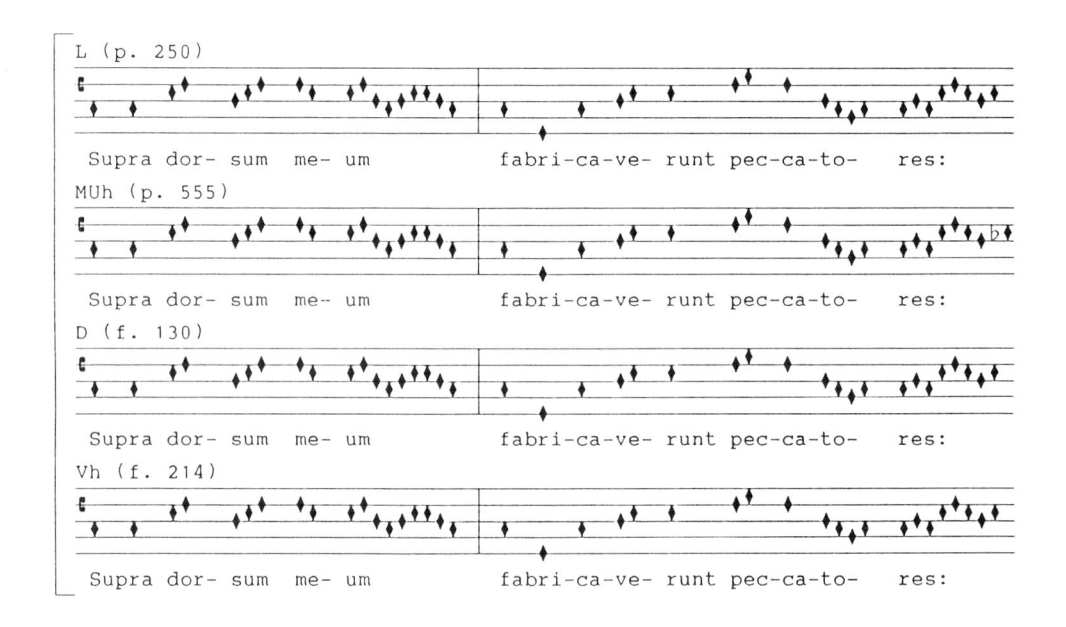

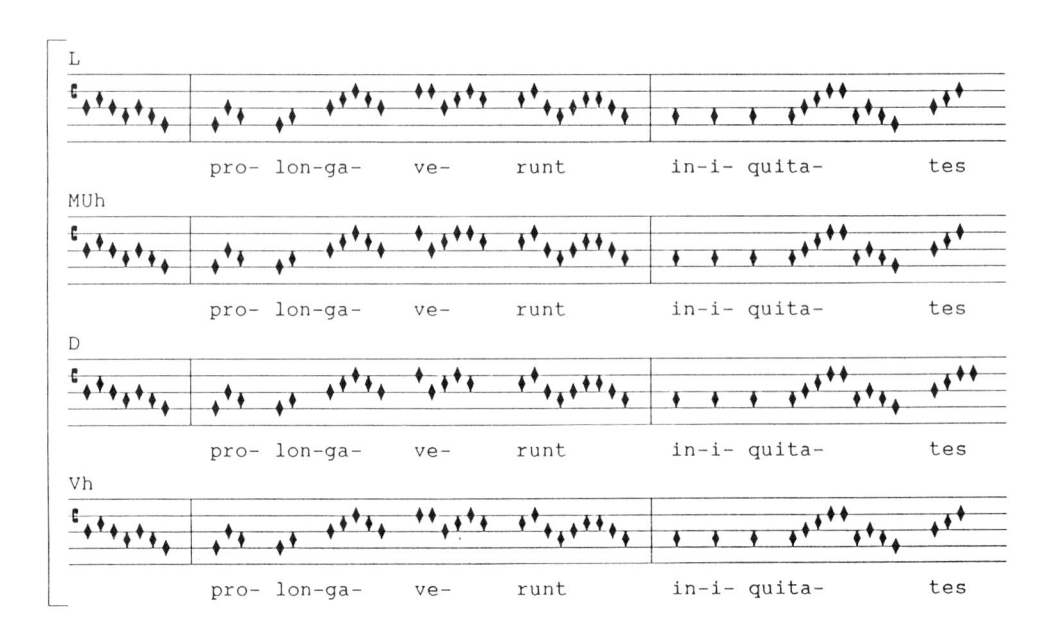

L (p. 250)
Supra dor- sum me- um fabri-ca-ve- runt pec-ca-to- res:

MUh (p. 555)
Supra dor- sum me- um fabri-ca-ve- runt pec-ca-to- res:

D (f. 130)
Supra dor- sum me- um fabri-ca-ve- runt pec-ca-to- res:

Vh (f. 214)
Supra dor- sum me- um fabri-ca-ve- runt pec-ca-to- res:

L
pro- lon-ga- ve- runt in-i- quita- tes

MUh
pro- lon-ga- ve- runt in-i- quita- tes

D
pro- lon-ga- ve- runt in-i- quita- tes

Vh
pro- lon-ga- ve- runt in-i- quita- tes

SUPRA DORSUM (continued)

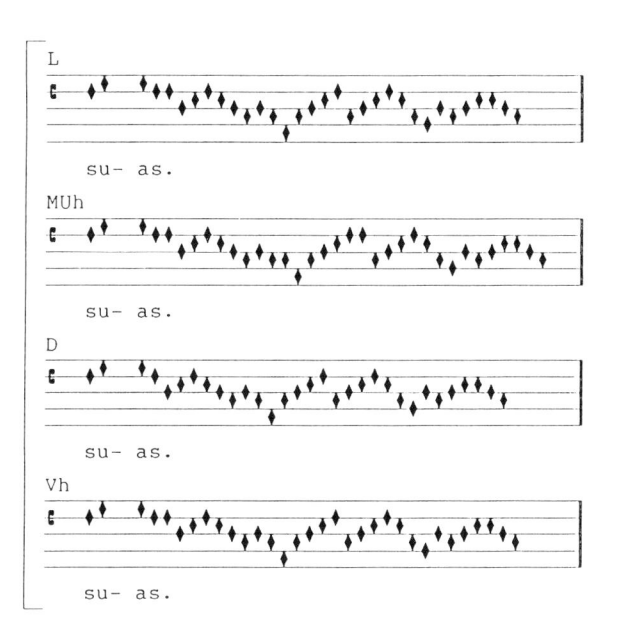

L

su- as.

MUh

su- as.

D

su- as.

Vh

su- as.

(ii) DOMINUS IUSTUS CONCIDET

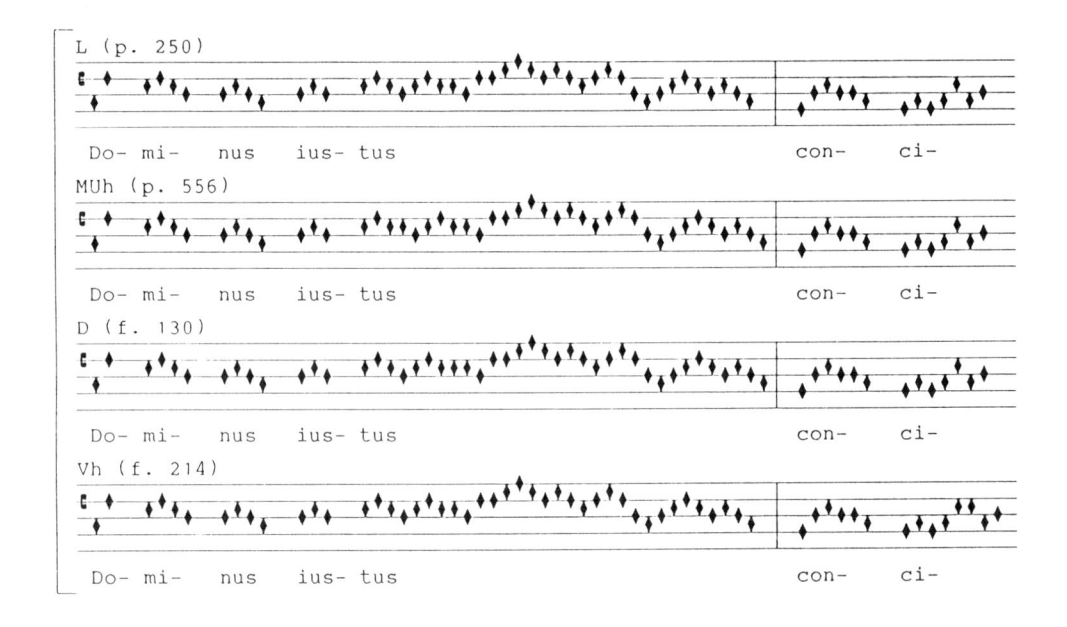

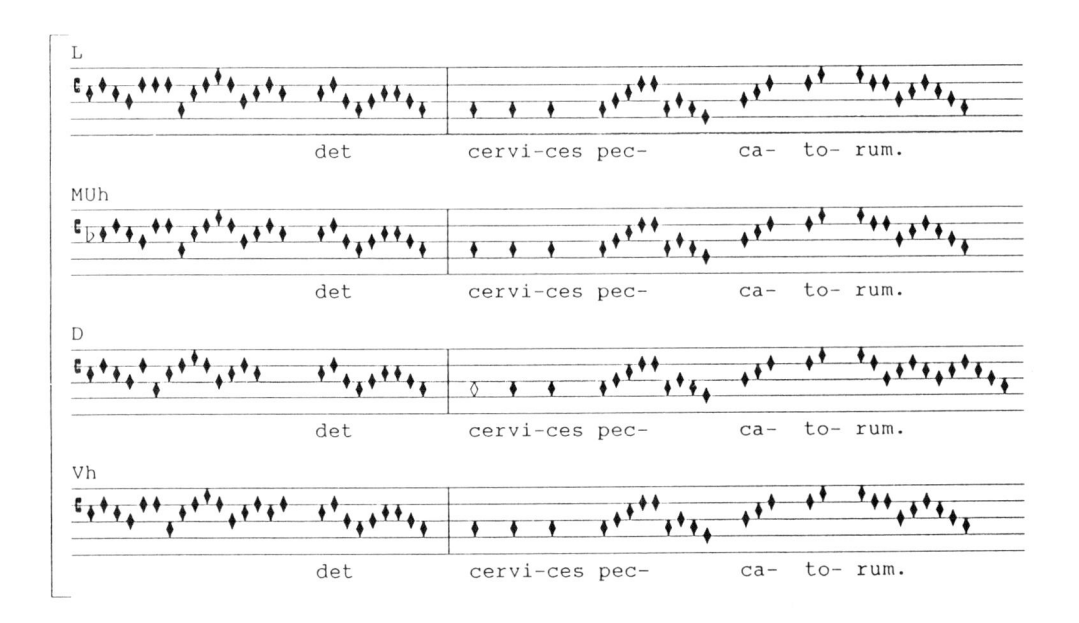

L (p. 250)

Do- mi- nus ius- tus con- ci-

MUh (p. 556)

Do- mi- nus ius- tus con- ci-

D (f. 130)

Do- mi- nus ius- tus con- ci-

Vh (f. 214)

Do- mi- nus ius- tus con- ci-

L

det cervi-ces pec- ca- to- rum.

MUh

det cervi-ces pec- ca- to- rum.

D

det cervi-ces pec- ca- to- rum.

Vh

det cervi-ces pec- ca- to- rum.

DOMINUS IUSTUS (continued)

SICUT CERVUS DESIDERAT

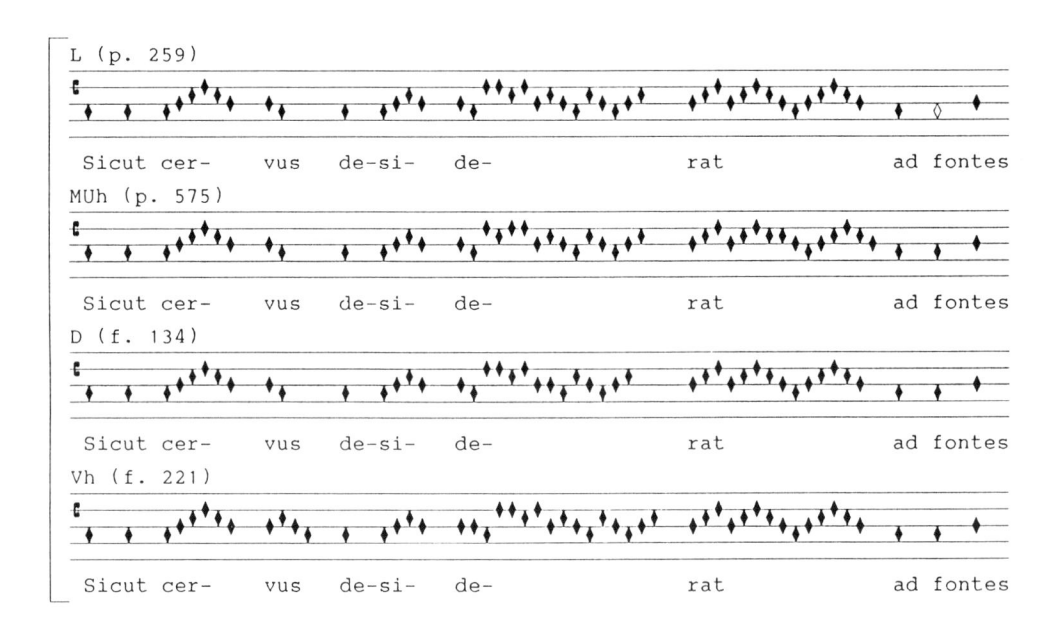

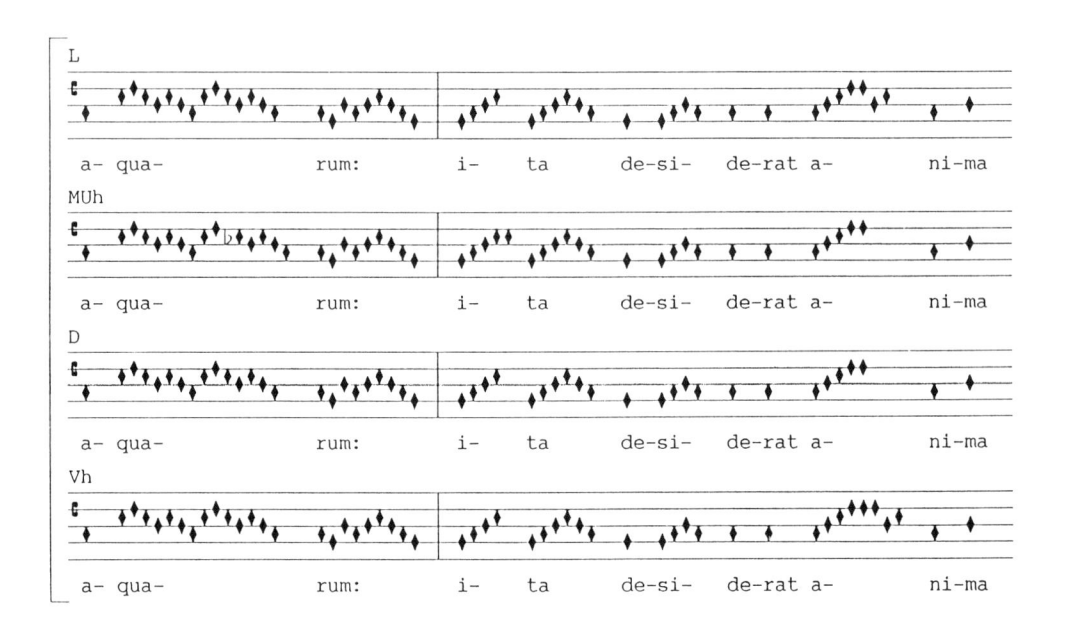

SICUT CERVUS (continued)

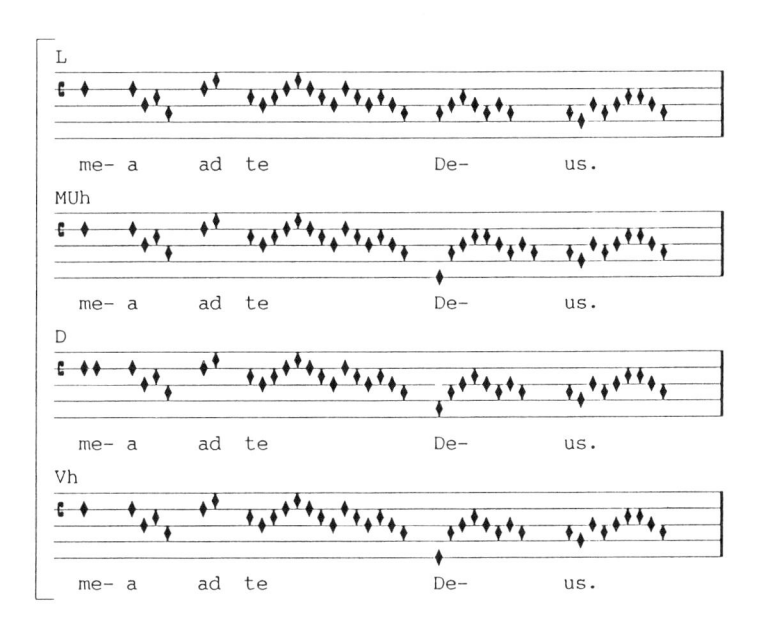

L
me- a   ad te   De-   us.

MUh
me- a   ad te   De-   us.

D
me- a   ad te   De-   us.

Vh
me- a   ad te   De-   us.

TUNC HI TRES

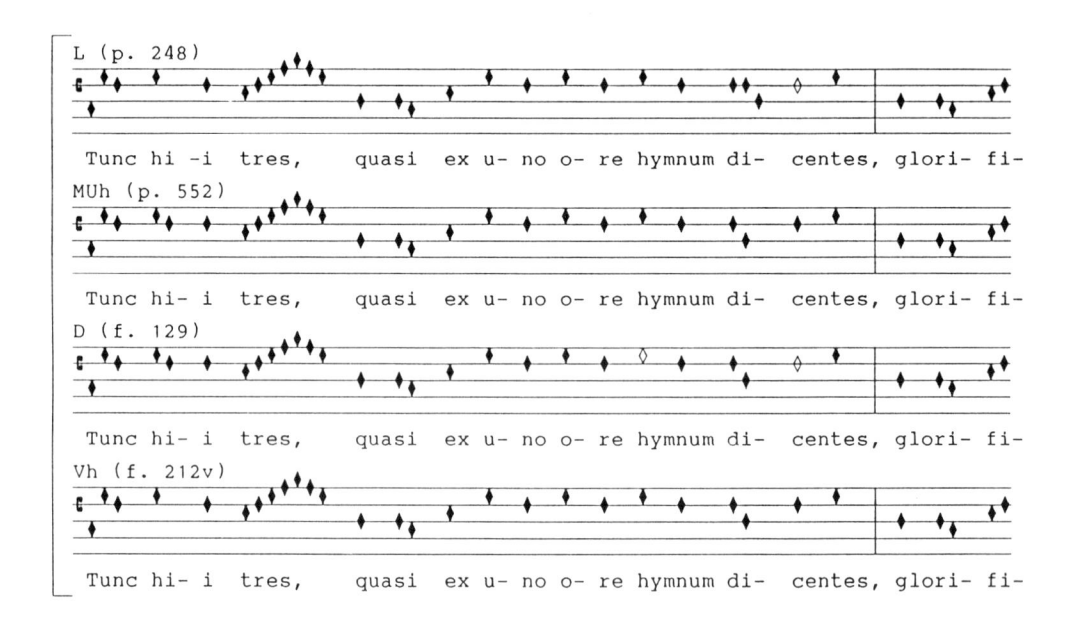

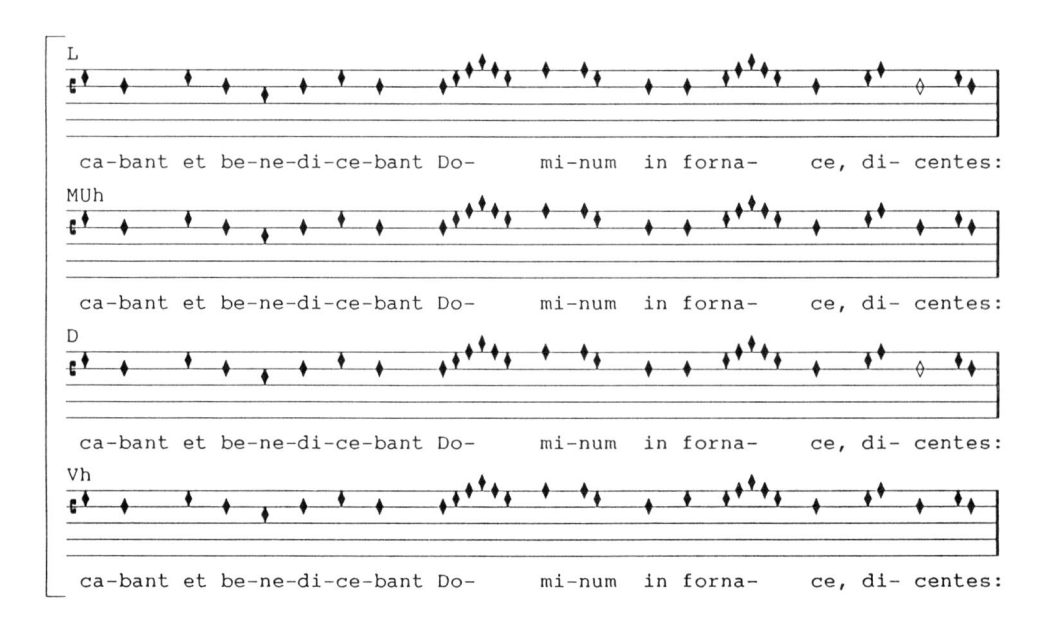

L (p. 248)
Tunc hi-i tres, quasi ex u-no o-re hymnum di-centes, glori-fi-

MUh (p. 552)
Tunc hi-i tres, quasi ex u-no o-re hymnum di-centes, glori-fi-

D (f. 129)
Tunc hi-i tres, quasi ex u-no o-re hymnum di-centes, glori-fi-

Vh (f. 212v)
Tunc hi-i tres, quasi ex u-no o-re hymnum di-centes, glori-fi-

L
ca-bant et be-ne-di-ce-bant Do-mi-num in forna-ce, di-centes:

MUh
ca-bant et be-ne-di-ce-bant Do-mi-num in forna-ce, di-centes:

D
ca-bant et be-ne-di-ce-bant Do-mi-num in forna-ce, di-centes:

Vh
ca-bant et be-ne-di-ce-bant Do-mi-num in forna-ce, di-centes:

BENEDICTUS ES DOMINE

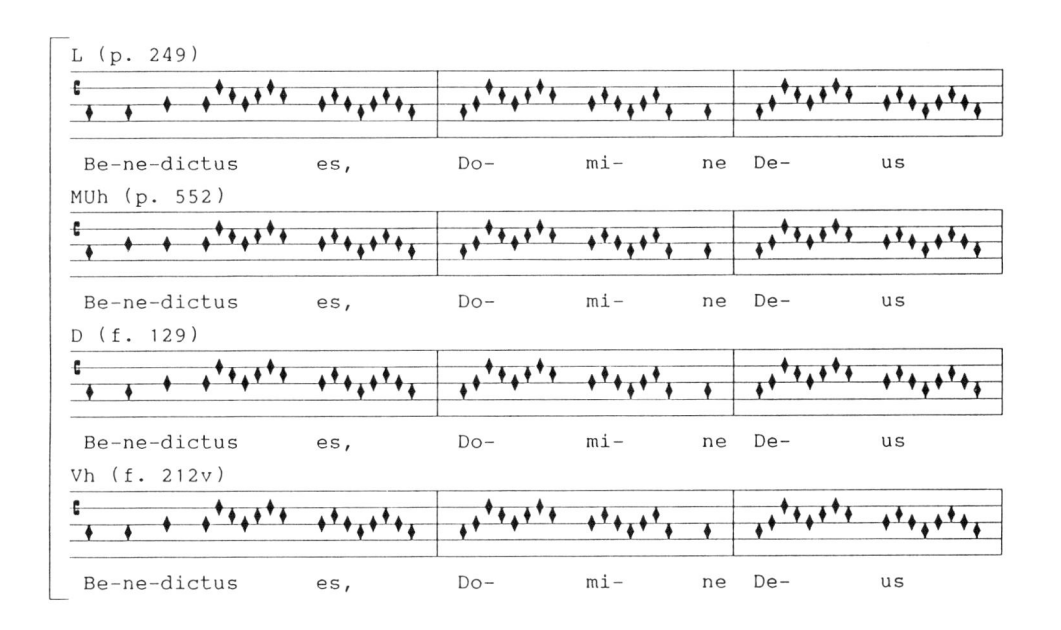

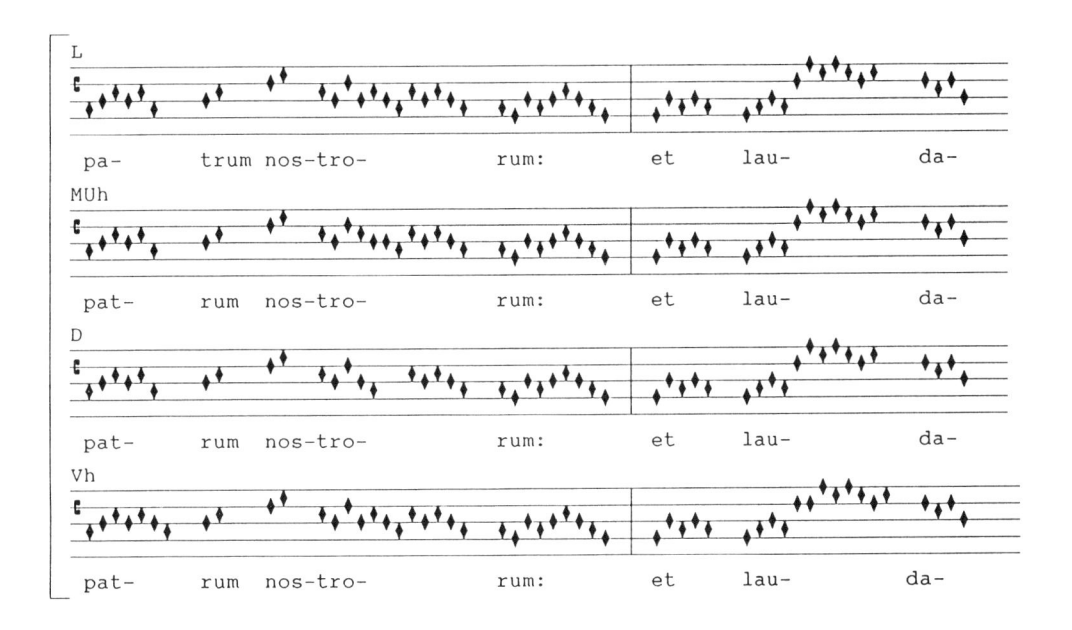

L (p. 249)

Be-ne-dictus es, Do- mi- ne De- us

MUh (p. 552)

Be-ne-dictus es, Do- mi- ne De- us

D (f. 129)

Be-ne-dictus es, Do- mi- ne De- us

Vh (f. 212v)

Be-ne-dictus es, Do- mi- ne De- us

L

pa- trum nos-tro- rum: et lau- da-

MUh

pat- rum nos-tro- rum: et lau- da-

D

pat- rum nos-tro- rum: et lau- da-

Vh

pat- rum nos-tro- rum: et lau- da-

BENEDICTUS ES DOMINE (continued)

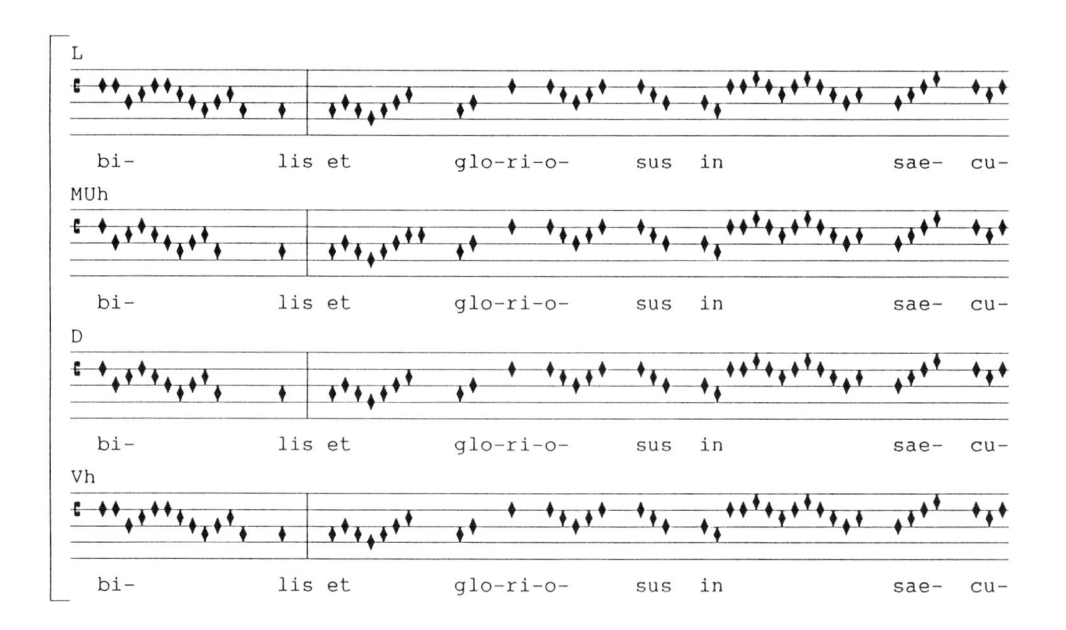

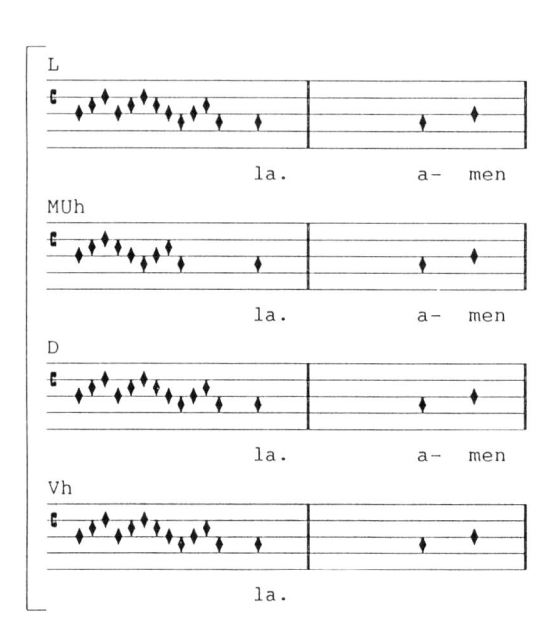

(ii) ET BENEDICTUM NOMEN

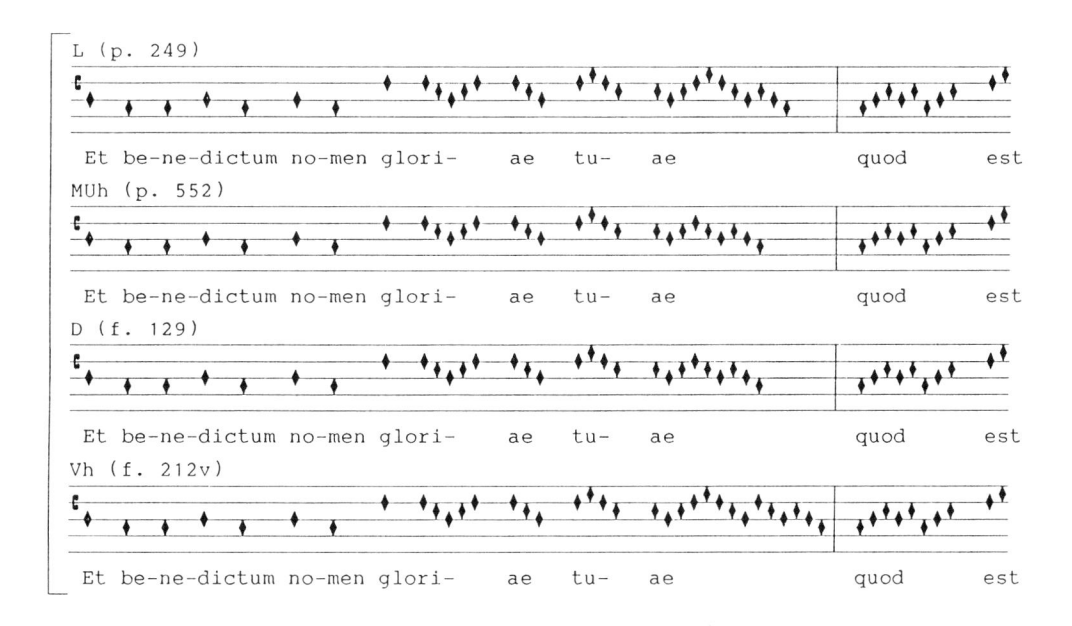

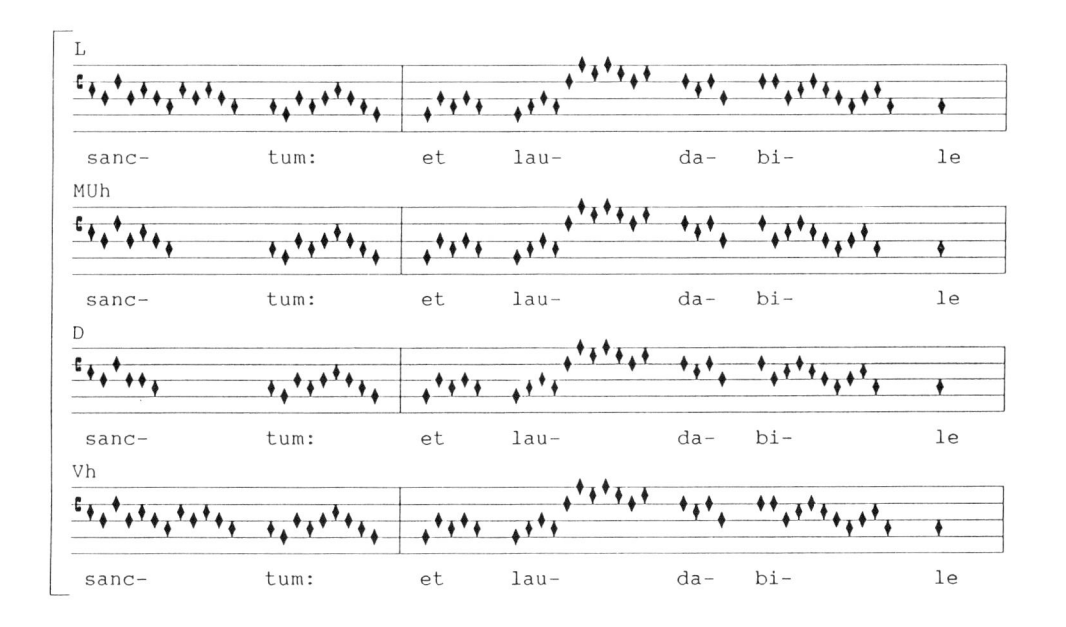

ET BENEDICTUM NOMEN (continued)

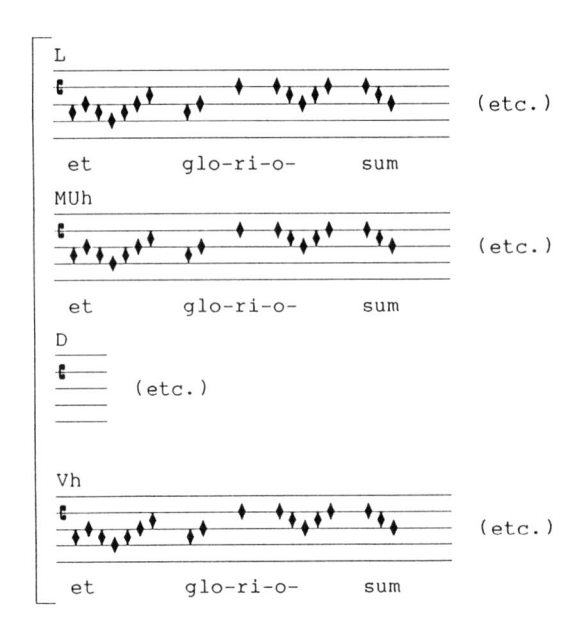

L

et glo-ri-o- sum (etc.)

MUh

et glo-ri-o- sum (etc.)

D

(etc.)

Vh

et glo-ri-o- sum (etc.)

(iii) BENEDICTUS ES SUPER SEDEM

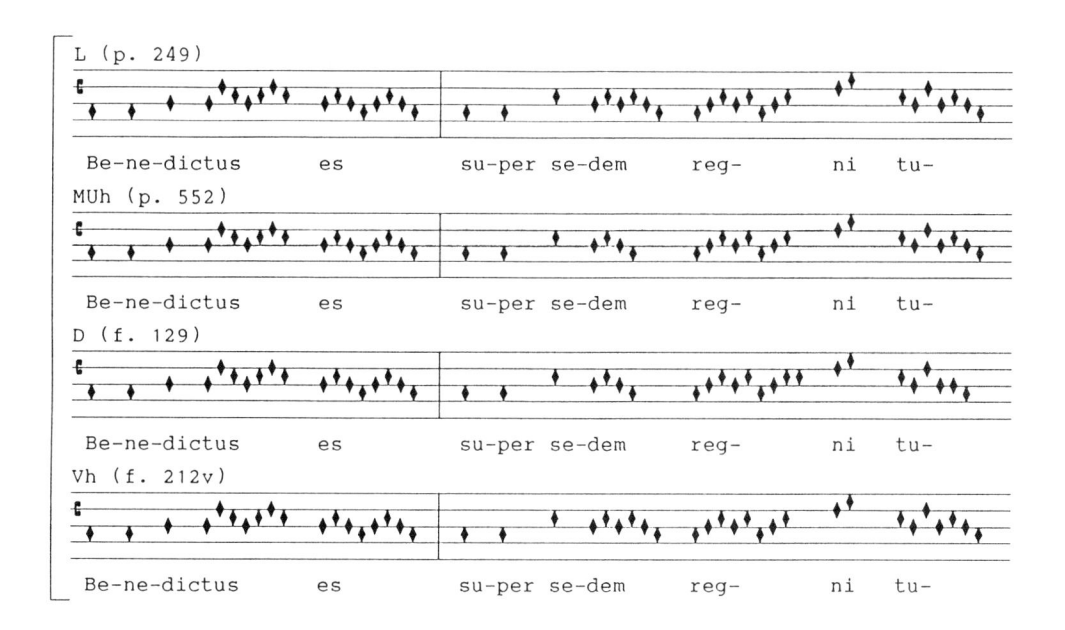

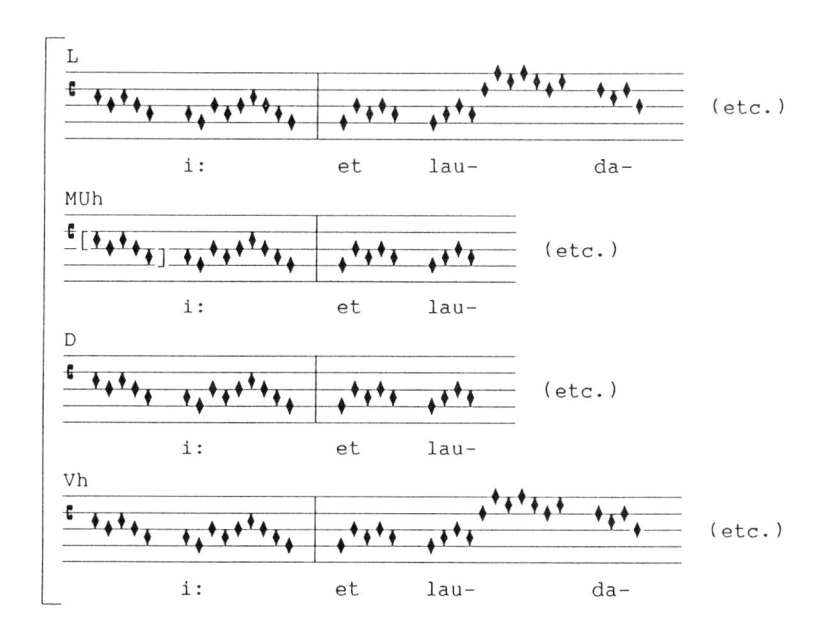

L (p. 249)
Be-ne-dictus   es   su-per se-dem   reg-   ni   tu-

MUh (p. 552)
Be-ne-dictus   es   su-per se-dem   reg-   ni   tu-

D (f. 129)
Be-ne-dictus   es   su-per se-dem   reg-   ni   tu-

Vh (f. 212v)
Be-ne-dictus   es   su-per se-dem   reg-   ni   tu-

L
i: et   lau-   da-   (etc.)

MUh
i: et   lau-   (etc.)

D
i: et   lau-   (etc.)

Vh
i: et   lau-   da-   (etc.)

(iv) BENEDICITE OMNIA OPERA

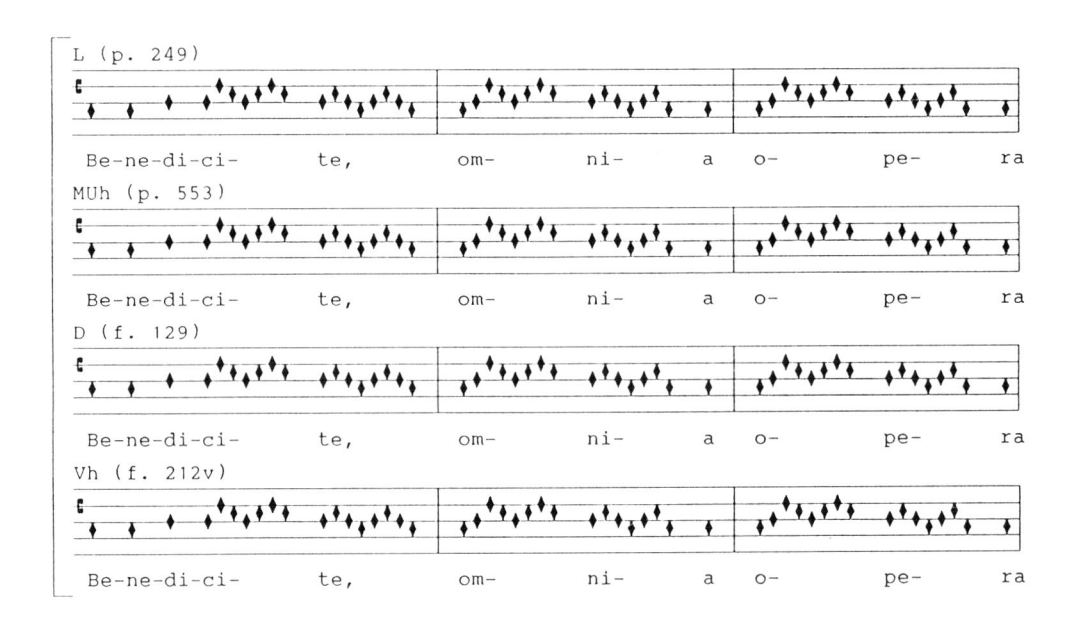

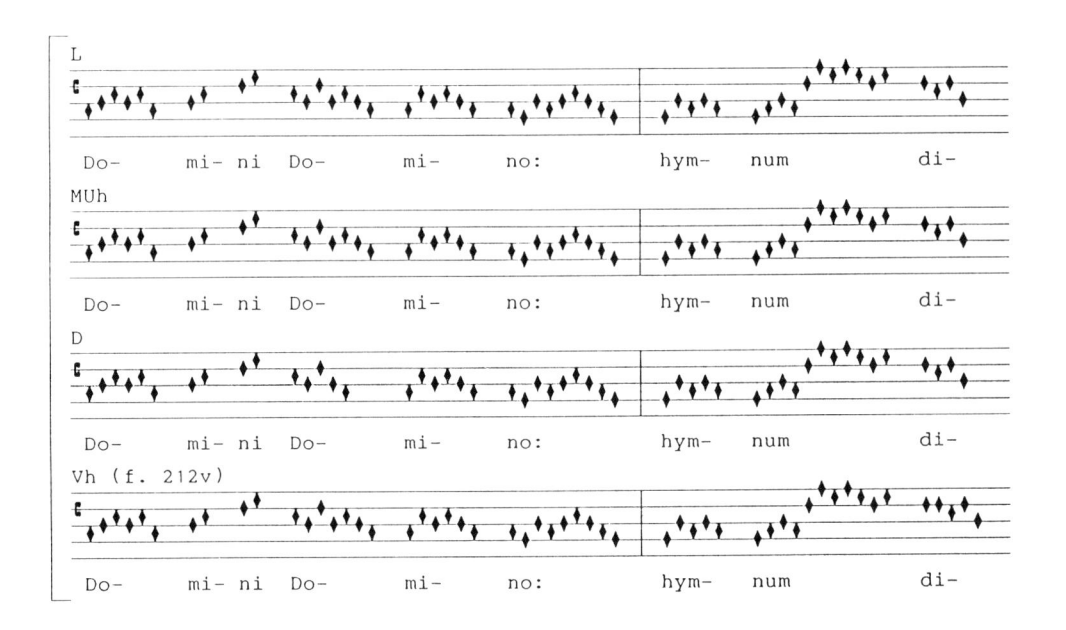

L (p. 249)

Be-ne-di-ci- te, om- ni- a o- pe- ra

MUh (p. 553)

Be-ne-di-ci- te, om- ni- a o- pe- ra

D (f. 129)

Be-ne-di-ci- te, om- ni- a o- pe- ra

Vh (f. 212v)

Be-ne-di-ci- te, om- ni- a o- pe- ra

L

Do- mi- ni Do- mi- no: hym- num di-

MUh

Do- mi- ni Do- mi- no: hym- num di-

D

Do- mi- ni Do- mi- no: hym- num di-

Vh (f. 212v)

Do- mi- ni Do- mi- no: hym- num di-

BENEDICITE OMNIA OPERA (continued)

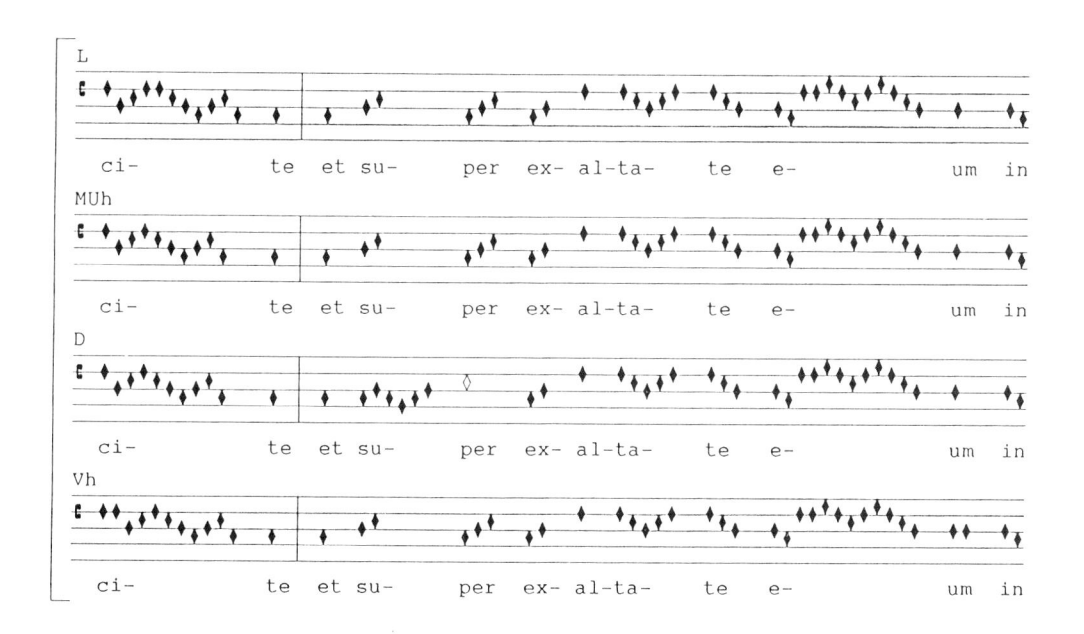

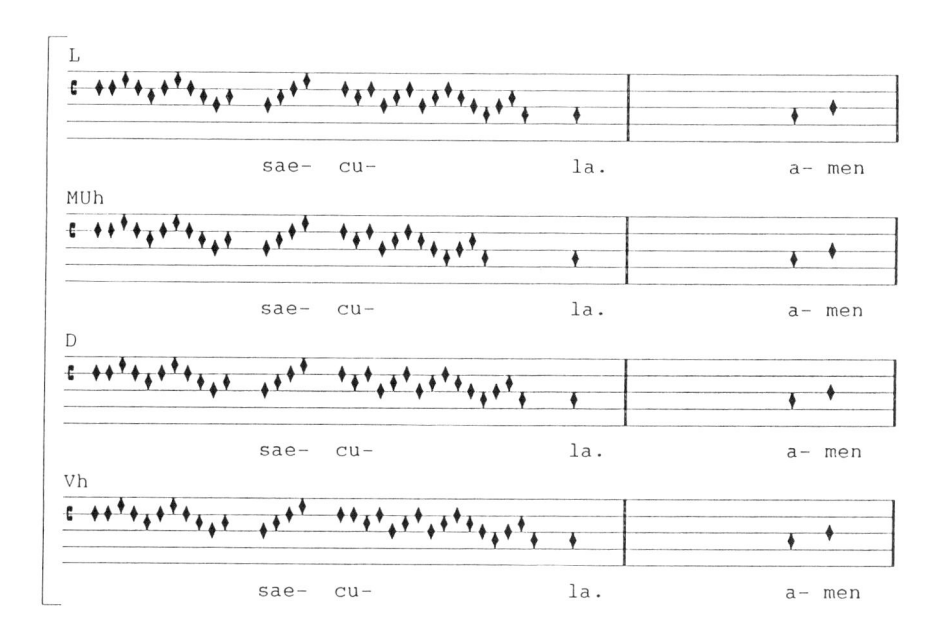

(v) BENEDICITE CAELI DOMINO

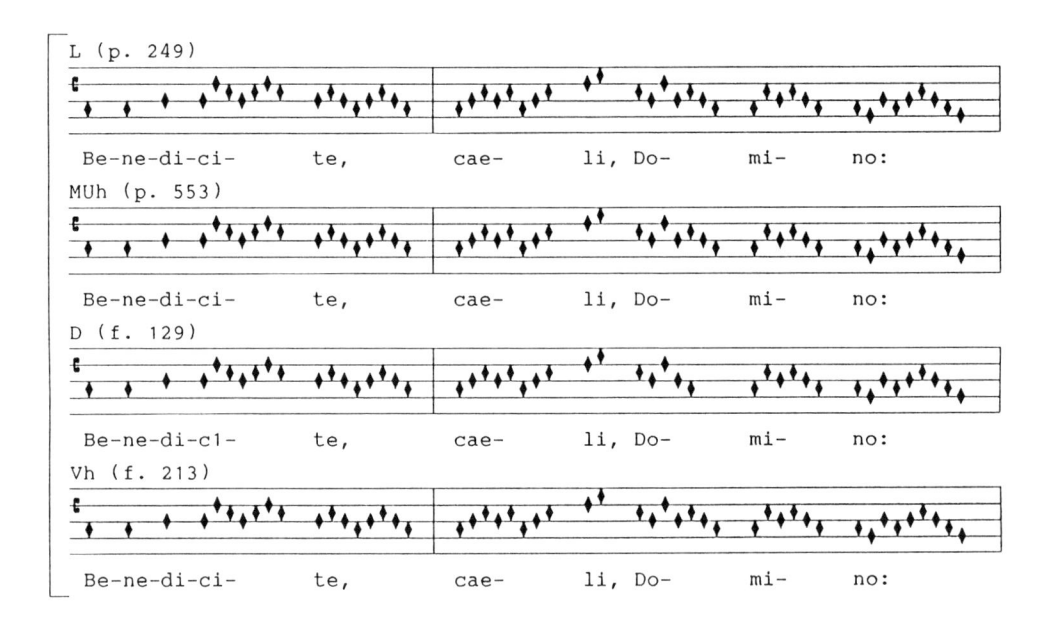

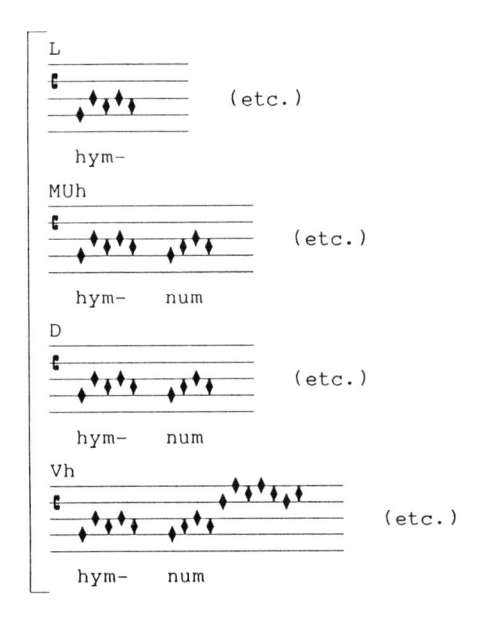

L (p. 249)
Be-ne-di-ci- te, cae- li, Do- mi- no:

MUh (p. 553)
Be-ne-di-ci- te, cae- li, Do- mi- no:

D (f. 129)
Be-ne-di-ci- te, cae- li, Do- mi- no:

Vh (f. 213)
Be-ne-di-ci- te, cae- li, Do- mi- no:

L
hym- (etc.)

MUh
hym- num (etc.)

D
hym- num (etc.)

Vh
hym- num (etc.)

(vi) BENEDICITE ANGELI DOMINI

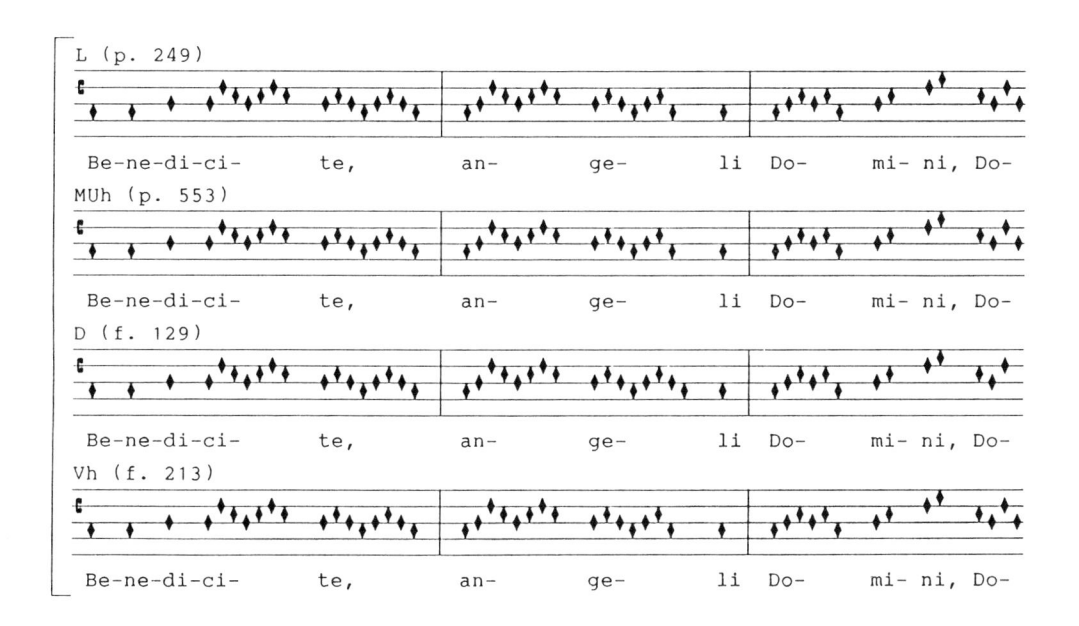

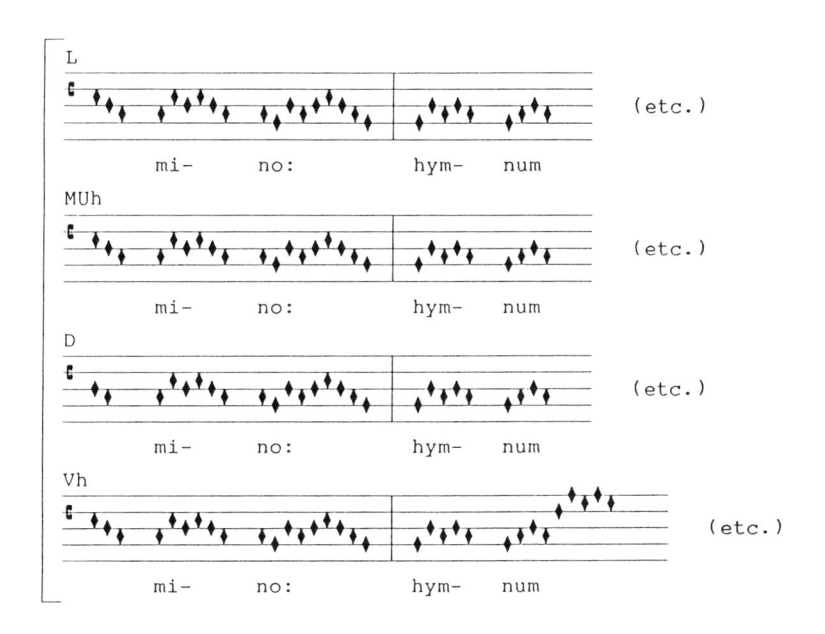

L (p. 249)

Be-ne-di-ci- te, an- ge- li Do- mi- ni, Do-

MUh (p. 553)

Be-ne-di-ci- te, an- ge- li Do- mi- ni, Do-

D (f. 129)

Be-ne-di-ci- te, an- ge- li Do- mi- ni, Do-

Vh (f. 213)

Be-ne-di-ci- te, an- ge- li Do- mi- ni, Do-

L

mi- no: hym- num (etc.)

MUh

mi- no: hym- num (etc.)

D

mi- no: hym- num (etc.)

Vh

mi- no: hym- num (etc.)

(vii) BENEDICITE OMNES VIRTUTES

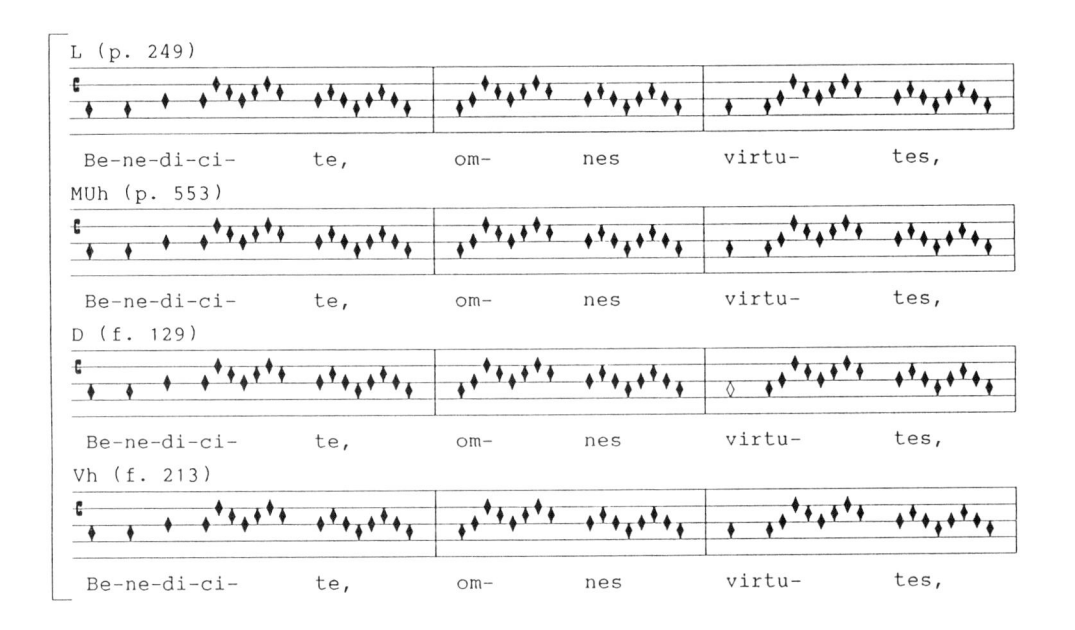

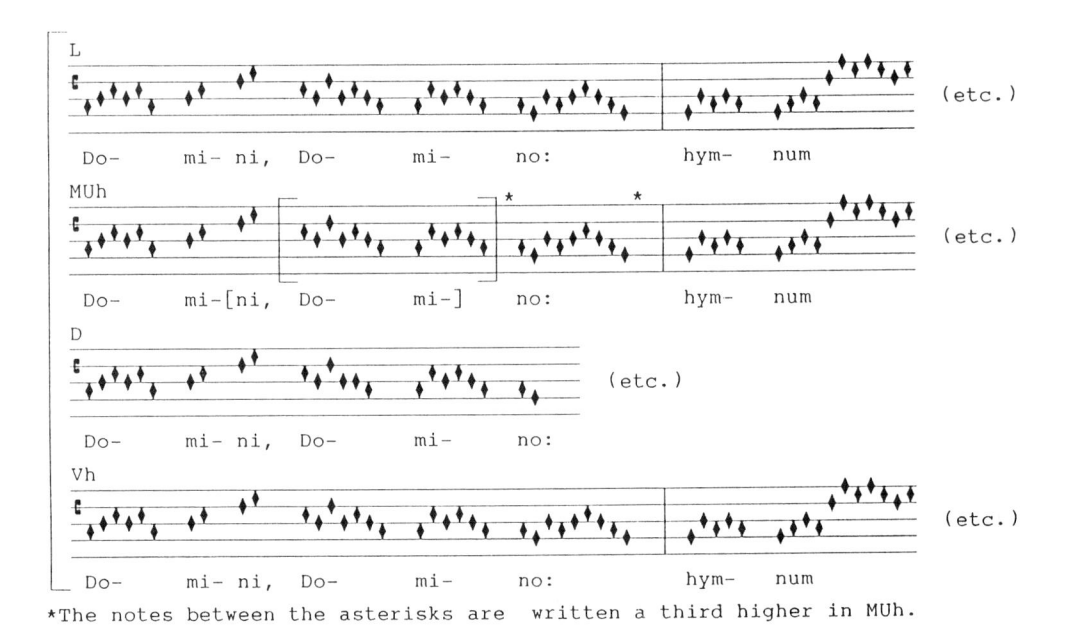

L (p. 249)

Be-ne-di-ci- te, om- nes virtu- tes,

MUh (p. 553)

Be-ne-di-ci- te, om- nes virtu- tes,

D (f. 129)

Be-ne-di-ci- te, om- nes virtu- tes,

Vh (f. 213)

Be-ne-di-ci- te, om- nes virtu- tes,

L

Do- mi- ni, Do- mi- no: hym- num (etc.)

MUh

Do- mi-[ni, Do- mi-] no: hym- num (etc.)

D

Do- mi- ni, Do- mi- no: (etc.)

Vh

Do- mi- ni, Do- mi- no: hym- num (etc.)

*The notes between the asterisks are written a third higher in MUh.

214

(viii) BENEDICITE SACERDOTES DOMINI

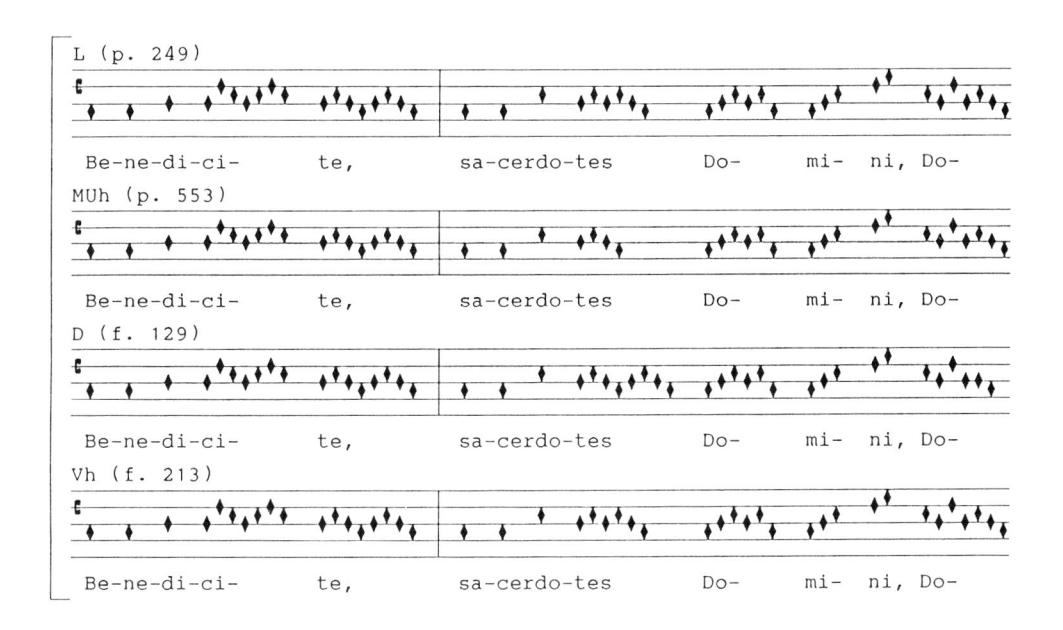

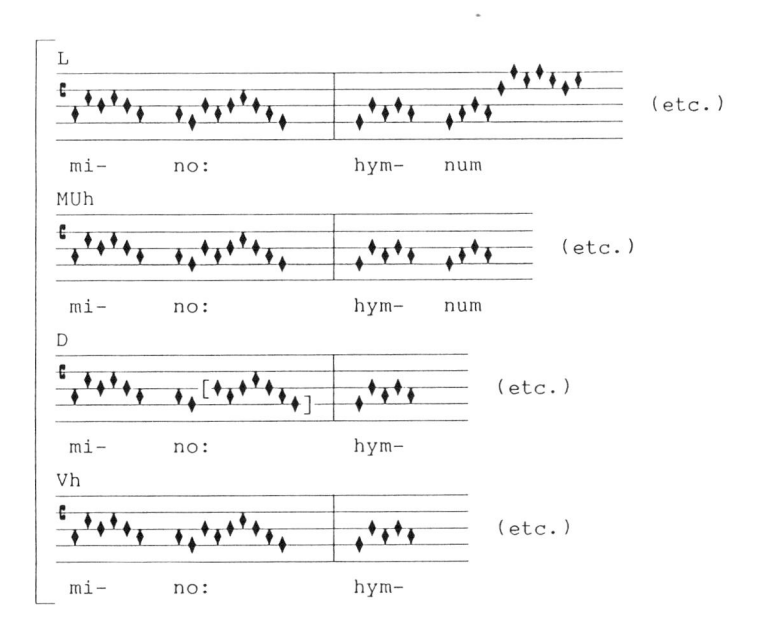

(ix) BENEDICITE SERVI DOMINI

L (p. 249)
Be-ne-di-ci- te, ser- vi Do- mi- ni, Do-

MUh (p. 554)
Be-ne-di-ci- te, ser- vi Do- mi- ni, Do-

D (f. 129v)
Be-ne-di-ci- te, ser- vi Do- mi- ni, Do-

Vh (f. 213)
Be-ne-di-ci- te, ser- vi Do- mi- ni, Do-

L
mi- no: hym- num (etc.)

MUh
mi- no: hym- num (etc.)

D
(etc.)

Vh
mi- no: hym- num (etc.)

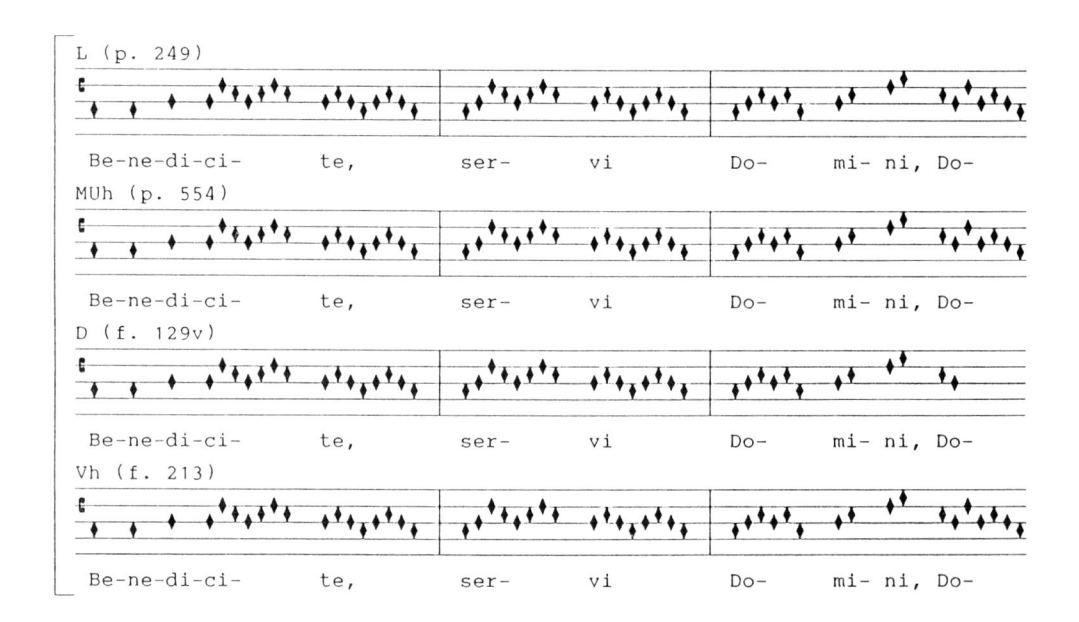

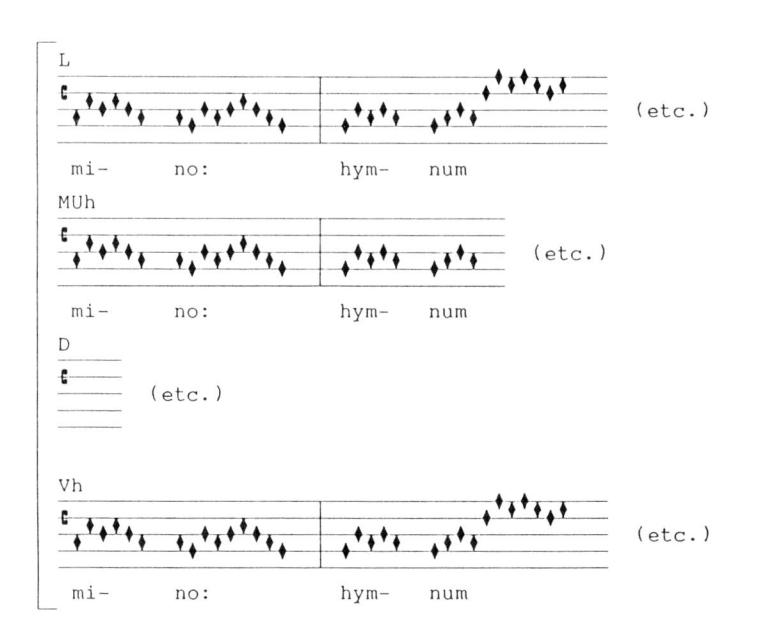

(x) BENEDICITE SPIRITUS ET ANIMAE

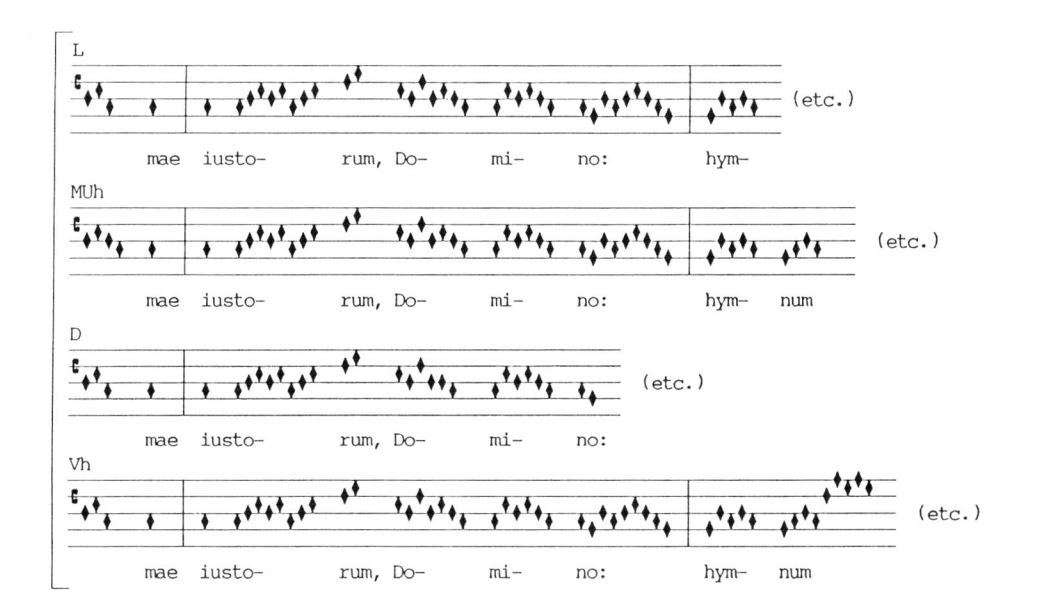

L (p. 250)

Be-ne-di-ci-te, spi- ri- tus et a- ni-

MUh (p. 554)

Be-ne-di-ci-te, spi- ri- tus et a- ni-

D (f. 129v)

Be-ne-di-ci-te, spi- ri- tus et a- ni-

Vh (f. 213v)

Be-ne-di-ci-te, spi- ri- tus et a- ni-

L

mae iusto- rum, Do- mi- no: hym- (etc.)

MUh

mae iusto- rum, Do- mi- no: hym- num (etc.)

D

mae iusto- rum, Do- mi- no: (etc.)

Vh

mae iusto- rum, Do- mi- no: hym- num (etc.)

(xi) BENEDICITE SANCTI ET HUMILES

L (p. 250)

Be-ne-di-ci-te, sanc-ti et hu- mi-

MUh (p. 554)

Be-ne-di-ci-te, sanc-ti et hu- mi-

D (f. 129v)

Be-ne-di-ci-te, sanc-ti et hu- mi-

Vh (f. 213v)

Be-ne-di-ci-te, sanc-ti et hu- mi-

L

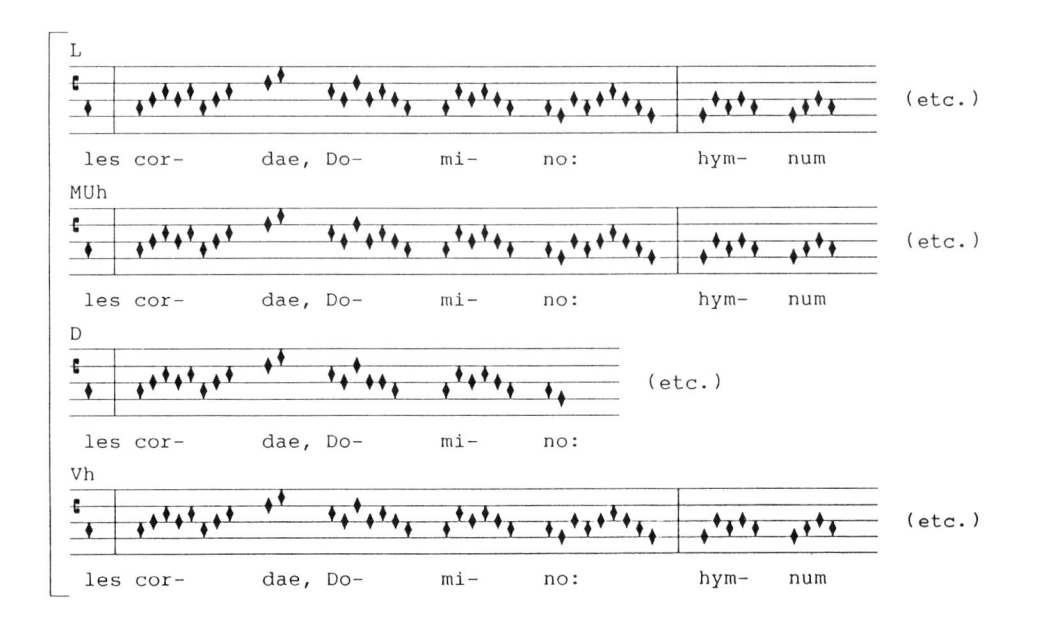

les cor- dae, Do- mi- no: hym- num (etc.)

MUh

les cor- dae, Do- mi- no: hym- num (etc.)

D

les cor- dae, Do- mi- no: (etc.)

Vh

les cor- dae, Do- mi- no: hym- num (etc.)

(xii) BENEDICITE ANANIA AZARIA MISAHEL

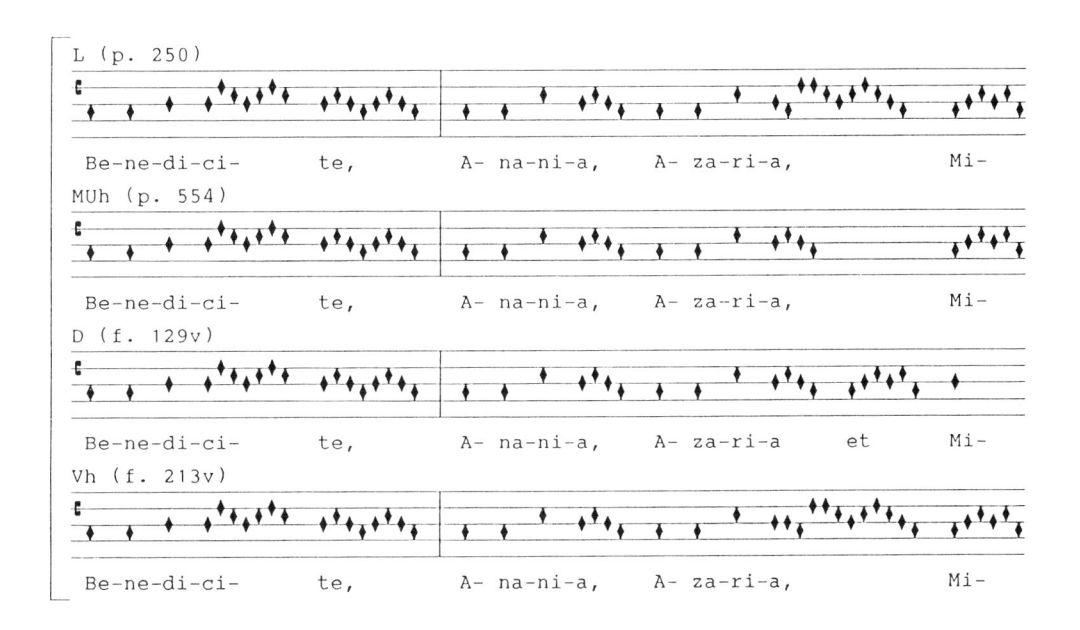

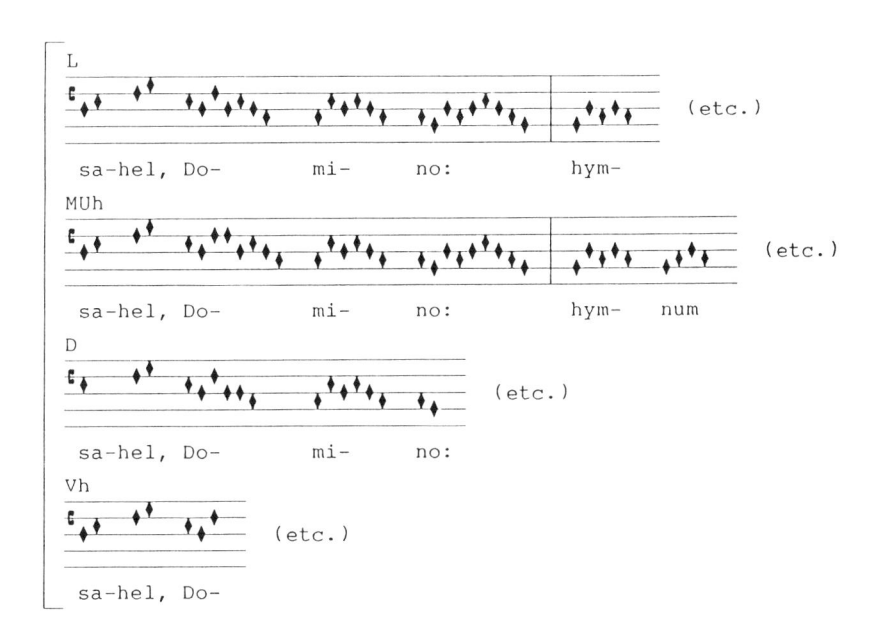

L (p. 250)

Be-ne-di-ci- te, A- na-ni-a, A- za-ri-a, Mi-

MUh (p. 554)

Be-ne-di-ci- te, A- na-ni-a, A- za-ri-a, Mi-

D (f. 129v)

Be-ne-di-ci- te, A- na-ni-a, A- za-ri-a et Mi-

Vh (f. 213v)

Be-ne-di-ci- te, A- na-ni-a, A- za-ri-a, Mi-

L

sa-hel, Do- mi- no: hym- (etc.)

MUh

sa-hel, Do- mi- no: hym- num (etc.)

D

sa-hel, Do- mi- no: (etc.)

Vh

sa-hel, Do- (etc.)

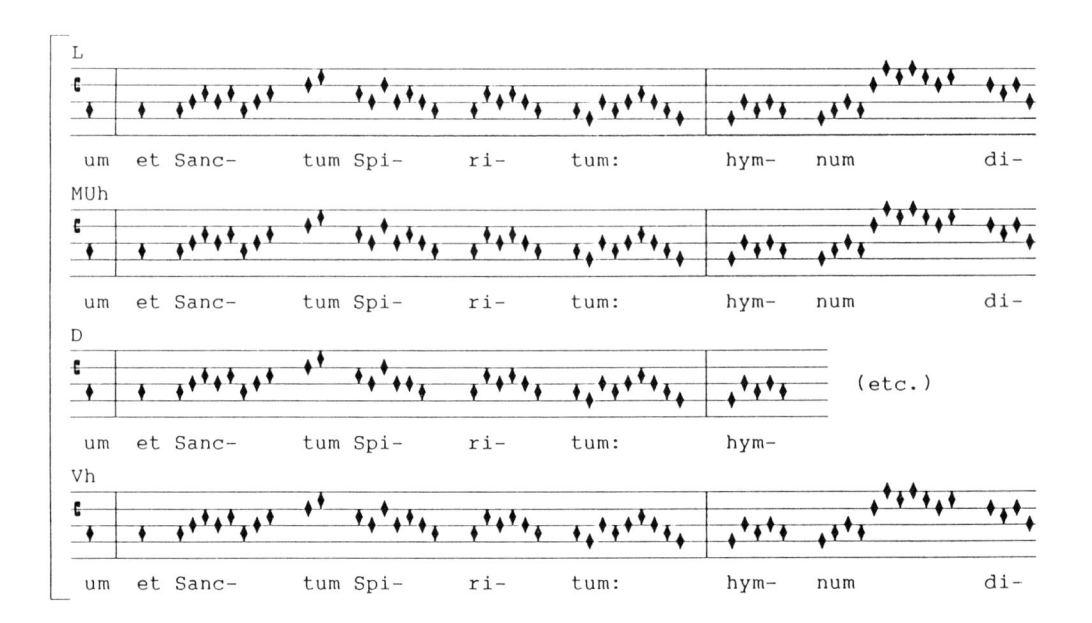

(xiii) BENEDICAMUS PATREM ET FILIUM

BENEDICAMUS PATREM (continued)

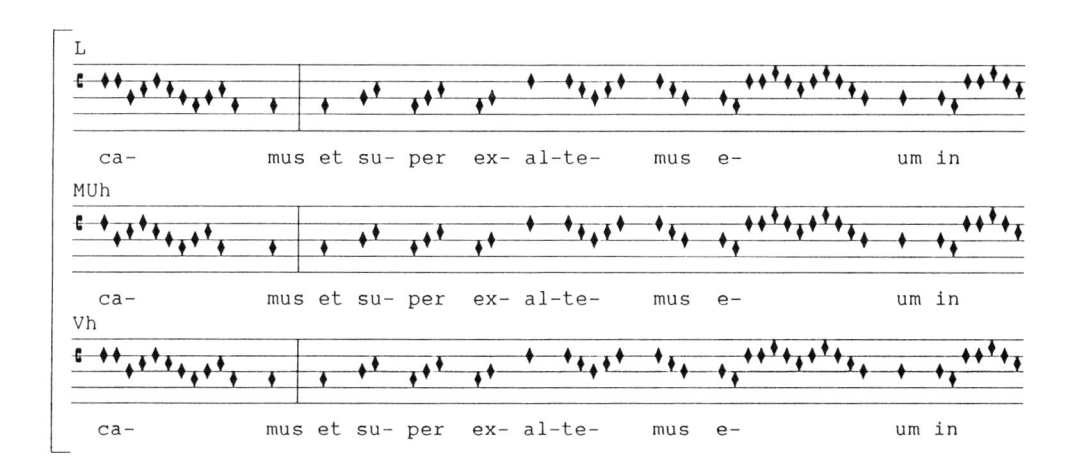

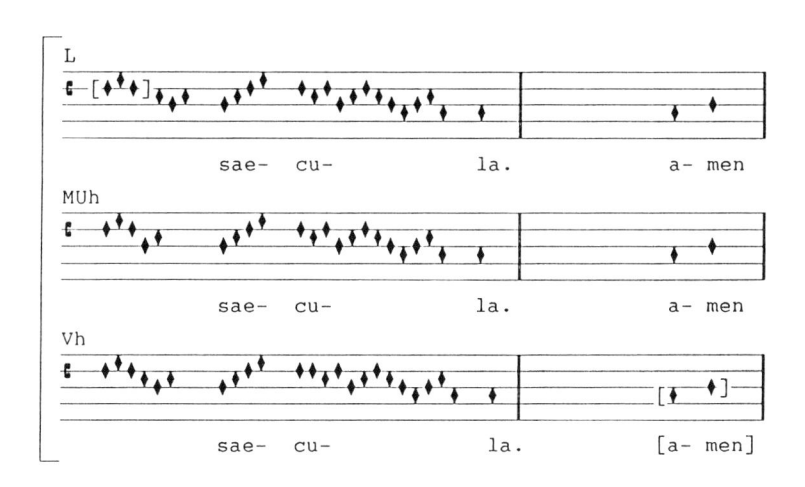

L: ca- mus et su- per ex- al- te- mus e- um in

MUh: ca- mus et su- per ex- al- te- mus e- um in

Vh: ca- mus et su- per ex- al- te- mus e- um in

L: sae- cu- la. a- men

MUh: sae- cu- la. a- men

Vh: sae- cu- la. [a- men]

QUONIAM ERIPUIT NOS

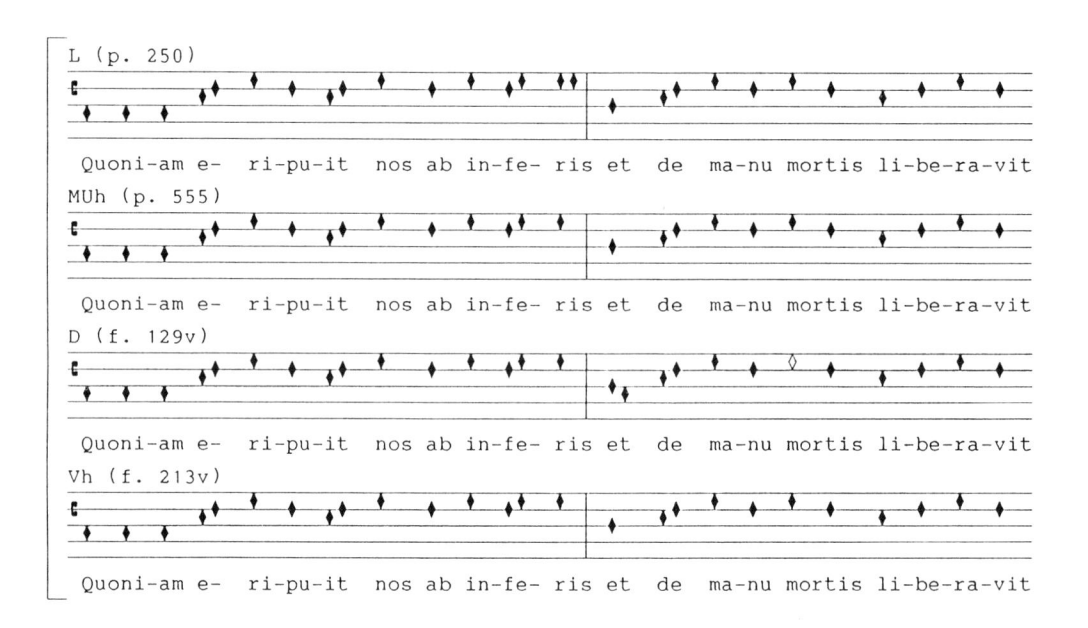

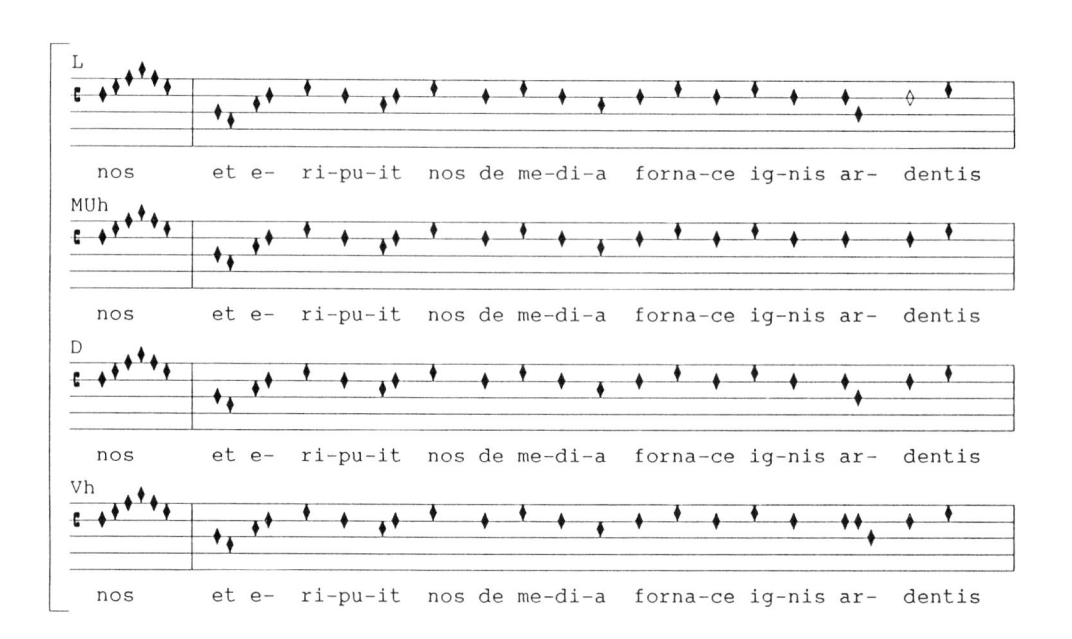

QUONIAM ERIPUIT (continued)

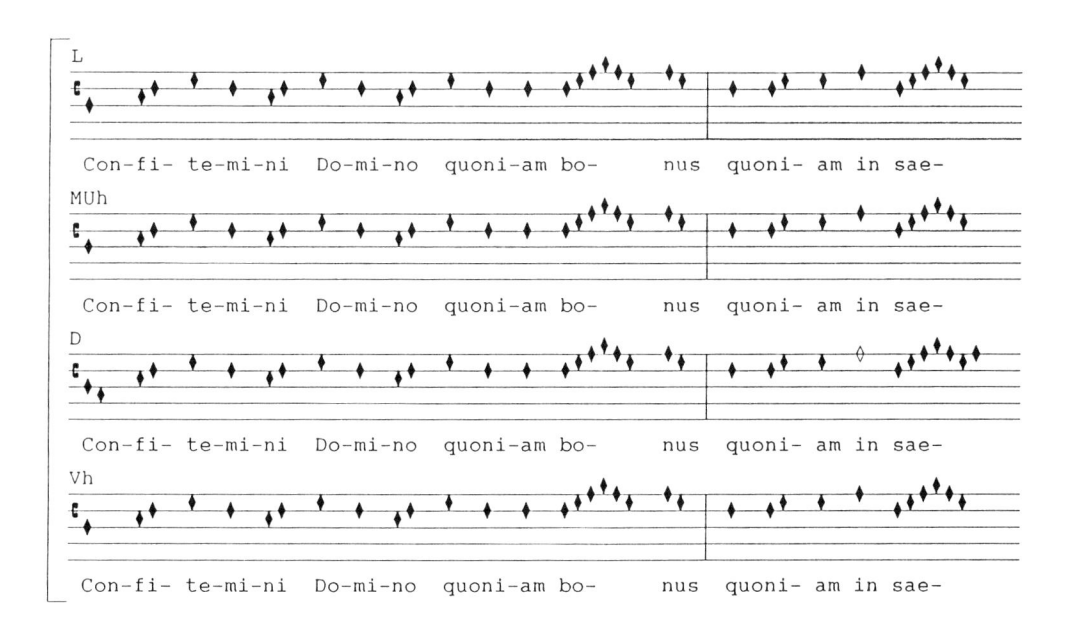

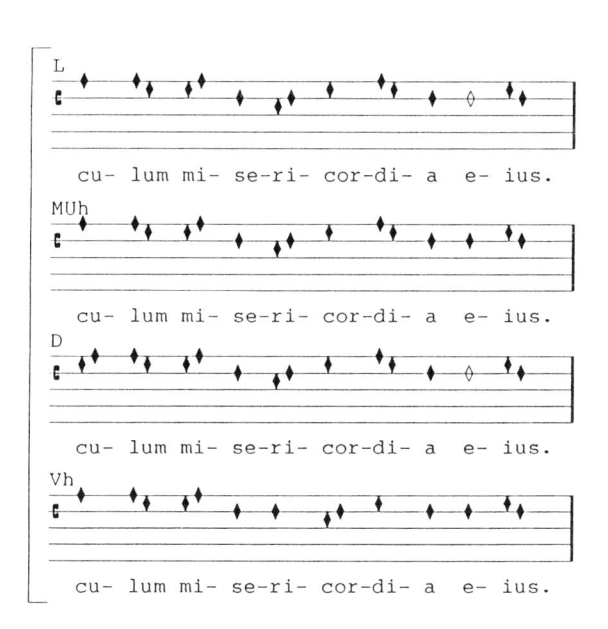

L: Con- fi- te-mi-ni Do-mi-no quoni-am bo- nus quoni- am in sae-
MUh: Con- fi- te-mi-ni Do-mi-no quoni-am bo- nus quoni- am in sae-
D: Con- fi- te-mi-ni Do-mi-no quoni-am bo- nus quoni- am in sae-
Vh: Con- fi- te-mi-ni Do-mi-no quoni-am bo- nus quoni- am in sae-

L: cu- lum mi- se-ri- cor-di- a e- ius.
MUh: cu- lum mi- se-ri- cor-di- a e- ius.
D: cu- lum mi- se-ri- cor-di- a e- ius.
Vh: cu- lum mi- se-ri- cor-di- a e- ius.

THE HOLY SATURDAY VERSION OF THE BENEDICTUS ES

For the verses sung in the shorter version of the BENEDICTUS ES canticle on Holy Saturday, the manuscripts usually provide only cues (of various lengths), and sometimes only text *incipits*. In a very few cases, the cues for the second occasion present minor variants of the melodies written out in full for Good Friday:

The verse BENEDICTUS ES DOMINE: in *MUh* (p. 552), the second syllable, (Be)NE(dictus, is sung to the same pitch as the first. In this case the cue probably gives the correct version.

For the verse BENEDICAMUS PATREM: in *L* (p. 258), the last note is omitted from the syllable SANC(tum); (also in *L*, on the same page) in the syllable (se)CU(la), the second, third and fourth notes are repeated. In these two cases the variants would seem to be inadvertent.

Following is the brief introduction to the Holy Saturday version of the Canticle, and the verse BENEDICITE FONTES DOMINI, which does not appear in the Good Friday version. In *Vh*, for the canticle proper, only text cues are provided. But since the verse BENEDICITE FONTES can be easily reconstructed from the examples of the other verses in the same manuscript, I have not thought it necessary to introduce another source to provide a fourth version.

HYMNUM DANIELIS

L (p. 258)

Hym-num Da- ni-e- lis

MUh (p. 570)

Hym-num Da- ni-e- lis

D (f. 133)*

Hym-num Da- ni-e- lis

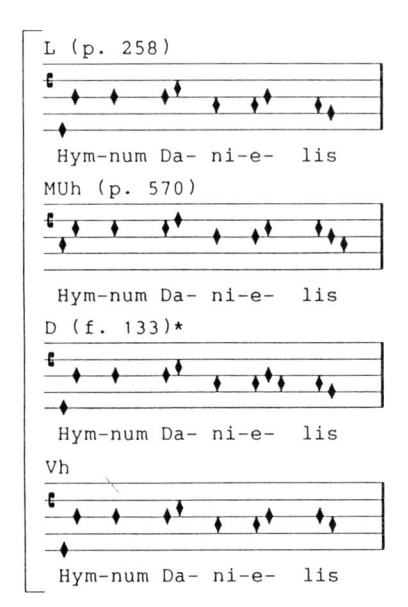

*The pitches for this phrase are uncertain.

Vh

Hym-num Da- ni-e- lis

(v) BENEDICITE FONTES DOMINI

L (p. 258)

Be-ne-di-ci- te, fon- tes Do- mi- ni, Do-

MUh (p. 571)

Be-ne-di-ci- te, fon- tes Do- mi- ni, (etc.)

D (f. 133v)

Be-ne-di-ci- te, fon- tes Do- mi- ni, Do-

L

mi- no: hym- num (etc.)

D

mi- no: hym- (etc.)

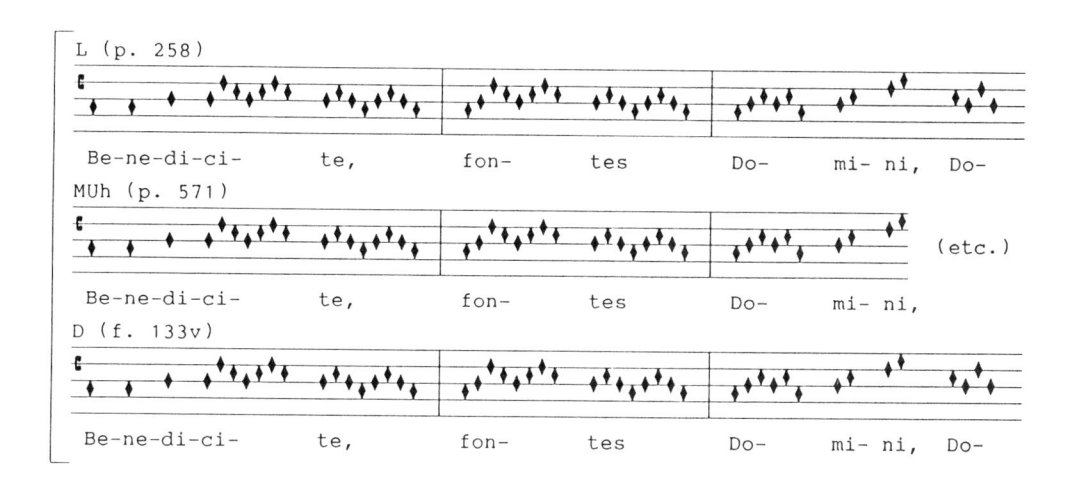

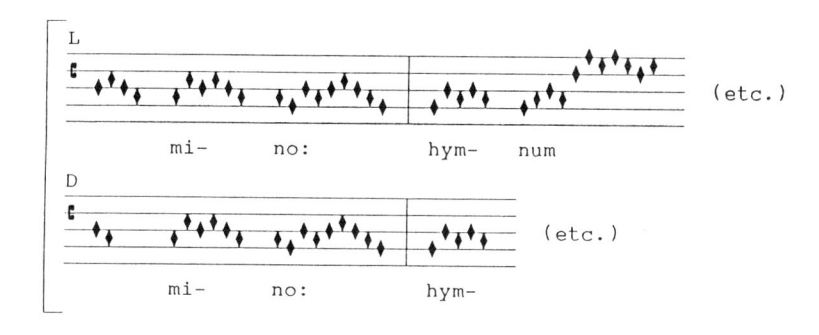

TUNC CANTABAT MOYSES

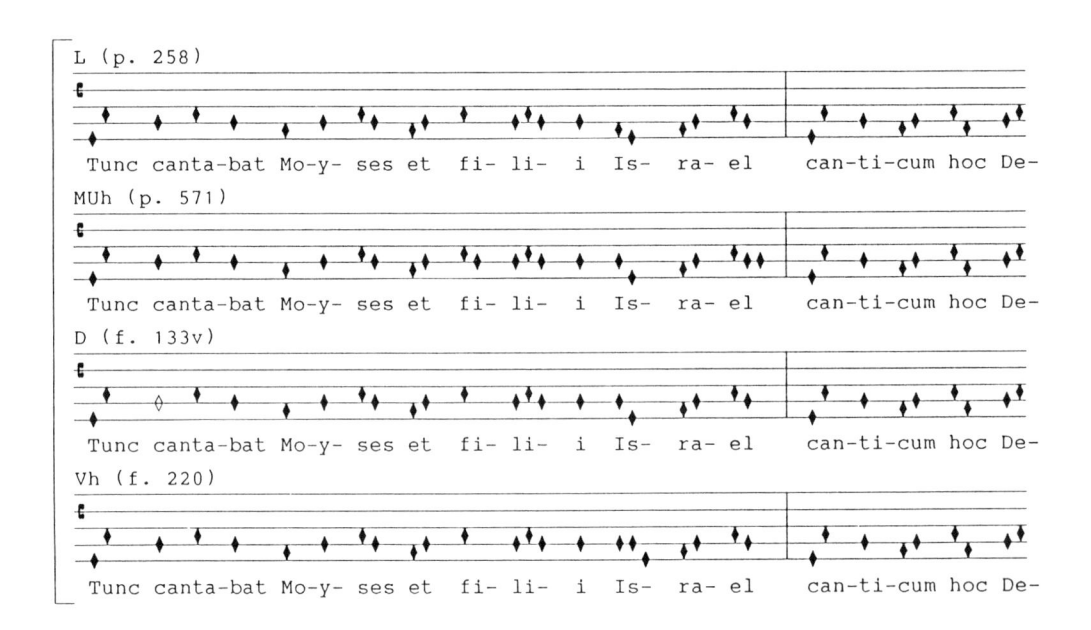

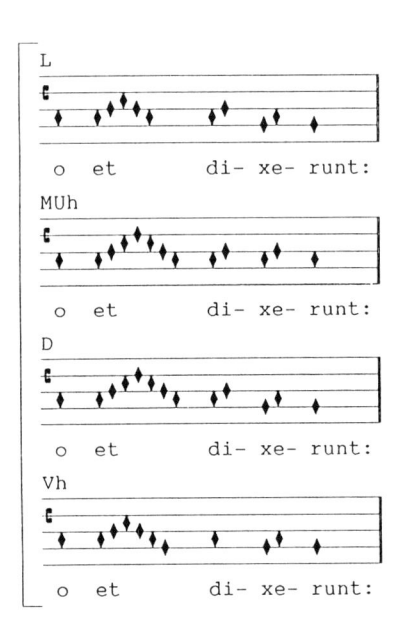

L (p. 258)
Tunc canta-bat Mo-y- ses et fi- li- i Is- ra- el can-ti-cum hoc De-

MUh (p. 571)
Tunc canta-bat Mo-y- ses et fi- li- i Is- ra- el can-ti-cum hoc De-

D (f. 133v)
Tunc canta-bat Mo-y- ses et fi- li- i Is- ra- el can-ti-cum hoc De-

Vh (f. 220)
Tunc canta-bat Mo-y- ses et fi- li- i Is- ra- el can-ti-cum hoc De-

L
o et di- xe- runt:

MUh
o et di- xe- runt:

D
o et di- xe- runt:

Vh
o et di- xe- runt:

CANTEMUS DOMINO GLORIOSE

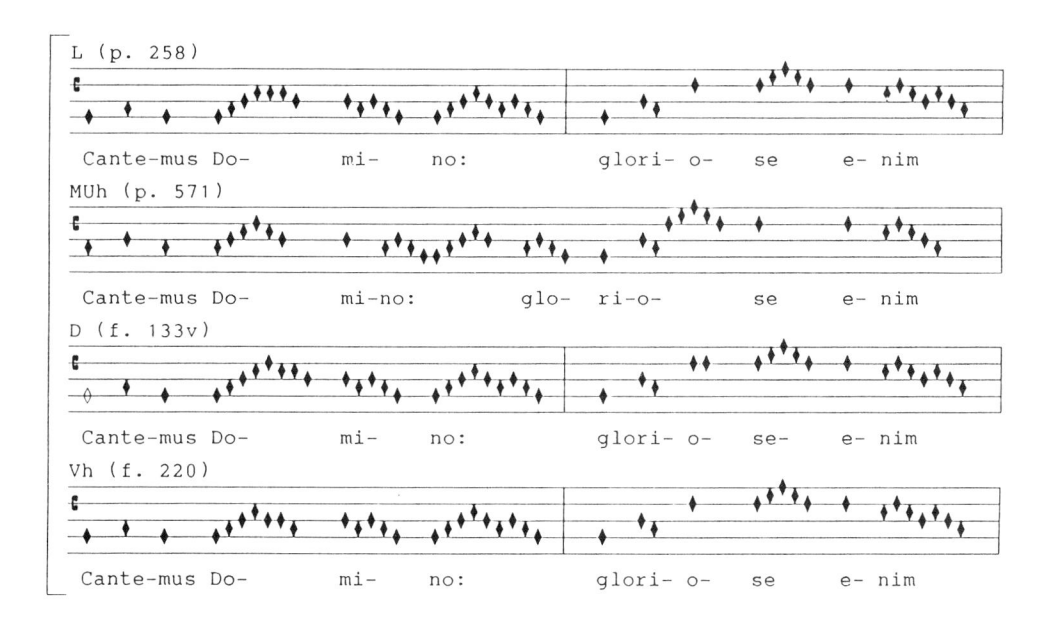

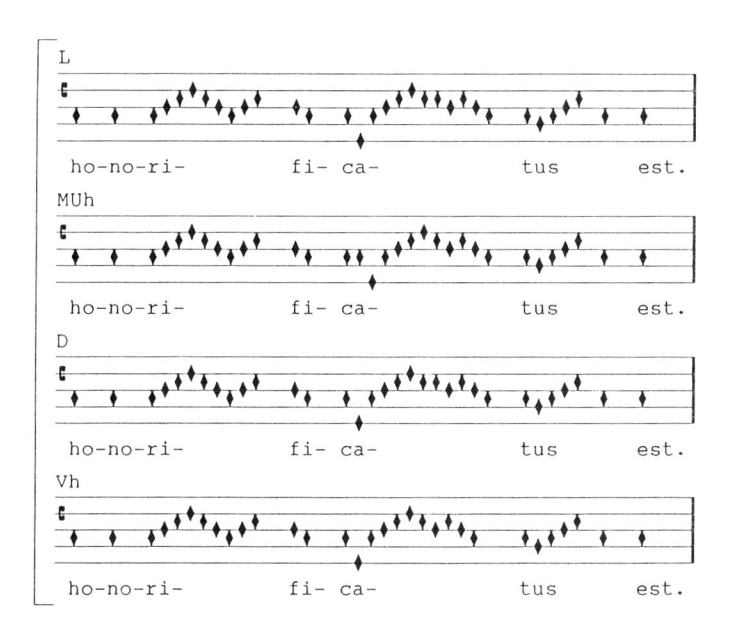

(ii) EQUUM ET ASCENSOREM

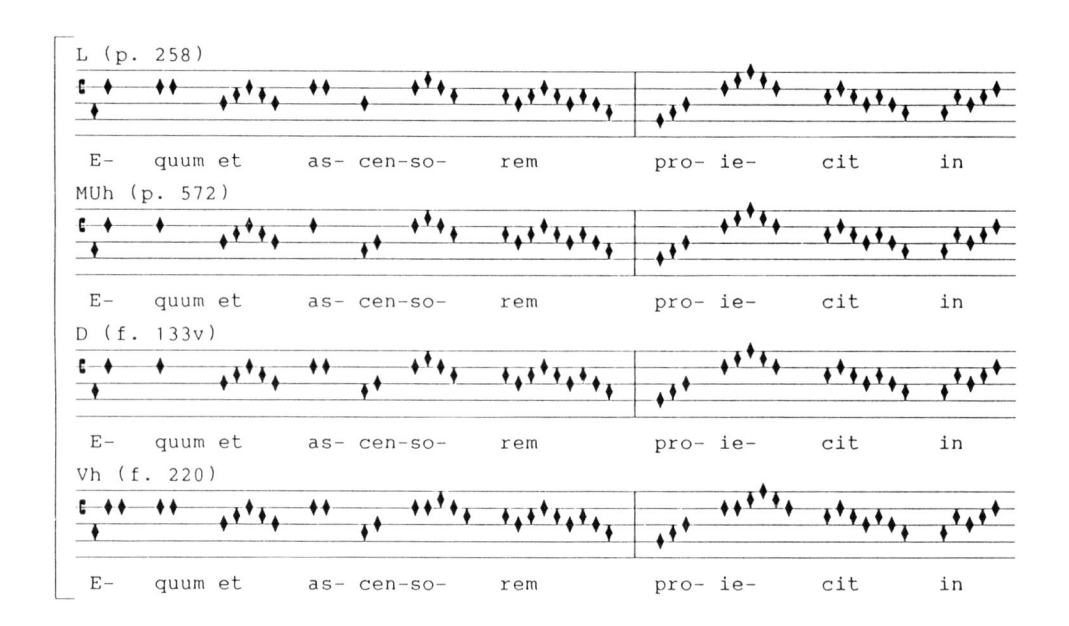

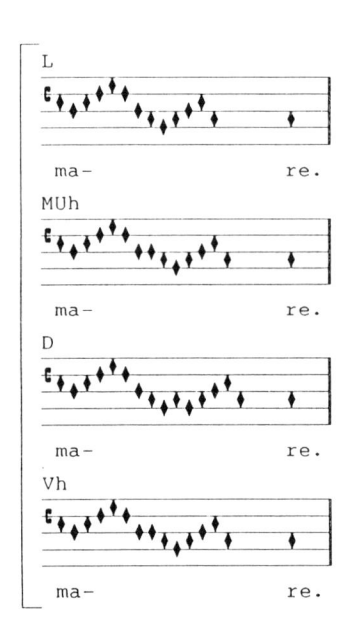

L (p. 258): E- quum et as- cen-so- rem pro- ie- cit in ma- re.

MUh (p. 572): E- quum et as- cen-so- rem pro- ie- cit in ma- re.

D (f. 133v): E- quum et as- cen-so- rem pro- ie- cit in ma- re.

Vh (f. 220): E- quum et as- cen-so- rem pro- ie- cit in ma- re.

(iii) ADIUTOR ET PROTECTOR

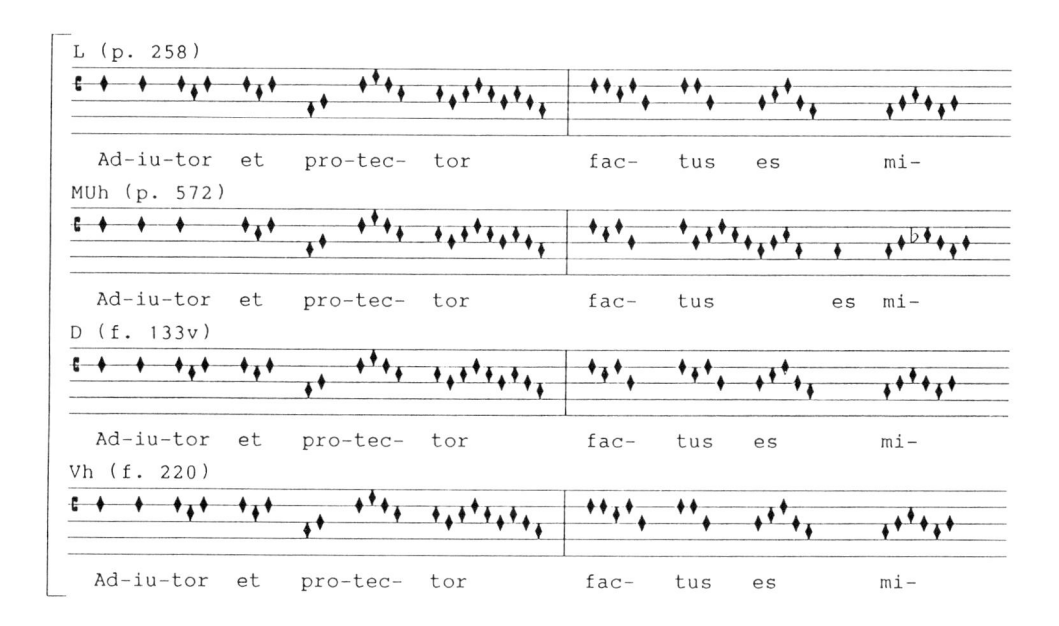

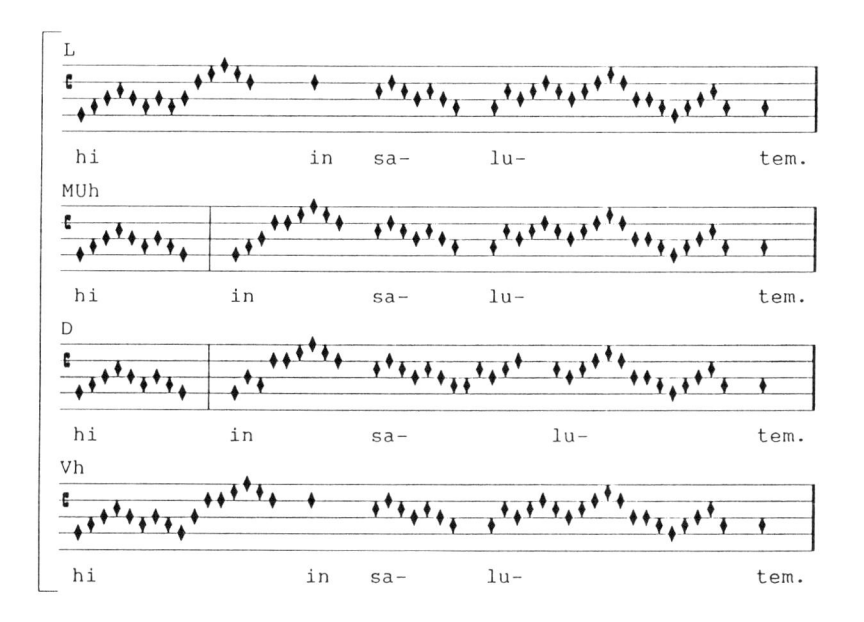

L (p. 258)

Ad-iu-tor et pro-tec- tor fac- tus es mi-

MUh (p. 572)

Ad-iu-tor et pro-tec- tor fac- tus es mi-

D (f. 133v)

Ad-iu-tor et pro-tec- tor fac- tus es mi-

Vh (f. 220)

Ad-iu-tor et pro-tec- tor fac- tus es mi-

L

hi in sa- lu- tem.

MUh

hi in sa- lu- tem.

D

hi in sa- lu- tem.

Vh

hi in sa- lu- tem.

(iv) HIC DEUS MEUS

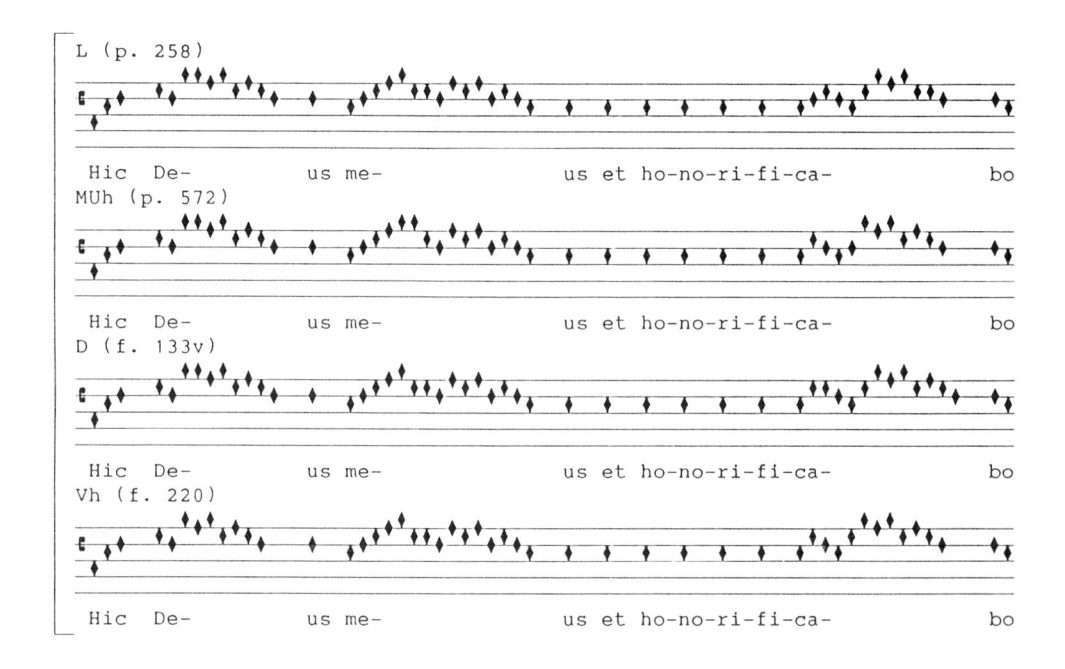

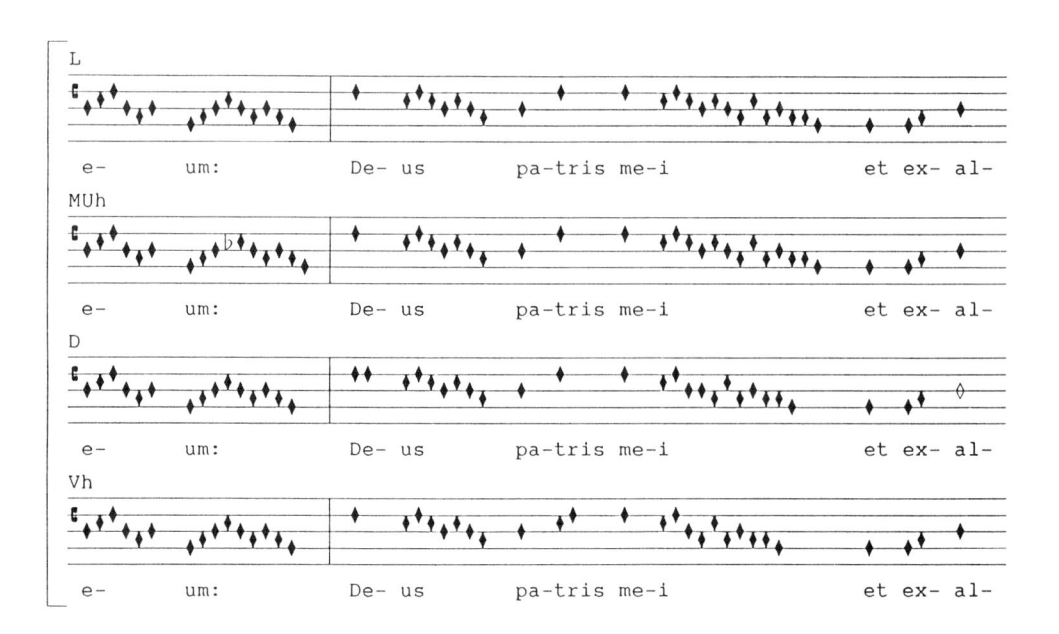

L (p. 258)

Hic De- us me- us et ho-no-ri-fi-ca- bo

MUh (p. 572)

Hic De- us me- us et ho-no-ri-fi-ca- bo

D (f. 133v)

Hic De- us me- us et ho-no-ri-fi-ca- bo

Vh (f. 220)

Hic De- us me- us et ho-no-ri-fi-ca- bo

L

e- um: De- us pa-tris me-i et ex- al-

MUh

e- um: De- us pa-tris me-i et ex- al-

D

e- um: De- us pa-tris me-i et ex- al-

Vh

e- um: De- us pa-tris me-i et ex- al-

HIC DEUS MEUS (continued)

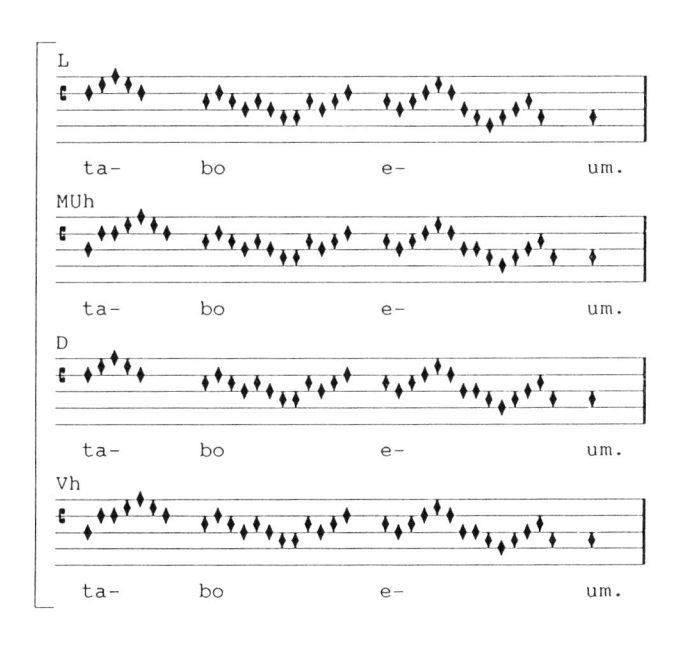

(v) DOMINUS CONTERENS BELLA

L (p. 259)
Do- mi- nus conte- rens bel- la: Do-mi-nus no-

MUh (p. 572)
Do- mi- nus conte- rens bel- la: Do-mi-nus no-

D (f. 133v)
Do- mi- nus conte- rens bel- la: Do-mi-nus no-

Vh (f. 220)
Do- mi- nus conte- rens bel- la: Do-mi-nus no-

L
men est e- i.

MUh
men est e- i.

D
men est e- i.

Vh
men est e- i.

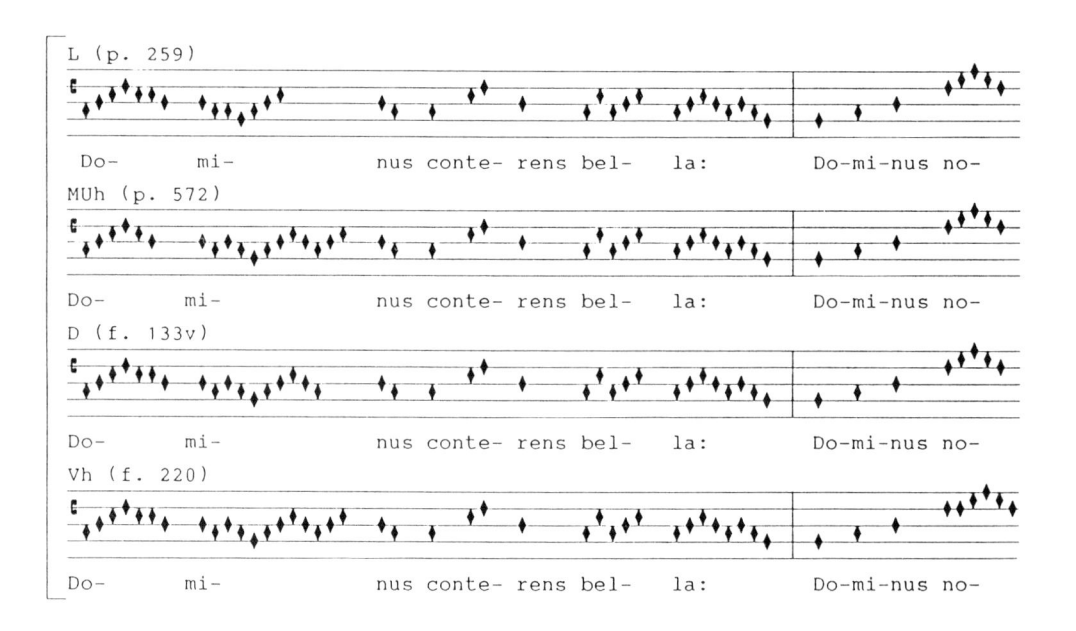

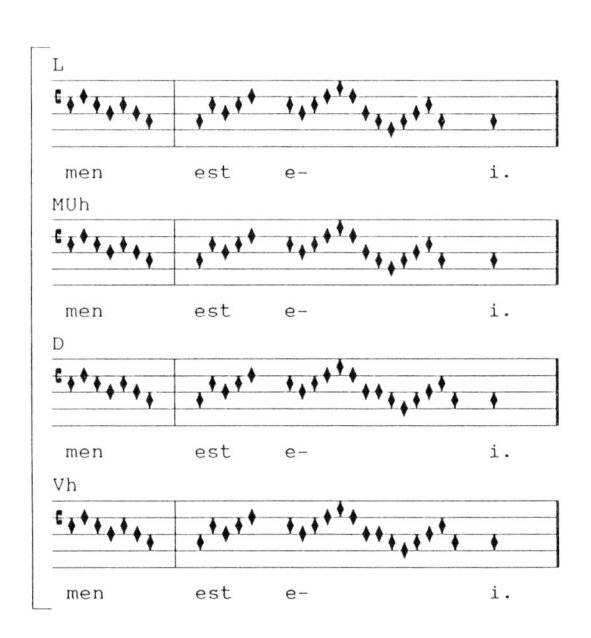

(vi) DOMINUS REGNANS IN AETERNAM

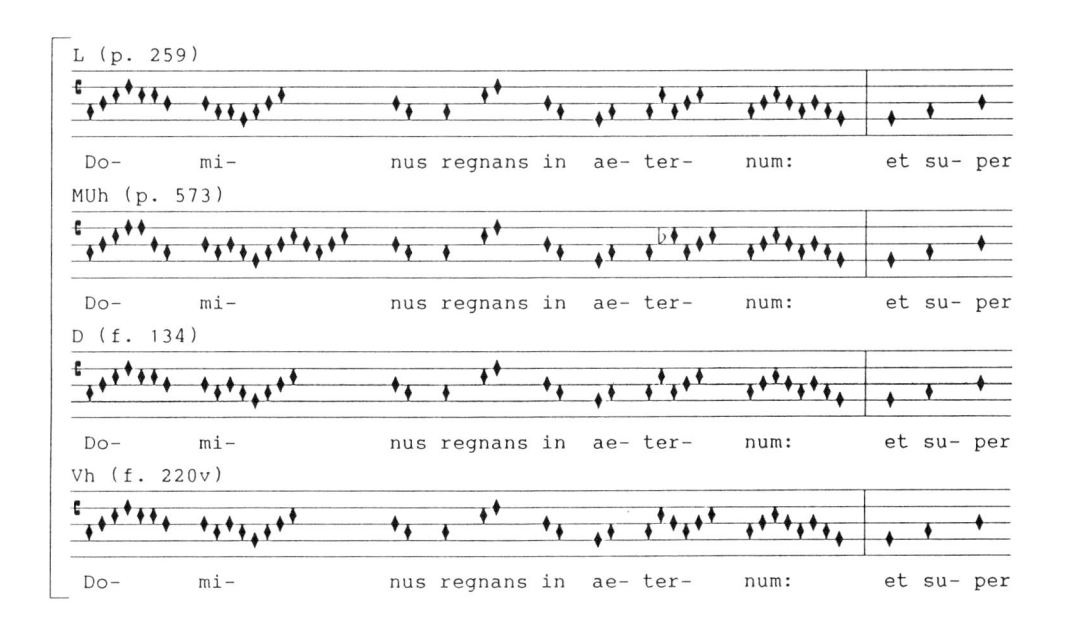

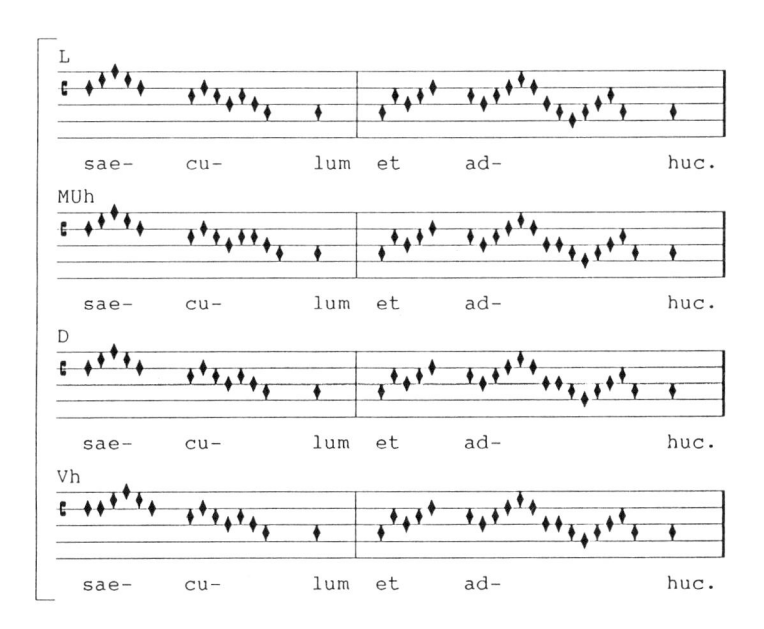

L (p. 259)

Do- mi- nus regnans in ae- ter- num: et su- per

MUh (p. 573)

Do- mi- nus regnans in ae- ter- num: et su- per

D (f. 134)

Do- mi- nus regnans in ae- ter- num: et su- per

Vh (f. 220v)

Do- mi- nus regnans in ae- ter- num: et su- per

L

sae- cu- lum et ad- huc.

MUh

sae- cu- lum et ad- huc.

D

sae- cu- lum et ad- huc.

Vh

sae- cu- lum et ad- huc.

(vii) FILII AUTEM ISRAEL

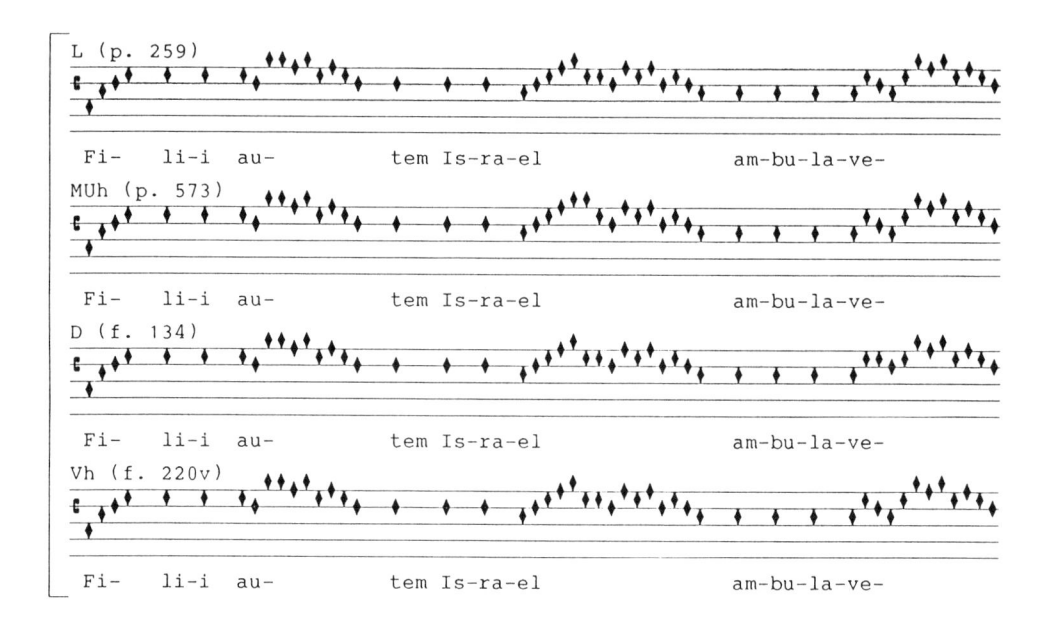

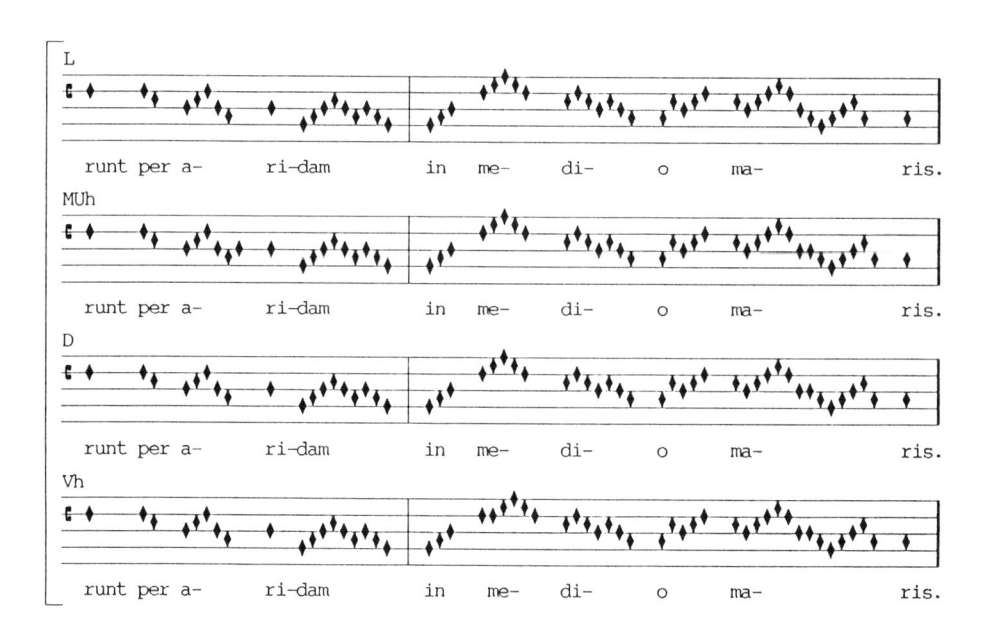

SUMPSIT AUTEM MARIA

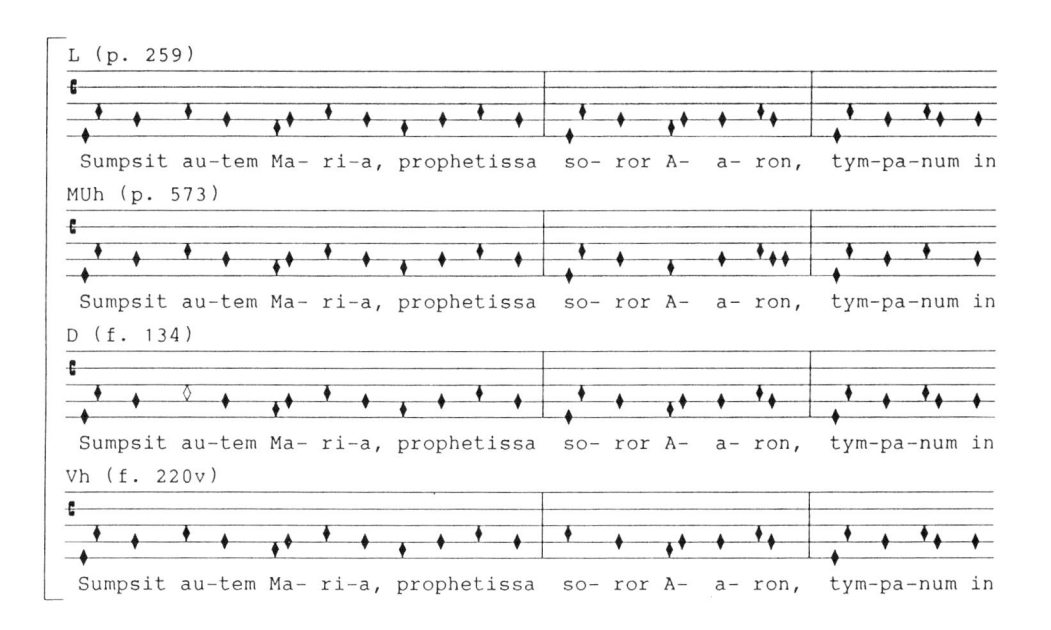

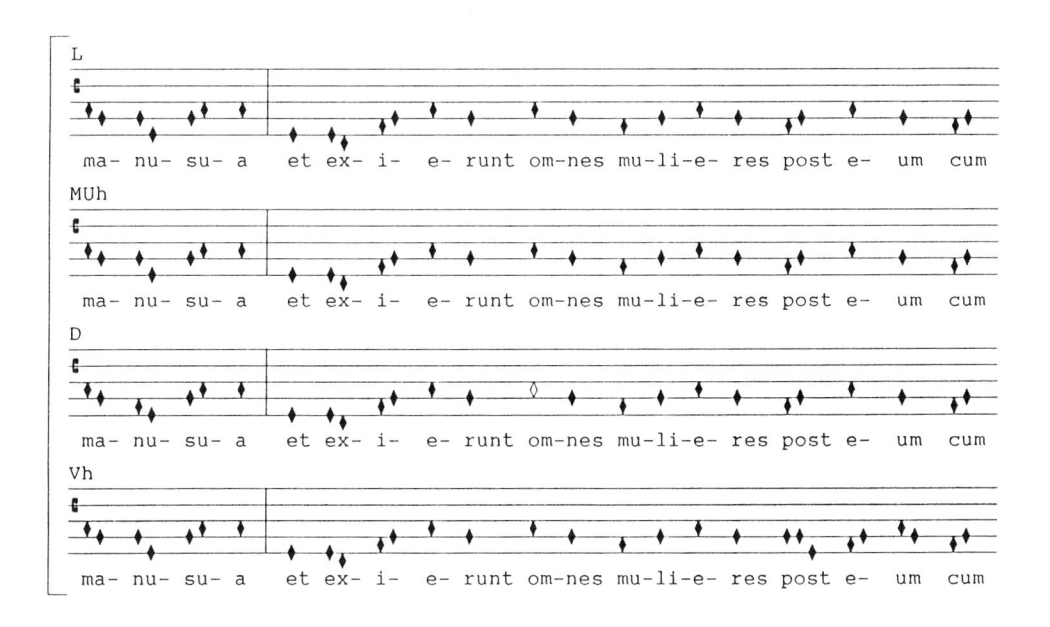

L (p. 259)
Sumpsit au-tem Ma- ri-a, prophetissa so- ror A- a- ron, tym-pa-num in

MUh (p. 573)
Sumpsit au-tem Ma- ri-a, prophetissa so- ror A- a- ron, tym-pa-num in

D (f. 134)
Sumpsit au-tem Ma- ri-a, prophetissa so- ror A- a- ron, tym-pa-num in

Vh (f. 220v)
Sumpsit au-tem Ma- ri-a, prophetissa so- ror A- a- ron, tym-pa-num in

L
ma- nu- su- a et ex- i- e- runt om-nes mu-li-e- res post e- um cum

MUh
ma- nu- su- a et ex- i- e- runt om-nes mu-li-e- res post e- um cum

D
ma- nu- su- a et ex- i- e- runt om-nes mu-li-e- res post e- um cum

Vh
ma- nu- su- a et ex- i- e- runt om-nes mu-li-e- res post e- um cum

SUMPSIT AUTEM MARIA (continued)

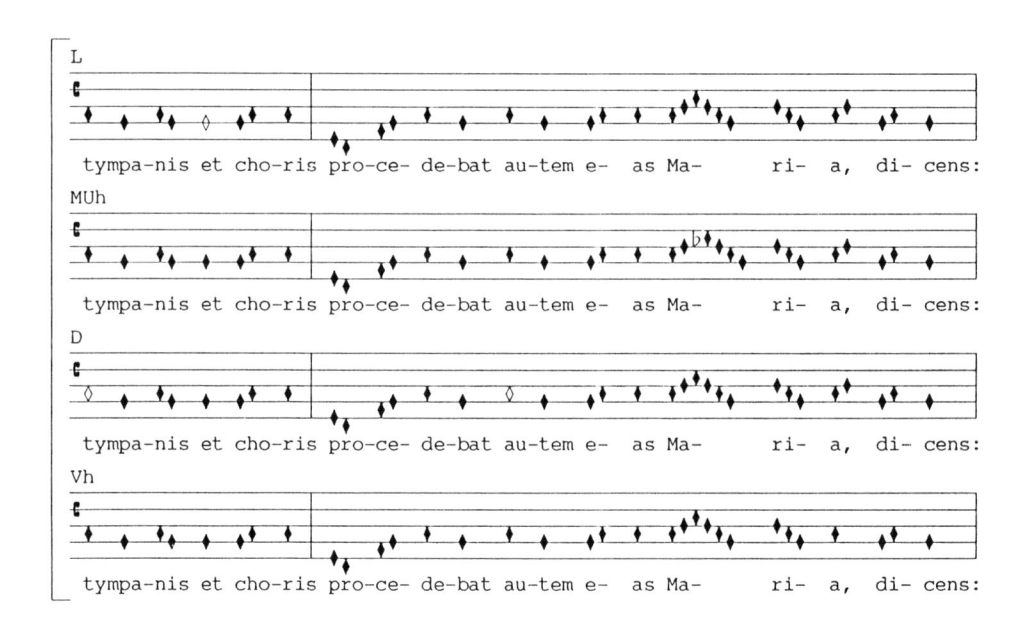

L

tympa-nis et cho-ris pro-ce- de-bat au-tem e- as Ma- ri- a, di- cens:

MUh

tympa-nis et cho-ris pro-ce- de-bat au-tem e- as Ma- ri- a, di- cens:

D

tympa-nis et cho-ris pro-ce- de-bat au-tem e- as Ma- ri- a, di- cens:

Vh

tympa-nis et cho-ris pro-ce- de-bat au-tem e- as Ma- ri- a, di- cens:

CANTEMUS DOMINO GLORIOSE

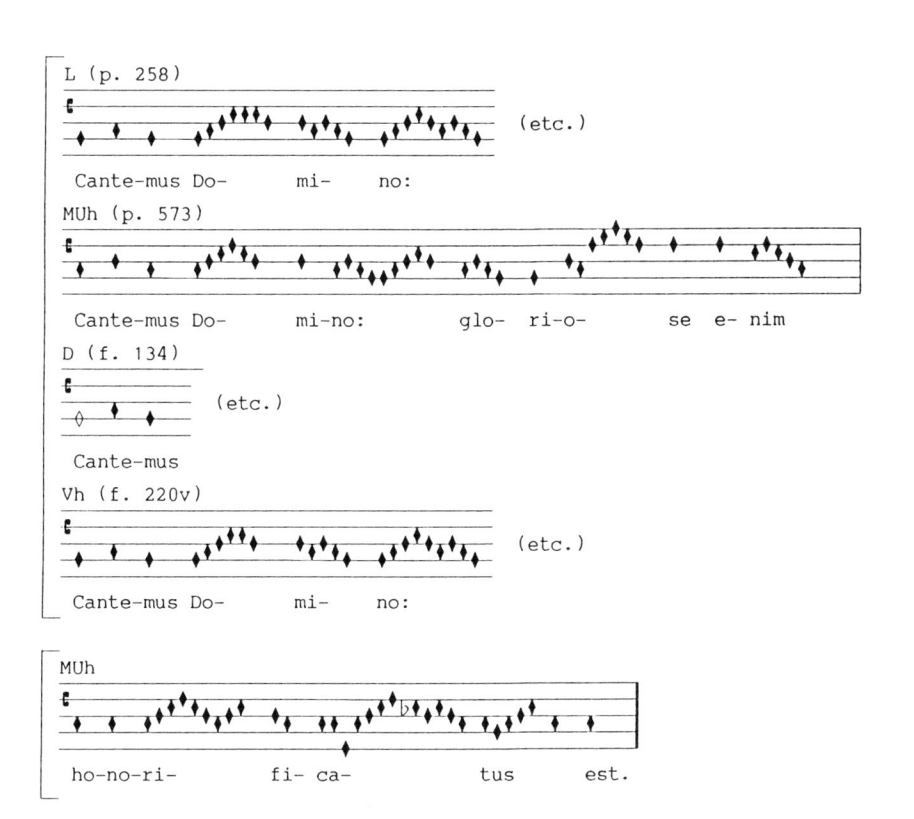

BIBLIOGRAPHY

Books and Articles Mentioned in the Text

Willi Apel, *Gregorian Chant* (Bloomington, 1958).

—— "Responsory," in *The Harvard Dictionary of Music* (edited by the same author, 2nd edition, Cambridge, 1969), 727.

Terence Bailey, *The Processions of Sarum and the Western Church* (Toronto, 1971).

—— *Commemoratio Brevis de Tonis et Psalmis Modulandis* (Ottawa, 1979).

—— "Ambrosian Psalmody: An Introduction," in *Rivista internazionale di musica sacra* I/1 (1980), 89.

—— "Ambrosian Choral Psalmody: The Formulae," in *Rivista internazionale di musica sacra* I/3 (1980), 316.

—— *The Ambrosian Alleluias* (Englefield Green, 1983).

Biblia sacra iuxta vulgatem clementinam, edited by professors of the Faculty of Theology of Paris and the Seminary of Saint-Sulpice (Rome, Tournai and Paris, 1947).

Bernard Botte (editor), *La tradition apostolique de saint-Hippolyte* (Münster, 1963).

Fernand Cabrol (editor), *Dictionnaire d'archéologie chrétienne et de liturgie* (15 volumes, Paris, 1903-1953).

Enrico Cattaneo, *Note storiche sul canto ambrosiano* (Milan, 1950).

Noël Denis-Boulet, "Analyse des rites et des prières de la messe (La liturgie de la parole)" in *L'église en prière* (edited by A. G. Martimort, Paris, 1961), 325.

Gregory Dix, *The Shape of the Liturgy* (second edition, Westminster, 1945).

Charles (Dufresne, Sieur) Du Cange, *Glossarium . . . mediae et infimae . . . latinitatis* (Paris, 1678, revised by Léopold Favre, Niort, 1883-1887).

Wilhelm Christ, *Über die Bedeutung von Hirmos, Troparion und Kanon . . .* (Leipzig, 1870).

Frank Cross and Elizabeth Livingstone (editors), *The Oxford Dictionary of the Christian Church* (Oxford, 1974).

Paolo Ferretti, *Estetica gregoriana* (Rome, 1934). French translation (by A. Agaësse), *Esthétique grégorienne* (Tournai, 1938).

Klaus Gamber, *Codices liturgici latini antiquiores* (Freibourg, second edition, 1968).

Noah Greenberg (editor), *The Play of Herod* (New York, 1965).

Graduale sacrosanctae romane ecclesiae (Tournai, 1945).

Jean Hanssens (editor), *Institutiones liturgicae de ritibus orientalibus* (in 2 volumes, Rome, 1930).

—— *Amalarii episcopi opera liturgica omnia*, (in 3 volumes, Rome, 1948-1950).

René-Jean Hesbert (editor), *Antiphonale Missarum Sextuplex* (Rome, 1935).

Richard Hoppin, *Medieval Music* (New York, 1978).

Helmut Hucke, "Tractusstudien" in *Festschrift Bruno Stäblein* (Kassel and Basel, 1967).

—— "Gradual (i)" (in the *New Grove Dictionary of Music and Musicians*, ed. Stanley Sadie (in 20 volumes, London and New York, 1980) VII, 599.

——— "Tract," in the *New Grove Dictionary of Music and Musicians* XIX, 110.

——— "Das Responsorium," in *Gattungen der Musik in Einzeldarstellungen: Gedenkschrift Leo Schrade* (Bern and Munich, 1973), 153.

Michel Huglo, "Le réponse-graduel de la messe, evolution de la forme, permanence de la fonction" in *Schweitzer Jahrbuch für Musikwissenschaft*, new series 2 (1982), 53.

Michel Huglo, Luigi Agustoni, Eugène Cardine, Ernesto Moneta Caglio, *Fonti e paleografia del canto ambrosiano* (Milan, 1956).

Ewald Jammers, *Das Alleluia in der gregorianischen Messe* (Münster, 1973).

Roy Jesson, "Ambrosian Chant: the Music of the Mass" (unpublished Ph.D. dissertation, Indiana University, 1955).

Joseph Jungmann, *Missarum Sollemnia* (fifth edition, in two volumes, Vienna, 1962).

Bruno Krusch and Wilhelm Levison (editors), the *Historia Francorum* of Gregory of Tours, in *Monumenta Germaniae historica: Scriptores rerum Merovingicarum* I (1951).

Margareta Landwehr-Melnicki (editor), *Die Gesänge des altrömischen Graduale* (volume 2 of *Monumenta monodica medii aevi*), introduction by Bruno Stäblein (Kassel and Basel, 1970).

Paul Lejai, "Ambrosien (Rit)," in *Dictionnaire d'archéologie chrétienne et de liturgie* (edited by F. Cabrol, H. Leclercq and H. Marrou, in 15 volumes, 1903-1953), I, 1392.

Marco Magistretti (editor), *Beroldus sive ambrosianae mediolanensis kalendarium et ordines saec. XII* (Milan, 1894).

——— *Manuale ambrosianum* (volume 2 of *Monumenta veteris liturgiae ambrosianae*), in 2 vols, Milan, 1905.

Jacques-Paul Migne (editor), *Patrologia latina* (in 221 volumes, Paris, 1844-1855).

Germain Morin, "Le plus ancien Comes ou lectionnaire de l'église romaine," in *Revue bénédictine*, XXVII (1910), 46.

Joseph-Louis d'Ortigue, *Dictionnaire liturgique, historique et théorique de plainchant et de musique d'église* (Paris, 1854).

Paléographie musicale. Les principaux manuscrits du chant grégorien, ambrosien, mozarabe, gallican. Publiés en fac-similés phototypiques, edited by the Monks of Solesmes, in 21 volumes in two series (Solesmes-Tournai, 1899-).

Johannes Quasten (editor), *Monumenta eucharistica et liturgica vetustissima* (Bonn, 1955).

Wunibald Roetzer, *Des heiligen Augustinus Schriften als liturgiegeschichtliche Quelle* (Munich, 1930).

Hermann Schmidt, *Hebdomada sancta* (2 vols, Rome, 1957).

William Scudamore, "Gradual," in *Dictionary of Christian Antiquities*, ed. W. Smith and S. Cheetham (in two volumes, Toronto, 1880), I, 747.

William Smoldon, "Liturgical Drama," in *The New Oxford History of Music* (edited by Anselm Hughes in 11 volumes, revised first edition, Oxford, 1955) II, 175.

Gregorio Suñol (editor), *Antiphonale missarum juxta ritum sanctae ecclesiae mediolanensis* (Rome, 1935).

Milos Velimirovic, "The Byzantine Heirmos and Heirmologion" in *Gattungen der Musik in Einzeldarstellungen: Gedenkschrift Leo Schrade* (Berne and Munich, 1973), 192.

Pierre-Patrick Verbraken, "Le psaultier des tropistes," in *Research on Tropes*, ed. Gunilla Iversen (Stockholm, 1983), 65.

Peter Wagner, *Einführung in die gregorianischen Melodien* (third edition, Leipzig, 1911).

Eric Werner, "The Origin of Psalmody," in *Hebrew Union College Annual* XXV (1954), 327.

INDEX TO THE EDITION

AD DOMINUM CUM TRIBULARER	164
ADIUTOR ET PROTECTOR	229
ADIUTORIUM NOSTRUM A DOMINO	162
ANIMA NOSTRA EREPTA	159
AUXILIUM MEUM A DOMINO	173
BENEDICAM DOMINUM	193
BENEDICAMUS PATREM ET FILIUM	220
BENEDICITE ANANIA AZARIA MISAHEL	219
BENEDICITE ANGELI DOMINI	213
BENEDICITE CAELI DOMINO	212
BENEDICITE FONTES DOMINI	225
BENEDICITE OMNES VIRTUTES	214
BENEDICITE OMNIA OPERA	210
BENEDICITE SACERDOTES DOMINI	215
BENEDICITE SANCTI ET HUMILES	218
BENEDICITE SERVI DOMINI	216
BENEDICITE SPIRITUS ET ANIMAE	217
BENEDICTUS ES DOMINE	205, 224
BENEDICTUS ES SUPER SEDEM	209
CANTEMUS DOMINO GLORIOSE	227, 237
CONSERVA ME DOMINE	187
DE PROFUNDIS CLAMAVI	191
DOMINE EXAUDI ORATIONEM	192

DOMINE LIBERA ANIMAM	165
DOMINUS CONTERENS BELLA	232
DOMINUS CUSTODIAT ANIMAM	176
DOMINUS IUSTUS CONCIDET	200
DOMINUS REGNANS IN AETERNAM	233
ECCE QUAM BONUM	179
EQUUM ET ASCENSORUM	228
ET BENEDICTUM NOMEN	207
FILII AUTEM ISRAEL	234
HEU ME QUOD INCOLATUS	168
HIC DEUS MEUS	230
HYMNUM DANIELIS	224
IN CONVERTENDO DOMINUS	189
LAUDATE DOMINUM OMNES GENTES	194
LEVAVI OCULOS MEOS	171
NISI QUOD DOMINUS	157
QUI EDEBAT PANES	197
QUI REGIS ISRAEL	153
QUIA ILLIC MANDAVIT	184
QUONIAM CONFIRMATA EST	195
QUONIAM ERIPUIT NOS	222
SICUT CERVUS DESIDERAT	202
SICUT UNGUENTUM IN CAPITE	181
SUMPSIT AUTEM MARIA	235

SUPER FLUMINA BABYLONIS	155
SUPRA DORSUM FABRICAVERUNT	198
TUNC CANTABAT MOYSES	226
TUNC HI TRES	204

LIST OF TABLES

TABLE 1. THE CANTUS AND THEIR LITURGICAL ASSIGNMENTS 24

TABLE 2. THE STRUCTURE OF THE MASS CANTUS 62

TABLE 3. THE STRUCTURE OF THE BENEDICTUS CANTICLES 63

TABLE 4. THE STRUCTURE OF THE CANTEMUS CANTICLE 64

TABLE 5. PHRASES "a," "B," "b." "B1," AND "B2"
IN THE MASS CANTUS 68

TABLE 6. PHRASES "A1," "A2," AND "B1" OF THE MASS CANTUS ... 76

TABLE 7. THE PHRASES "c," "D," "D1," "D2" AND "d"
IN THE MASS CANTUS 87

TABLE 8. THE PHRASES "w," "X" AND "x" OF THE MASS CANTUS ... 99

TABLE 9. GREGORIAN TRACT-VERSES WITH AMBROSIAN
COUNTERPARTS 133

LIST OF MUSICAL EXAMPLES

Example 1. The Most Common Ambrosian Reciting-Tone
and a Frequently-found Alternate Termination 56

Example 2. The Structural Tones of the Ambrosian
Cantus Melody 58

Example 3. Phrases "a," "B," "b," and "B2"
in the Mass Cantus 69

Example 4. Phrases "A1," "A2" and "B1" of the Mass Cantus 77

Example 5. Phrases "A," "a" and "B" of the
BENEDICTUS Canticles 81

Example 6. The A and B Phrases of the CANTEMUS 83

Example 7. The Phrases "c," "D," "D1," "D2" and "d"
in the Mass Cantus 88

Example 8. The Phrases "C1," "C2" and "D2"
in the Mass Cantus 93

Example 9. The Phrases "C," "C1" and "D"
　　　　　　of the BENEDICTUS Canticles 96

Example 10. The Phrases "C," "c" and "D"
　　　　　　 of the CANTEMUS Canticle 97

Example 11. The Phrases "w," "X" and "x" of the Mass Cantus 100

Example 12. The Phrases "W1," "(W1)" and "X1"
　　　　　　 in the Mass Cantus 106

Example 13. The Phrases "W" and "X"
　　　　　　 of the BENEDICTUS Canticles 108

Example 14. The Phrase "W" of the CANTEMUS 109

Example 15. The Phrases "Y," "(Y)," "y," "(y)"
　　　　　　 and "Y1" in the Mass Cantus 111

Example 16. The Phrases "Z," "Z1," "(Z1)" and "Z2"
　　　　　　 in the Mass Cantus 114

Example 17. The Phrases "Y," "Y1" and "Z"
　　　　　　 in the BENEDICTUS Canticles 115

Example 18. The Phrases "Y," "Y1" and "Z" in the CANTEMUS .. 116

Example 19. The Various Forms of the Cadential Flourish,
　　　　　　 the B, D, X and Z Phrases 118

Example 20. Ambrosian, Gregorian, Old-Roman and
            Old-Beneventan Chants Compared

   (a) DE PROFUNDIS CLAMAVI 136
   (b) LAUDATE DOMINUM 137
   (c) QUONIAM CONFIRMATA 138
   (d) QUI REGIS ISRAEL 139
   (e) SICUT CERVUS 140

INDEX

Entries for the Cantus verses are in Capital letters; other chant incipits are given in italics.

Abbreviation of the Cantus-Tract **36, 38**
Accentual forms **75, 82, 105, 108, 115, 122**
AD DOMINUM **28, 73, 92, 94, 104**
ADIUTORIUM NOSTRUM **79**
Afferentur regi (the Psalmellus) **19**
Agustoni, Luigi **145**
Alcuin **42**
Aliturgical assemblies **42, 50,51**
Alleluia(s) **8, 13, 20, 26, 38, 39, 44, 49, 52, 94, 113, 120, 122, 123, 129**
All Saints (the feast) **144**
Amalarius of Metz **13, 14, 21, 23, 36, 42**
Ambrosian Chant (the age) **9**
Ambrosian Psalter **24, 26, 27**
Ancient Vigils **44, 50, 51**
ANIMA NOSTRA **72, 73, 75, 79, 80, 104, 126**
Annunciation **13, 19, 133**
Antiphona in laudate **55**
Antiphonale missarum **51**
Apel, Willi **8, 42, 43, 123, 127, 130, 131**
Apostolic Constitutions **32, 35**
Apostolic Tradition of St Hippolytus **31, 34**

Assumption (the feast)   19
Athanasius   36
Augustine, St   31, 33, 34, 35, 36, 38, 39
Aurelian of Réôme   13
AUXILIUM MEUM   79, 95

Bailey, Terence   30, 44, 48, 55, 60, 103, 120, 121
Bellini and Chopin   119
Bémolisation   147, 148
BENEDICAM DOMINUM   27, 28, 60, 65, 72, 74, 75, 80, 143
BENEDICAMUS PATREM   47
BENEDICITE ANANIA   149
BENEDICITE FONTES   47, 82
BENEDICITE SERVI   47
BENEDICTUS ES   27, 35, 45, 46, 47, 54, 73, 82, 83, 84, 92, 96, 98, 108, 115, 119, 122, 132, 148
Benedictus dominus (the Psalmellus)   19
Beroldus, the compiler of the Milanese ordinal   16
Bipartite Cantus verse   141
Blessing of the Font   50
Botte, Bernard   31

Cabrol, Fernand   50
Cadenza   80, 94
CANTEMUS DOMINO   27, 60, 82, 83, 84, 85, 92, 98, 104, 109, 110, 116, 119, 122, 127, 132
Cantemus domino (the Gregorian Tract)   132, 134
Canticum   16, 17, 18, 35, 39, 45, 47, 48, 53
Cantus, musical relationships owing to textual similarities   66, 123, 125
Cantus sung originally throughout the year   30
Cantus texts appropriate to the occasion   41, 42
Cantus, not responsoria, in the Office   40
Cantus-Tracts as Mass readings   36
Cardine, Eugène   145
Centonization technique   9

Chants alternating with lessons 39
Christ, Wilhelm 15
Christmas 53
Clavicularii 53, 54
Codification of Ambrosian Chant 9
Comes of Würzburg 37
CONSERVA ME 28, 72, 75, 112
Correction of the melodies 110
Cross, Frank 28

D'Ortigue, Jean-Louis 12
DE PROFUNDIS 73, 90, 91, 92, 94, 103, 104, 113, 141
De profundis (the Gregorian Tract) 133
Denis-Boulet, Noël 7
Deus manifeste (the Psalmellus) 21
Dilexisti iustitiam (the Psalmellus) 19
Distinctive opening figure of the phrase "W1" 74, 105
Divinae lectiones 32, 36
Dix, Gregory 50
DOMINE EXAUDI 19, 60, 72, 73, 75, 105, 107, 123, 143
Domine exaudi (the Gregorian Tract) 133
DOMINE LIBERA 113
DOMINUS CONTERENS 134
Dominus conterens (the Gregorian Tract) 134, 135
DOMINUS CUSTODIAT 123, 149
DOMINUS IUSTUS 60, 90, 105, 107, 123, 143
Dominus justus (the Gregorian Tract) 133
Du Cange, Charles 12
Duchesne, Louis 32, 37, 43, 50

ECCE QUAM 79, 84, 92, 94, 106, 107, 112, 126, 144
Elaboration of the melodies in the course of time 121
Ember Days 29, 133
Epiphany 53
Eripe me (the Gregorian Tract) 42

Etenim potuerunt (the Gregorian Tract)   **133**
Extra Masses   **30**

Fatio de Castoldis, the scribe of *MUh*   **145**
Faulty adaptation of Cantus phrases   **110**
Ferretti, Paolo   **20, 129, 130, 131**
Flex   **60**
Foreign phrases   **84, 98, 122, 126, 127**
Friday Masses in Lent   **21**

Good Friday   **18, 25, 26, 41, 42, 45-47, 50, 51, 53, 54, 63, 64, 73, 82, 83, 91, 123, 148**
Gregorian   **8, 9, 11, 13, 15, 17-21, 28-30, 34, 37, 39, 40, 42, 45, 46, 48-51, 56-59, 74, 80, 91, 103-105, 113, 119, 121-123, 128-135, 141, 142, 144**
Gregorian influence   **80**
Gregorian Sacramentary   **46**
Gregory of Tours   **35**

Hanssens, Jean   **14, 32, 42**
Heirmos   **15**
Hesbert, René-Jean   **11, 17, 20, 42, 46**
HEU ME   **29, 72-75, 79, 80, 113, 125, 126**
HIC DEUS MEUS   **134**
Hic Deus meus (the Gregorian Tract)   **134**
Holy Innocents (the feast)   **13, 123**
Holy Thursday   **19, 20, 25, 41-44, 50, 52, 123**
Holy Week   **41**
Honorius of Autun   **12**
Hoppin, Richard   **37**
Hucke, Helmut   **8, 12, 20, 38, 132**
Hugh of St Victor   **12**
Huglo, Michel   **36, 43, 145**
Hymnum Danielis (the introduction to the canticle)   **54, 126**

Idiosynchratic opening of the W phrase **95, 103**
In capite quadragesimae (the Sunday) **26**
IN CONVERTENDO **74, 90, 91, 92, 94, 104, 113, 125**
In tempore (the neuma) **20**
Isidore, St **14, 36**

Jammers, Ewald **44**
Jerome, St **39**
Jesson, Roy **8**
Jubilate Domino (the Gregorian Tract) **13**
Jungmann, Joseph **37, 43, 46**

Kinship of the Gregorian and Milanese assignment for Holy Saturday **48**

Landwehr-Melnicki, Margareta **128**
Late adaptations of the Cantus melody **122**
Later additions to the repertory **123, 124**
LAUDATE DOMINUM **13, 29, 90, 113, 114, 123, 124, 141**
Laudate dominum (the Gregorian Tract) **129, 133**
Lector **45, 53**
Lejai, Paul **13**
Leo, St **34, 35, 38**
LEVAVI OCULOS **30, 79, 81, 112, 143, 144**
Liquescents **135**
Liturgical dramas **126**
Local differences **112**

Magister **53, 54**
Magistretti, Marco **16, 19, 30, 40**
Major Litany **40**
Manuale **18**
Melisma(s) **29, 60, 61, 65, 75, 80, 94, 105, 107, 112, 113, 114, 125, 125, 126, 132, 134, 141, 146**
Melodiae **20, 94, 113**

Manuscripts (other than those of the Edition)
    Bedero, S. Vittore B **20**
    Benevento VI.40 **135**
    Cannobio, S. Vittore (no number) **20**
    Milan, Trivulziana MS A.14 **20**
    St Gall 359 **11, 17**
Moneta, Caglio, Ernesto **145**
Murbach Lectionary **46**

Nativity of the Virgin (the feast) **19, 144**
Neumae **20**
Neume groupings **146**
Neutral character of the Cantus texts **13, 27, 29, 30**
NISI QUOD **73, 75, 90, 91, 92, 94, 103, 112, 113, 124, 125, 144**
Normalization **105, 112, 122, 124, 132**
Nuances **148**

Occurrerunt Maria (the Psalmellus) **19**
Office lessons, the late introduction **50**
Old-Beneventan **9, 11, 58, 129, 130, 131, 135, 141, 142**
Old-Roman **9, 11, 128, 130, 131, 135, 141, 142**
Oral tradition **9, 18, 72, 120, 121, 124**
Orationes solemnes **50**

Pacifice loquebantur (the Psalmellus) **19, 30**
Palm Sunday **19, 29, 30**
Pars aestiva **144**
Pars hiemalis **144**
Pentecost **133**
Processional psalm **48, 49**
Prolongaverunt iniquitates (the Gregorian Tract) **133**
Proper procedure for semiverses that were too short to be divided **104**
Psalmellus **13, 18, 19, 20, 21, 30, 38, 42-44, 47, 49, 52, 53, 83, 144**
Psalmodic titles **27**
Psalms between lessons **32**

Psalmus tractus and congregational refrains 35
Psalter of St Germain **36**
Puer magistri scholarum **52**
Punctuation **148**

QUI EDEBAT **20, 41, 42, 43, 50, 90, 91, 92, 94, 123**
QUI REGIS **65, 72, 74, 105, 107, 119, 141**
Qui regis (the Gregorian Tract) **131, 133**
Qui regis (the Old-Roman Tract) **143**
QUIA ILLIC **79, 95**
Quilismas **135, 146**
QUONIAM CONFIRMATA **72, 81, 90, 123, 141**
Quoniam confirmata (the Gregorian and Old-Roman Tracts) **141**
Quoniam confirmata (the Gregorian Tract) **133**
Quoniam eripuit (extra verse concluding the canticle) **53**

Readings from Genesis and Proverbs **20, 40, 41**
Recent liturgical reforms **10**
Reges (the neuma) **20**
Relationship of text and music **66**
Requiem **19, 144**
Respond-Gradual(s) **14, 18, 20, 30, 37, 38, 49**
Responsories, the function of **43**
Responsorium **18, 23, 44, 45, 49, 50, 133**
Rex (the neuma) **20**

St Agnes (the feast) **19**
St Ambrose (the feast) **144**
St James (the feast) **144**
St John the Baptist (the feast) **144**
St Joseph (the feast) **19**
St Lawrence (the feast) **144**
St Martin (the feast) **144**
Sts Nazarius and Celsus (the feast) **144**
Sts Peter and Paul (the feast) **144**

Sts Protasius and Gervasius (the feast)   144
Schmidt, Hermann   42
Schubert, Franz   120
Scudamore, William   37
SICUT CERVUS   18, 41, 48, 49, 84, 92, 104, 113, 119, 141
Sicut cervus (the Gregorian Tract)   134, 135
Sicut cervus (the Old-Beneventan Tract)   141
SICUT UNGUENTUM   79, 113, 149
Speciosus forma (the Psalmellus)   21
Successive repetition   94, 113, 120, 125
Sumpsit autem (the introduction to the canticle)   84
Suñol   9, 10, 18, 83, 146, 149
Suñol's Antiphonale, its scholarly indadequacies   9
SUPER FLUMINA   53, 73, 75, 90, 92, 94, 123
SUPRA DORSUM   41, 44, 45, 53, 84, 90, 123, 124
Supra dorsum (the Gregorian Tract)   133
Suscipiant domine (the Psalmellus)   19
Symmetry of lessons separated by chants   38
Syntactical interchangeability of the Cantus phrases   58, 80, 131

Tamquam ad latronem (the Psalmellus)   19, 42, 52
Tenebrae factae (the Psalmellus)   18
Text variants   149
Timentes autem (the Psalmellus)   19
Tommasi, Giuseppe   14
Tract, its position in the Mass   37
Tracts   7-18, 20, 21, 23, 30-32, 34-40, 42, 44, 45, 48-51, 57, 58, 73, 80, 91, 103, 105, 119, 122, 123, 128-135, 141-143
TRACTUS CANTUS   11, 18
Traits verts   147
Transcription of the notation   148
Tunc cantabat (the introduction to the canticle)   47, 54, 83, 84, 126
Tunc hi tres (the introduction to the canticle)   46, 53, 83, 126

Uncurtailed Cantus psalmody   47

Uniformity of the canticle settings **122**

Velimirovic, Milos **15**
Verbraken, Pierre-Patrick **28**
Vigil(s) **13, 19, 24, 29, 44, 47, 48, 50, 51, 53, 133, 134, 144**

Wagner, Peter **12, 14, 20, 34, 35, 37**
Werner, Eric **32**
Word painting **66, 125, 126**